CULINARY TEA

More Than 150 RECIPES
STEEPED IN TRADITION *from* AROUND *the* WORLD

CYNTHIA GOLD *and* LISË STERN

RUNNING PRESS
PHILADELPHIA · LONDON

Cover and interior design by Amanda Richmond
Edited by Kristen Green Wiewora
Typography: Requiem, Chronicle Text, and La Portentia
Food Styling by Katrina Tekavec
Special thanks to Monica Parcell, Virginia Villalon,
Mariellen Melker, and Andrea Monzo

The publisher would like to thank the following retailers for their
invaluable assistance in the production of this book: Ruka,
Philadelphia, PA; Manor Home & Gifts, Philadelphia, PA; Foster's
Homeware, Philadelphia, PA; Scarlett Alley, Philadelphia, PA;
Open House, Philadelphia, PA; Crate & Barrel, King of Prussia, PA;
and Kitchen Kapers, King of Prussia, PA

Running Press Book Publishers
2300 Chestnut Street
Philadelphia, PA 19103-4371

Visit us on the web!
www.runningpresscooks.com

CONTENTS

ACKNOWLEDGMENTS

So MUCH GOES INTO THE CREATION OF A book, and so many people helped make a possibility become a reality. We are very grateful.

From Cindy:

To Donald Saunders and the tea crew at the BPPH who made it possible for my passion for tea to be shared with so many. Thanks Nicky, Vi, Amber, Fega, Ming, Joe, and George, among others. Also, everyone at the BPPH who put up with the unusual schedules created by my teaching, speaking, and travel itineraries.

To Roy Fong and Norwood Pratt, who patiently guided me on that first formative trip to China, which truly changed my life.

To John Romkey and the staff and patrons of Tea-Tray in the Sky as well as the tea patrons at the Park Plaza for endless inspiration and feedback.

To Chef Roberta Dowling and the Cambridge School of Culinary Arts, who long recognized the importance of tea training in culinary education. My gratitude to all the cooking schools who permitted me to introduce students to the gastronomic potential of tea.

Several people have done much for tea education. To trailblazer Pearl Dexter of *TEA: A Magazine*, and to Donna, Richard, Phil (thanks for the jasmine photos), Ken, and all the volunteers involved with the Specialty Tea Institute and their passionate commitment.

To Frank Sanchez and Tom Eck of Upton Tea for their ongoing support of tea education and the principals of culinary tea.

To Kumar and Glendale Estates for introducing the concept of culinary tea in India, and for sharing with me the beauty of Southern India.

To Elaine, Penny, Emily, Ashley, and all those at *Santé Magazine* (past and present) for recognizing the need to expose the culinary world to the potential of tea.

To George and everyone involved with the World Tea Expo for allowing priceless opportunities for networking and sharing tea knowledge.

To so many extraordinary people throughout the tea world who have generously shared their knowledge and time with me, hosting me on farms and estates, taking me to auctions and broker houses, and revealing myriad insider details.

To all my friends and family who have put up with my obsessive focus on tea and my almost complete unavailability to meet normal social obligations. Holidays, family gatherings—what are those?

And most of all, to my husband Julian for endless tea photography, for tolerating schedule and life disruptions, and for being my number one recipe taster.

From Lisë:

Special thanks to my family: my amazing children Gabriel, Eitan, and Shoshanna, who put up with late meals and delayed vacations all in the name of culinary tea, and gave honest feedback on recipes; my parents Joyce and Michael, who provide profound support, for which I am eternally grateful, and to my Grandlady. And to Shabbat dinner mainstays Tante Raya and Carolyn Faye Fox.

I'm blessed with wonderful tea-drinking and non-tea-drinking friends who have been here for me through sunshine and rain, including Katherine Ellin, Jill Eskenazi, Naava Frank, Jesse Gordon, Lisa Horvitz, Lisa Howe, Steve Kaufer, Lisa Link, Kimberly Mayone, Elizabeth Rosenzweig, Judi Roth, Jill and David Segal, and all the wonderful King Open parents. A special raise of the cup to Caroline Kaufer, who loved the accoutrements of afternoon tea. To Moms Jen Bump, Karin Conn, Kelly Katz, Julie Rochlin, Claudia Stearns, and Gail Williams. To fellow food writers extraordinaire, the Ladies Who Lunch Andrea Pyenson, Clara Silverstein, Rachel Travers, Cathy Walthers, and Lisa Zwirn.

Hugs, kisses, and thanks to my dear Larry Kletter, for being here, there, and everywhere. And for reading through the entire manuscript, asking important questions, and giving me the chance to try yellow tea.

From both of us:

A huge thank you to our agent Clare Pelino, whose diligence and enthusiastic encouragement turned a proposal into an actual book. Warm thanks to everyone at Running Press for making *Culinary Tea* a reality.

To Joe Simrany for his ongoing leadership and his efforts to help others enjoy the beauty of the world's tea fields and the value of specialty teas.

To all the participants in and sponsors of the 2009 New England Culinary Tea Competition. Their embrace of the culinary tea concept demonstrates that chefs and home cooks everywhere will enjoy cooking with tea. Thanks too to all the chefs who contributed recipes.

To Ronnie Almeida and Ananda Fernando of New Vithanakande Tea Estates for the beautiful nineteenth-century photographs of the Kandy region in Sri Lanka.

To Malik and Dilhan, and everyone at Dilmah Tea for educating the chefs of Sri Lanka and beyond about the culinary side of fine teas, and for publicizing cooking with tea via international competitions. We thank participants in those contests for demonstrating the universality of culinary tea.

Ongoing studies connecting the health benefits of tea have done much to popularize our favorite beverage and culinary ingredient. For sharing their extensive research regarding the health aspects of tea, thanks to Dr. Jeffrey Blumberg, Dr. C.S. Yang, and Dr. Lenore Arab. And thanks to Maggie Moon, MS, RD, for compiling much of the ongoing tea and health research. It's great to know that something we enjoy so much just so happens to be very, very good for us!

PART I: UNDERSTANDING TEA

What is Culinary Tea?

TEA IS ONE OF THE OLDEST INGREDIENTS USED IN THE KITCHEN—AND AT THE SAME TIME, ONE of the newest. Within the various tea-producing regions of the world, tea has long been consumed as a food as well as a beverage, yet more often than not, these culinary preparations have stayed hidden within their cultural niches.

Tea as a beverage is fast gaining popularity in the West, thanks in part to a greater availability of wonderful loose-leaf varieties and also to a growing body of research that supports the historic understanding of the health benefits of tea. As large segments of our population embrace healthier lifestyles and eating habits, tea is a part of this. And for us, it followed naturally that tea should make the leap from cup to plate.

Culinary Tea is all about cooking with tea—bringing this remarkably versatile, healthful, and flavorful ingredient into modern kitchens. We offer fresh ways of looking at tea—approaching it from way outside the cup, as it were—by drawing on classic ways of cooking with tea, such as the centuries-old Chinese Tea-Marbled Eggs (page 91), as well as developing new recipes using innovative approaches in the techniques employed and the flavors and textures achieved, such as Tea-Rubbed Short Ribs with Smoky Barbecue Sauce (page 152) or Assam Shortbread Diamonds (page 186)

There are myriad ways in which tea can enhance a dish, and a variety of techniques that bring out the best flavor in both the tea and the complementary ingredients in a dish. Tea can be added dry, steeped in water, steeped in other liquids, smoked, brined, or infused. And the many styles of tea complement foods in different ways. Within the four basic categories of tea—green, black, oolong, and white—specific *styles* of tea can enhance various dishes in different ways. Among black teas, for example, a delicate Darjeeling will work better in one kind of dish, a hearty Keemun in another, a smoky Lapsang Souchong in a third.

The enchantment of tea, too, is its backstory. Tea is literally steeped in history, a history that spans the world. China, India, and Japan are the most well-known tea countries today, but other Asian countries such as Sri Lanka (formerly called Ceylon) and Korea have their tea traditions, as do European countries such as Britain and France. This cultural history affected the development of different tea traditions, and different teas.

Culinary Tea is divided into two parts. In part one, we give an overview and background on tea in general, with a history of cooking with tea, and detailed descriptions of more common styles of tea. While all tea comes from the same plant, *Camellia sinensis*, different handling and processing techniques create a wide array of distinctive flavors. We explain why black tea is called black, and what makes a tea green, white, oolong, Pu-erh, scented, or blended. We give an overview on flavor profiling. Just as certain wines harmonize with certain foods, teas complement foods in more and less satisfying ways, and we explain how. Part two begins with a chapter describing the various techniques we recommend for cooking with tea. We continue with over one hundred fifty recipes demonstrating the many methods of cooking with tea, organized by course.

As you explore *Culinary Tea*—forward, sideways, inside-out, as is often the way with cookbooks—you'll learn how to easily incorporate tea into your culinary repertoire. Ultimately, we hope you'll be inspired to create your own original culinary tea recipes.

Notes on Ingredients

TEA: We prefer loose-leaf tea. Loose-leaf offers the greatest variety, while tea bags are limited to a handful of blacks and greens, with an occasional white or oolong, as well as artificially flavored teas (peach, mango, etc.). Loose-leaf teas are now widely available outside specialty tea shops—you can even pick them up at coffee bars like Starbucks. At the end of the book, we list sources for both loose-leaf teas and tea equipment.

That said, you can use commercial teabags for culinary tea. Because the tea in teabags is usually finely broken or ground (unless you are using the new breed of teabags, containing whole leaves) you will need less tea if using teabags than the amount called for in our recipes. Here's the standard rule of thumb:

1 standard teabag = 1 teaspoon loose-leaf tea leaves

EGGS: We use large eggs in all recipes.

FLOUR: Unless otherwise stated, use all-purpose flour. We prefer unbleached flour, as bleached flour often has a chlorinated taste that can especially interfere with the subtle flavors of tea.

SALT: For baking and most cooking, we generally prefer fine sea salt, though some recipes call for coarse sea or kosher salt. Regular table salt may be substituted for any recipe calling for fine sea salt.

CHAPTER 1

THE ROOTS OF TEA & CULINARY TEA

Our Personal Histories with Culinary Tea

BOTH OF US CAME TO COOKING WITH TEA after years of simply enjoying it as a beverage. More than a decade ago, Cindy opened the first of two tea restaurant-cafés called Tea-Tray in the Sky in Cambridge, Massachusetts, in which she promoted her love of all things tea, and offered a menu of more than three hundred loose-leaf varieties. Lisë met Cindy when she was writing an article on masala chai for the *Boston Globe*. While she had tried several chais, Cindy's version converted Lisë from a tea *drinker* to tea *aficionado*.

As a chef, Cindy began creating foods in her restaurant that would complement the teas she served. Being surrounded by flavorful and aromatic teas— they screamed to be given their due! Soon customers started asking for pairing suggestions, wondering which of the many teas would best go with the food items on the menu. Cindy began to pay more attention to the flavor profiles; it then occurred to her that pairing a tea and food *within* a dish shouldn't be that different from pairing *alongside* a dish.

Cindy's first culinary tea creation was the Fresh Fruit Tart with Jasmine Tea Pastry Cream (page 214). Other dishes quickly followed, like the Jasmine Tea-Cured Gravlax (page 93) and the Flourless Keemun-Cherry Chocolate Torte (page 204).

Lisë, who was already a fan of Cindy's cooking, was inspired by Cindy's enthusiastic embrace of culinary tea. And as you discover the teas and recipes in this book, we think you will be, too. It's not a new concept: As we soon discovered, the concept of cooking with tea has a history as long (or longer) as the concept of drinking tea.

A Brief History of Tea

Tea is believed to have originated in China, or in the Assam region of northern India—the base of the Himalayas. Beyond that, its historical origins as food and drink are steeped in myth and legend. The Chinese have a legendary ancestor, shennong, known as the father of Chinese agriculture (*shennong* means "divine farmer") who is credited with, among other things, "discovering" tea. Descriptions of his first encounter with tea vary. Some say tea leaves blew into water he was boiling, others say he chewed on the leaves. Some claim he was feeling ill at the time from sampling other plants and the tea cured him, others say the tea simply imparted a good feeling and tasted delicious. Regardless, the year of his encounter with tea is oddly precise: 2737 B.C.E. According to *The True History of Tea* by Victor H. Mair and Erling Hoh, "Curiosity and gluttony being two hallmarks of our species, it is easy to surmise that humans discovered the nourishing, salubrious effects of the tea leaf much earlier than the Shennong myth claims. And when they did, it was certainly by chewing the raw leaf—a custom practiced to this day by people in its native region."

In *The Empire of Tea*, Alan MacFarlane agrees that people were enjoying tea long before they thought to add water. He writes, "No one on earth drank tea a few thousand years ago. A few small tribal groups in the jungles of southeast Asia chewed the leaves of the plant, but that was the nearest anyone came to tea drinking. Two thousand years ago it was drunk in a handful of religious communities. By a thousand years ago it was drunk by millions of Chinese. Five hundred years ago over half of the world's population was drinking tea as their main alternative to water."

According to Indian tradition, it was the Buddhist monk Bodhidharma who discovered the stimulating effects of tea: He found he was able to meditate with renewed attention after chewing on some tea twigs. The gorier Japanese twist on this legend is that Bodhidharma was attempting to meditate for seven (some accounts say nine) years, and after five years, dozed off. He was so upset, he cut off his eyelids and threw them on the ground; where they fell, tea trees grew.

Regardless of the legendary source, tea trees do go way back—and can live a long time. Tea trees assessed to be more than one thousand years old have been discovered in China. In 2007 at the Third China International Cultural Industry Fair, a brick of Pu-erh tea weighing about a pound was on display (and for sale for $38,961.04). The tree that commanded this price is said to be the oldest cultivated tea tree, estimated to be over three thousand years old.

The tea culture in China is similar to the wine culture in France, with hundreds of specialized regional teas and closely guarded production methods. China established a strong tea trade with surrounding countries. Tea was traded and used for currency, usually pressed into bricks and cakes for transport. Agnes Repplier writes in her 1931 volume *To Think of Tea!*, "The world drinks tea, but its history and traditions are indisputably Chinese. Japan has the ritual, England the pure comfort and delight, Tartary and Thibet the needed stimulant in a land of snows. But the 'China drink' is China's child, and China's inspiration."

Surrounding countries that became nations of tea drinkers include Japan, Tibet, Russia (Siberia), and Myanmar (Burma). Oddly, India was not much of a tea-drinking country until the British arrived. In regions where tea grew wild, such as Assam, native tribes might have had some tea here and there, but there is little documented history.

Tea did not arrive in Europe until the seventeenth century—namely to Britain, Holland, and France. As in China and Japan, it was initially lauded for its curative powers. The British famously took to tea more than anyone else, and as demand in that country grew, the British East India Company, which had been importing tea from China, saw India as a goldmine of tea possibilities. At the end of the eighteenth century, what started as a business deal turned into a colony, as the East India Company began buying up more and more land in India. A few decades later, after a coffee blight wiped out that industry in Sri Lanka (then called Ceylon) tea plantations were planted there as well.

The British may have lost the American Revolution, but they played a significant role in the spread of tea—taxed or not—all around the world.

Each country that adopted tea developed its own rituals. In the 1968 Time Life *Foods of the World* series volume on China, Emily Han writes, ". . . most of us have taken to tea. We each have our special ways of using it. The Chinese drink it straight without sugar, cream, or lemon; the Moslems put in mint; the British, when faced with crises, rush to make a nice strong cup of 'Indian' mixed with milk; the Irish like it so strong that—to use their own expression—'a rat couldn't sink its foot in it'; and the Australians probably brew it longer than anyone else."

Mair and Hoh, in an appendix to *The True History of Tea,* write extensively about the etymology of the word *tea*. They propose that the very word is a linguistic account of the spread of tea:

Just as the trade routes for tea may be traced, so may the paths of transmission for the various types of words for tea be tracked. Not surprisingly, the two systems—economic and linguistic—closely coincide. Of the three main

branches of the family of tea words, te, cha, and chai, the first commenced its voyage from the southeast coast of China . . . the second went overland from northern China to neighboring territories, but also by sea from Canton in the south, while the third journeyed by pack animals (camels, horses, mules, but also often humans) and carts across steppes and deserts and over mountains. To study the history of words for tea is thus what might be called an exercise in geolinguistics. In the end, goods produced and named by human beings, from start to finish, are ineluctably linked to the land. The evolution of tea usage is a prime example of the intimate interface between Homo sapiens and Mother Earth.

Tea and Health

THERE IS NO OTHER DRINK IN THE WORLD like tea. What other elixir is simultaneously relaxing and energizing? "First and foremost, tea gives you a high, a buzz," says James Norwood Pratt, author of *New Tea Lover's Treasury*. "You don't notice it, because tea is subtle. You never feel a jolt from it—it's so subtle, that you don't feel the liftoff—and you don't notice the letdown a couple hours later. At the same time, other constituents in the tea leaves are acting on the human system to calm you down."

Modern medicine has caught on relatively recently to kitchen wisdom passed down through generations. Probably the single factor that has most contributed to the growing popularity of tea is its healthful reputation. In the past decade, the number of studies examining the health benefits of tea has increased exponentially. Each study conclusively demonstrates that tea benefits heart, mind, and body in numerous ways. In an introduction to the Second International Scientific Symposium on Tea & Human Health in 1998, Richard P. Phipps, Dean's Professor of Environmental Medicine, Oncology, Pediatrics, and Microbiology & Immunology at the University of Rochester, wrote "It is fascinating to reflect that tea, the world's most widely consumed beverage next to water, began in Chinese antiquity not as a beverage but as a medicine. Several millennia later, modern scientific research is confirming that such ancient intuition has relevance to contemporary health concerns including cancer, heart disease, and antibiotic-resistant bacteria."

Of course, while healthfulness might initially prompt people to try tea, it's not necessarily enough to keep them in the tea camp. This is where taste comes in. Health can pique an interest; taste can create a devotee. The more people try tea, the more they discover that they actually like the stuff, and a new aficionado is born.

Tea as Food Around the World

CHINA

EARLY RECORDS OF CHINESE TEA CONsumption indicate it was used more as a food than a beverage. Mair and Hoh describe a third century document on tea preparation, which states that those who "wish to brew the tea first roast [the cake] until it is a reddish color, pound it into a powder, put it into a ceramic container, and cover it with boiling water. They stew scallion [spring onion], ginger, and orange peel with it." For centuries, tea has been used in China for classic dishes such as Tea Smoked Duck (page 142). In some regions, especially near the West Lake District, fresh unprocessed young tea shoots and buds were lightly wok-cooked for dishes such as Tung Ting Shrimp (page 97), and whole fish were stuffed with tea leaves before steaming.

While Shennong's existence is not entirely historical, another important figure to tea in China is. In *Ch'a Ching*, translated as *The Classic of Tea*, which was published in 780, author Lu Yu describes all aspects of tea, from farming to production to preparation to medicinal benefits. He was very precise about where water should be drawn for making tea, and he also was definitive about what tea should—or rather, should not—be prepared with. Namely, no scallions, ginger, mint, or anything other than salt.

Still, Repplier describes accounts of tea leaves being steamed and pounded into a paste, then mixed with rice, spices, milk, and salt. "The mixture must have been more like a *pot au feu* than liquid jade," she observes.

In China today, cooks are starting to use tea in contemporary dishes, as well as adding it to traditional ones. In Chinese bakeries, you can find moon cakes, bean-filled pastries served for an autumn holiday, flavored with different teas, including green and oolong.

The Chinese Hakka minority today still prepare a dish called *lei cha* ("pounded tea") that dates to the third century. A cultural legend describes the curative powers of an early version, which was often served at lunch, or for the arrival of honored guests. Lei cha consists of a soupy herb-and-tea "pesto" served over rice and sautéed vegetables, topped with nuts and sunflower or sesame seeds. The dish is also served in Malaysia by the Hakka population there, and for many it's a daily staple.

JAPAN

The Japanese have long used tea in broths and when making rice. More recently, many Japanese sweets incorporate *matcha*, a finely powdered brilliant green tea—an "instant" tea of sorts that is synonymous with *chanoyu*, the ritualistic Japanese tea ceremony. Matcha is one of the oldest styles of tea in Japan: The Japanese Buddhist priest Eisai is credited with bringing tea to Japan from China in 1191—and the tea he brought was a powdered tea.

Matcha is produced in several different grades. A culinary-grade matcha is a popular ingredient especially in many Japanese sweets. It is used to flavor and color *wagashi,* candy-like confections made from bean paste and rice powder, which resemble marzipan. It is also used in a number of other Japanese desserts, which tend to be less sweet than their American counterparts, including green tea mousse cakes and green tea ice cream.

TIBET

The standard historic tea preparation in Tibet is tea blended with salt and yak butter. Brick tea is boiled, then blended with cream—actually churned, in an instrument that looks just like a butter churn, till the mixture is smooth. Sometimes this *ja* is mixed with barley flour, called *tsamba,* and sometimes the tsamba is further steeped with pig bones, for a substantial *rera ja,* or meat tea.

The British explorer Henry Savage Landor recounts in his 1898 volume, *In the Forbidden Land: An Epic Equestrian Journey through 19th Century Tibet,* being captured by "lamas" (bandits, in this context) in Tibet. His captors were evidently looking forward to a ritual execution the next day; when he threatened to perish from starvation, they brought him tsamba and a large *raksang* of tea to ensure that he'd still be around for the execution. He partook of the feast; ultimately his life was spared and he lived to tell the tale.

MYANMAR (BURMA)

There is an old Burmese saying, "Mango is the best among fruits and laphet is the best among leaves." The leaves here are tea leaves—but not just any tea leaves. Laphet are pickled, fermented fresh tea leaves. This dish was—and is—so revered that ancient Burmese kings appointed an official to oversee the production and to serve them laphet and green tea.

Tea leaves from the interior mountains of the Northern Shan State or Namsan, and from Mogok in Mandalay, harvested after March but before the monsoon season, are considered to be the best leaves for laphet. After harvest, as in green tea production, the leaves go through a period similar to a wither period (see page 20). They are then steamed lightly until wilted, mixed with oil, and packed into urns, hollow bamboo, or a variety of different containers. Originally they were then buried for three to seven months, but in modern commercial production this is less common. The resulting fermented leaves vary from paste-like to the texture of cooked spinach with complex, pungent flavors: salt, bitterness, smoke, and tea.

Laphet is often finished into a salad, Laphet Thote (page 66), which is the national dish of Myanmar. Variations on the salad components and ratios are as numerous as variations on masala chai recipes in India, but some of the common ingredients include raw cabbage, diced tomato, fried garlic chips, toasted sesame seeds, roasted peanuts, dried shrimp, roasted or fried beans or peas, and chili peppers. When the fermented and seasoned leaf paste is combined with the chosen ingredients, the result is a complex melding of textures and flavors.

INDIA

The Singpho tribe in Assam, who are believed to have been the first to discover tea in India, as well as the Khamti (also known as Hkamti) tribe of Assam and northwest Burma (now Myanmar) have been consuming tea since the twelfth century. In 1598, the Dutch traveler Jan Huyghen van Linschoten observed that the Indians ate the leaves as a vegetable with garlic and oil, as well as boiling the leaves to make a beverage. This early example of culinary tea in India is particularly significant, since cooking with tea in India is not as old or as widespread a tradition.

Left: Modified hand plucking at Glenmorgan Estate, the Nilgiri Blue Mountains, India; *Right:* The famed Hupao Spring, or Running Tiger Spring in Hanzhou China, revered by Lu Yu in the eighth century as an ideal water source for tea preparation.

Modern Culinary Tea

TODAY, MANY MORE RESTAURANTS ARE featuring quality teas as beverage options. And as soon as a restaurant stocks quality teas, it's not surprising to find chefs recognizing their culinary potential, using them as ingredients in everything from appetizers to desserts. (In our experience, having those teas around leads to some inspired new dishes.) It is our hope that eventually the concept of cooking with tea will go mainstream—that tea, like wine or garlic or pepper, will be a pantry staple in every kitchen.

To that end, Cindy teaches seminars and classes around the country on basic concepts of how to cook with tea. There also are some noteworthy pioneers in this effort, including chefs Robert Wemischner and Joanna Pruess. Dilmah Tea, a visionary Sri Lankan tea company, is also now leading that effort in promoting cooking with tea by educating chefs. They started by creating the National Dilmah Tea Sommelier Competition, held in Colombo, Sri Lanka, in 2007. This led to an International Tea Sommelier Competition, which looked at a central piece of a tea sommelier's focus, steeping and serving fine teas, as well as creating tea cocktails and other drinks that can enhance guests' appreciation of the diverse potential of tea. From the first competition involving twenty-five hotels and restaurants, Dilmah then went on to sponsor Thé Culinaire competitions, again beginning in Sri Lanka, and an event with Australian chefs, called the Chefs and the Tea Makers.

We are grateful to Dilmah Tea for their ongoing efforts to deepen the respect and appreciation of fine teas world wide, and we are pleased to include some of the winning recipes from these competitions in this book.

As Dilmah Tea recognized, competitions are a great way to stimulate interest and creativity. In the United States, the 2009 New England Culinary Tea Competition, sponsored by the Boston Park Plaza Hotel and Towers, the Tea Board of India, the Cambridge School of Culinary Arts, Upton Tea Imports, and *TEA: A Magazine*, brought together student and alumni competitors from culinary schools throughout New England. Over one hundred entries vied for the Best Tea Cuisine Savory Dish, Best Tea Cocktail, Best Tea Cuisine Dessert, and the Best Culinary Use, any category, of Indian Tea. Some of the finalists' recipes, as well as the winning recipes, are included in this book.

Additionally, several chefs in India are making great strides now cooking with tea, and we have included some of their recipes as well.

CHAPTER 2:

TYPES OF TEA

ALL TRUE TEA IS FROM THE SAME PLANT, *Camellia sinensis.* (We use the term "true" tea to refer to tea from this plant—often herbal infusions such as chamomile or rooibos are erroneously called "tea"; see page 28.) While several teas may appear and taste quite different—a delicate white, a toasty green, an assertive black—they all start from this same plant. How and where the plants are grown, and how the leaves are treated once harvested is what turns seemingly identical leaves into vastly different products.

Both nature and nurture play a part. Geographical circumstances affecting the tea include regional location, soil type, elevation, and weather patterns. Processing factors include levels of oxidation, when and how the leaves are harvested, if and how the leaves are rolled, and the source of heat when the leaves are fired or dried. Tea production methods have in some cases been passed down virtually unchanged for centuries, while in other cases have evolved over time with new technology.

A note on our terminology: To explain the basic types of tea, we'll trace the path these versatile leaves take from the field to the kitchen. Within each basic *type* of tea, there are many *styles* of tea, often relating to a specific region. For example, black tea is a *type* of tea, while

Keemun, Darjeeling, and Ceylon we refer to as *styles* of black tea. We discuss several more common specific tea styles in chapter 3: the Flavor Profiles of Tea" (page 29).

Let's start with the plant. *Camellia sinensis* is the species that produces tea. There are two main varietals, *Camellia sinensis sinensis* (China bush, native to China) and *Camellia sinensis assamica* (Assam bush, native to the Assam region of northern India). There are a tremendous number of local cultivars developed to thrive under particular conditions, but all are essentially the same plant. In theory, any tea plant in any tea-growing region can be processed to be any type of tea. Theory aside, however, specific styles of tea are often produced in specific regions, as certain regional conditions and cultivars tend to produce superior examples of certain styles of tea. Historic preferences and regional expertise play an equally important role in linking a style of finished tea to a locale. Globalization and changing market preferences have blurred these traditional region-specific styles, however, and we continue to see more and more diversification of tea production in regions that had previously specialized in very distinct localized styles.

Now consider the climate. *Camellia sinensis* prefers

tropical or subtropical weather and grows best in a light, sandy, acidic soil with good levels of nitrogen and excellent drainage. Good humidity and temperatures around 85°F/30°C will aid growth, as will a minimum annual rainfall of 80 to 90 inches, with no lengthy drought periods. In addition to China and India, other tea-producing countries include Taiwan, Nepal, Sri Lanka, Kenya, Japan, Korea, Turkey, Indonesia, and Argentina. Small amounts of tea are even cultivated in the mainland United States (primarily in South Carolina) and Hawaii, with new plantings going in each day. These domestic farms will provide easier access to fresh tea leaves for culinary use as well as processing them for harvest. Tea plants are evergreen; depending on the growing region, there may be year-round harvests (as in Sri Lanka) or there may be several distinct harvest seasons or "flushes" during the year, each yielding harvests with different characteristics (as in Darjeeling in northern India).

In some regions, tea is still harvested completely by hand. In China and Sri Lanka, the steep and varied terrain means automated harvesting equipment is not feasible.

In areas where the fields are flat, such as Japan, the United States, and South America, harvesting is often automated. In other regions, a combination of hand-plucking and machine-harvesting is used.

After harvesting, the tea leaves are weighed, sorted, and cleaned. The leaves then go through a series of steps that determine the color and style of the finished tea.

- Withering is a resting period during which the leaves lose some of their moisture and become soft and pliable.
- Rolling is a repetitive manipulation of the tea leaf, either by hand or using other equipment that shapes the leaf as well as ruptures or bruises the cell walls.
- Oxidation refers to a chemical change that happens to the leaves once their cell walls are ruptured and exposed to the air.
- Firing is when heat is applied in one of various forms, ranging from steam to ovens, in order to remove the "green" flavor, stop or prevent oxidation, and eventually, dry the leaves.

Early Tea Cultivation

CAMELLIA SINENSIS ASSAMICA GREW WILD IN THE Assam region of northern India long before *Camellia sinensis sinensis*, or the "China bush" was transplanted there by Robert Fortune, a Scottish botanist working for the British East India Company. When early attempts at growing the China bush proved challenging, they found that the native Assamica was far better suited to the region.

Unoxidized: White Tea

WHITE TEAS ARE THE LEAST PROCESSED teas, and in certain ways remain the closest to the original fresh tea plant. Only budsets (immature leaves, shoots, or tips) are harvested to produce white tea. The budset is covered with a beautiful white down; for the top grades of white tea, it is harvested when fully developed, but before the buds have begun to open. It then goes through a very minimal wither period, basically just the time it takes to bring the leaves in from the fields, varying slightly by weather conditions. The leaves are then dried, ideally sun-dried. In the original, classical definition, white tea could be produced only from specific cultivars in certain regions of China. Increased demand had led other regions and other countries to produce white tea as well, although some purists do not consider these teas to be true white tea.

Unoxidized: Green Tea

IF THE TEA LEAVES ARE TO BE FINISHED INTO a green tea, the wither period is a little bit longer than that for white tea. This step is sometimes called "primary drying." As with white tea, green tea does not go through a bruising and oxidation stage, but is finished through additional drying and optional rolling. Depending on the region and the type of green tea being produced, this final drying can be any one or more of the following methods: air-drying, pan- or wok-firing, basket-firing, oven-drying, or steaming. Wok- or pan-firing originated in China and is considered the classic method of firing green tea leaves.

In wok-firing, tea makers place small batches of the leaves in the woks, then begin a repetitive process of pulling the leaves up the side of the wok, with either bare hands or a broom-like tool, then gently dropping them back to the bottom. For Lung Ching Dragonwell tea, the leaves are pressed into the wok and "ironed," resulting in its distinctive flat appearance. The pressure applied is considered a form of rolling, even though a rolled shape is not created. For other styles of green tea, the leaves may be literally rolled as they are manipulated in the wok. In all cases, the leaves are kept constantly moving to prevent burning.

The entire process—from plucking to finished leaves—is quite brief, measured in hours rather than days.

Minimally Oxidized: Yellow Tea

Yellow tea is produced exclusively in China in very limited quantities, and is often difficult to find in the United States—and hence very expensive. It exhibits a flavor profile that is a cross between a white and a green, without any of the grassiness associated with green teas, and its aroma is flowery, fresh, and mild. Like white tea, it is usually harvested at the bud stage, then lightly wok-fired like green tea, but not initially fired completely. It undergoes hand-rolling, and then a very slow final air-drying over the course of more than a day, during which the tea literally yellows and undergoes a slight amount of oxidation. Yellow tea is not recommended for cooking due to its very high price, limited availability, and because its special subtlety is likely to be lost.

Partially Oxidized: Oolong Tea

Oolong tea is any tea that has been partially oxidized—as little as 10 percent or as much as 90 percent. The name derives from *wulong*, the Chinese word for dragon, because the look of the rolled leaf of early oolong styles was reminiscent of the serpentine Chinese dragon. From plucking through withering, all tea leaves should be handled with the utmost care, to minimize any bruising that would initiate oxidation. For tea that is to be partially or fully oxidized, the wither period is longer. Instead of being fired to prevent oxidation, as with green tea, the leaves for oolong teas are intentionally bruised. They are typically shaken or tumbled to bruise them and bring on consistent oxidation throughout the full batch of leaves.

After bruising, the oxidation continues until the desired level for the particular oolong is achieved. The production process for oolongs is elaborate, with multiple firing and resting periods. Oolong teas are the most complex to produce of any style of tea; the tea maker must juggle an incredible set of variables in order to produce these aromatic signature teas.

STYLES *of* UNOXIDIZED *or* LIGHTLY OXIDIZED TEAS

CEYLON ADAMS
PEAK WHITE

GLENDALE HANDMADE

CHINA YIN ZHEN
WHITE POINT RESERVE

FORMOSA TUNG TING
OOLONG

JASMINE PEARL GREEN

LUNG CHING
DRAGONWELL GREEN

BING YEN ZHEN
GREEN

GENMAI CHA
GREEN

JAPANESE SENCHA
GREEN

STYLES *of* BLACK *and* AGED TEA

PARK PLAZA
AUTUMN REVERIE
BLENDED BLACK

CHINA LYCHEE
CONGOU BLACK

SHOU CHA PU-ERH
TOUCHA

KEEMUN BLACK

YUNNAN SPIRAL
TIP BLACK

15 YEAR-OLD
SHENG CHA PU-ERH

PRESSED SHOU CHA
PU-ERH

NEW VITHANAKANDE
FBOPF EX SP BLACK

ASSAM CTC BLACK

Fully Oxidized: Black Tea

TEA LEAVES THAT ARE FULLY OXIDIZED are black teas. In China, they are called red teas or *congou,* because of the color of the steeped tea or liquor (not to be confused with the herbal infusion rooibos, or redbush, which is often incorrectly labeled as "red tea"). In China (and often in tea shops located in Chinese neighborhoods in North American cities) the terms "black tea" or "dark tea" are reserved for the fermented and aged Pu-erh teas produced in Yunnan Province.

Because the withering stage for black tea production is longer and more involved than for other styles of tea, it is typically done in dedicated withering troughs or trays with good air circulation from above and below, often supplemented by ceiling fans and blowers under burlap or mesh troughs or trays. This way, air circulation speed and direction can be carefully controlled and leaf handling may include periodically fluffing or turning the leaves in the troughs.

At the end of the extensive withering period, the leaves are pliable enough to undergo more extreme handling than that for bruising oolong leaves, without excessively tearing the leaf itself. Many factors, such as the amount of moisture in the leaves, the size of the leaves, and the ambient temperature and humidity, will affect the amount of time required during wither.

At this stage, tea production can be divided into Orthodox Style or CTC (cut-tear-curl or crush-tear-curl) style. For Orthodox tea production, one of two methods is used: the traditional hand production established in China, or, more commonly, using specialized machinery designed to mimic hand production. In both cases, the goal is to maintain the integrity of the whole leaf. Rolling machines have ribbed disks that turn to simulate the repetitive movements of hand-rolling the leaf on a flat surface. There may be some leaf breakage in this rolling, but the extended withering (softening of the leaf) reduces this. Further down the production line, the leaves will be sorted and graded, allowing the full-leaf and broken-leaf teas to be sold separately.

More leaf breakage is desired for producing more assertive, full-bodied teas, and for this the CTC method is used. The same extended wither period is typical, but for CTC teas, instead of a delicate and controlled rolling of the leaf, it is run through a Rotorvane, automated equipment that results in heavily cut leaves. This increases the surface area for oxidation and later steeping, yielding a more assertive tea.

When the oxidation is essentially complete, the tea

is fired to halt any additional oxidation, caramelize residual sugars, and dry the leaves. It is then sorted and graded by leaf size and appearance (Orthodox only).

The finished teas are then packaged and sold. In most regions of the world this means supplying samples to a tea broker, who then offers those samples at wholesale tea auctions.

Packaging Tea

THERE IS SOMETHING ROMANTIC ABOUT THE traditional tea chests used to pack bulk loose-leaf teas for storage and shipping—they have gone virtually unaltered for generations. But that is now changing, for good reasons. In the name of preserving trees, many wine bottles now have synthetic stoppers, rather than true cork, and this does not reflect the quality of the wine in the bottle. Similarly, increased awareness of the need to preserve trees, and a desire for more efficient and effective packaging, has caused more and more tea producers to switch to the far less traditional, and certainly far less beautiful—but far more practical—heavy paper sack, and the tea inside can be just as good as tea packed in wooden chests and crates (see page 140).

Aged Tea: Pu-erh

AGED TEA GENERALLY REFERS TO THE unique, rich, and earthy tea from the Yunnan Province in China called Pu-erh. Pu-erh production is a complicated process that is not fully known outside of the specific producers in Yunnan, who have a financial incentive to keep this knowledge proprietary. Pu-erh is the only style of tea where true fermentation occurs.

There are two stages involved in the production of Pu-erh. The first stage is the creation of *mao cha*, or "rough tea." This stage is similar to the production of green tea: the leaves go through the steps of careful plucking, sorting, withering, wok-firing, rolling, sun-drying, secondary rolling, and sorting. The wok-firing is not done to the final dry stages (as it is with green tea) but just to remove the grassiness of the leaves, similar to the wok-firing used in yellow teas.

The finishing stage of Pu-erh production depends on the type of Pu-erh to be made. *Sheng cha*, or "raw" Pu-erh, is very slowly aged, taking at least ten years to develop depth of flavor and smoothness, and can take twenty to thirty years or more to reach peak aging. Various organic molds, such as gourds, bamboo, and even grapefruit rinds, can also be used; as the tea ages, the container imparts a unique flavor. Pu-erh is either finished in loose-leaf form, or compressed into molds to produce cakes, or *beeng cha*, often of substantial size.

The compressed forms of Pu-erh come in a wide assortment of shapes and sizes, including large, flat bricks (often with bas relief pictures or words) disks of various sizes, or small bowl-shaped individual *tou-cha,* which can offer a single portion of Pu-erh, ready to be crumbled into a cup, gaiwan, or Yixing pot (see page 48).

Fine, well-aged *sheng cha* Pu-erhs are becoming more and more difficult to find, and when they are available, they can be quite pricey. To offer a more quickly produced and affordable version of Pu-erh, a process with some similarities to composting was developed in the 1970s. Known as *Wo Dui,* this process made it possible to accelerate the aging and produce a dark, rich tea in just a few months rather than a decade or more. This accelerated version of Pu-erh is known as *shou cha* or "cooked" Pu-erh and is much more affordable than the well-aged raw Pu-erhs; you should therefore use *shou cha* in recipes calling for Pu-erh. Pu-erhs are prized for their digestive qualities as well as their complex and unique flavors and can be steeped multiple times.

Blended Teas

BLENDED TEAS ARE COMBINATIONS OF several teas that yield a flavor greater than, or at least different from, the sum of its parts. Some blends are specialized styles, such as breakfast or afternoon teas. Blends are also created by large tea companies, such as Lipton, Twinings, and Bigelow; the blending process ensures that the "house" flavor profile is consistent from year to year.

As with wines, the highlights of each tea season are a unique result of local *terroir* (soil composition, elevation, general weather, and wind patterns) the talent of the tea maker, and Mother Nature's temperament in a given year. It can be exciting to savor the results of a particularly good harvest, or noteworthy Single Estate tea; however, in the commercial world, buyers typically look for consistency. The endless variables that are beyond the control of the tea maker make it impossible to produce a tea that is exactly the same every year. In order to achieve that season-to-season, year-to-year consistency, teas from several sources are blended. It takes true talent to be able to re-blend and rebalance a signature proprietary tea regardless of the conditions of the growing season.

Teas such as PG Tips, Taylors of Harrogate Yorkshire Gold, or Lipton's Original Blend are each teas that are very carefully blended to achieve a predictable flavor. The blend may consist of teas from different regions, countries, and even different seasons, but the goal is always to maintain their unique proprietary taste offered at a consistent price.

There are also blends that are created for a specific purpose, and the flavor will vary depending on the brand. Breakfast blends are full-bodied enough to support milk and they have adequate tannins to stand up to hearty cheeses, breakfast meats, eggs, and other traditional breakfast foods. English Breakfast is the most familiar, but there's also Irish Breakfast and Scottish Breakfast. These teas most commonly consist of Assam, African teas, Indonesian teas, and sometimes Keemuns and Ceylons.

Afternoon blends are lighter and more complex than breakfast blends, unscented or lightly scented. They can often support milk as well.

Scented or Flavored Teas

BLENDING ALSO CAN BE USED TO CREATE new and different teas, often by adding non-tea components or scents. Classic examples include Chinese floral blends like jasmine, rose, chrysanthemum, and lotus, which can be made using black, and or green tea bases. Lychee fruit is another flavoring that has been used for centuries in China. In Japan, *genmai cha* includes toasted (and sometimes popped) brown rice added to green tea. Earl Grey, a popular black tea scented with oil from the citrus fruit bergamot, was developed in England in the early nineteenth century. In Morocco, tea drinkers would add fresh mint leaves to Gunpowder green tea, which led to developing a blended tea with dried mint. Indian masala tea (chai) is flavored with warm spices such as cinnamon, cardamom, and black pepper.

There are also more modern flavored teas, made by adding high-quality essential oils to highlight the natural flavors of the tea. Others simply have scented chemicals added to them to make them taste like cherries, strawberries, or chocolate truffles. In such cases, the flavor can dominate any infusion made from the leaves, rather than support the special qualities of the tea itself.

Herbal Infusions or Tisanes

TEA WITH FLORAL OR OTHER COMPONENTS added is still very much a tea. When the blend does not contain any *Camellia sinensis*, it is not truly tea, but rather an herbal infusion or tisane. A wide variety of botanicals, such as chamomile, hibiscus, rosehips, yerba mate, rooibos, and honeybush, are often erroneously called herbal "tea." While these infusions are still very valid and popular beverages, they are not true tea.

CHAPTER 3:

THE FLAVOR PROFILES OF TEAS

Pairing Tea and Food

THERE ARE TWO WAYS TO PAIR TEA WITH food: within and alongside. When cooking with tea, certain types of tea go better with different ingredients. A partner to incorporating tea *within* a dish is sipping tea *alongside* it, just like pairing wine with a meal. Although we're used to the afternoon tea concept of hot tea served with scones and sandwiches, or as an after-dinner drink, pairing tea with different dishes might seem like a new idea. But the right tea can improve any meal as a complementary partner.

There is never just one correct pairing: Tea is a flexible beverage, both forgiving and complementary. Ideally, the drink enhances the food, which enhances the drink, making the total experience more than the combination of the separate components. To devise the best pairing, take into account various factors: the season, the style of food, the occasion, and most of all, personal preferences.

When pairing tea with a dish that has been prepared with tea, there are a few different options. The tea used in the dish may be sipped alongside if its flavor in the food is subtle and would not become redundant. You can use a beverage to highlight or tease out secondary flavors, or contrast or balance against more dominant aspects; the goal is to bring something new and not have the drink get lost in the food (or vice versa) by either being overpowered or merging completely.

When you're pairing a tea with a dish that was not cooked with tea, consider the flavor profiles, aromatics, and textures of the tea and of the dish. To start with, familiarize yourself with the characteristics of the tea. A more astringent tea, such as a first flush Darjeeling, is wonderful paired with richer foods for a textural pairing. An earthier tea like a Yunnan goes well with meat or chocolate in a pairing of complementary flavors, and sweeter teas like certain oolongs may balance nicely against a salty or a spicy dish, as an example of pairing for contrast.

Another approach (also used with wines) is to pair a regional dish with a tea from that region. This is partially due to terroir equally affecting the tea and the other indigenous ingredients; if there is a strong wine- or tea-making tradition in a given region, the cuisine tends to develop in parallel. (This guideline only applies to cuisines that come from tea-producing regions.)

The final pairing decision is best made by tasting for yourself. Below, you will find information on some of the more commonly available styles of tea with recommended pairings for each, organized by type of tea (white, green, and so forth.). These guidelines are for both types of pairings, within and alongside dishes.

WHITE TEAS

THIS IS THE LEAST PROCESSED STYLE OF TEA, with a mild, subtle, natural sweetness, velvety flavor, and a rounder, fuller mouthfeel, often exhibiting delicate nuttiness or toastiness. The finest quality Yin Zhen or Silver Needle white teas are often too subtle to cook with or effectively pair with food. Open-bud styles such as Shou Mei or Mutan are less subtle but can still be challenging to cook with effectively, although we include some examples.

CULINARY PAIRINGS: The delicate flavors and subtle sweetness can go well with mildly flavored sweets, such as light shortbread or butter cake, but the finest white teas are best savored alone.

GREEN TEAS

UNOXIDIZED GREEN TEAS GENERALLY PAIR WELL with seafood and fish, but there is quite a bit of varia-tion. Green teas can be broadly characterized as brothy, nutty, earthy, briny, vegetal, or sweet, and it is important to note which of these characteristics a particular tea exhibits when choosing your pairings.

DRAGONWELL (CHINA)

Dragonwell, also called Lung Ching green tea, is originally from Hanzhou in the Zhejiang Province Lake Region; it is now produced in other regions as well, and comes in many different quality levels. The finest Lung Ching can be absolutely stunning. It exhibits a unique flat shape because it is literally ironed during wok-firing. It has a slightly sweet, vegetal aroma, a mellow, smooth, chestnut-like flavor, beautiful jade green color, and lingering sweet finish.

CULINARY PAIRINGS: Dragonwell has the astringency to pair particularly well with many cheeses, such as Brie and Camembert. It has a nutty quality that combines deliciously with a well-aged Gruyère. It also goes well with seafood, fish, fruits, and custards, and steeps well into vodka.

GENMAI CHA (JAPAN)

This sun-grown green tea (usually sencha or bancha) is combined with toasted brown rice. Sometimes powdered matcha is also added. When toasted, some of the brown rice pops, giving it the nickname "popcorn tea." It is a soothing tea. A Japanese friend once explained that it was the Japanese comfort equivalent to chicken

Facing the Dragon:

MY FIRST EXPOSURE TO MAKING TEA

I HAVE BEEN VERY FORTUNATE TO HAVE THE OPPORTUNITY TO VISIT A WIDE VARIETY OF TEA farms, tea gardens, and tea estates throughout the world. Each time is a pleasure and an honor, as well as being a tremendous learning experience. But nothing will ever match my first experience literally making tea.

It was in Hanzhou, China, on a small family-owned tea farm producing Lung Ching Dragonwell tea. A cool morning mist hovered over the fields as we harvested tea leaves. I carefully worked on maintaining the right flicking motion to pluck the leaves without bruising them, and on not picking too far down the stem as I filled my basket. By mid-day, I was soaked from the mist, but very happy—I had actually picked tea! We brought our baskets of leaves in from the fields and laid them out for a brief wither. While waiting, the farmer lit a fire outside and we huddled around it to warm up and dry off. I couldn't think of a single place on earth that I'd rather be.

Then it was time to fire the leaves. After several demos, I sat down at my wok and began to wok-fire the leaves. The gentleman who had loaned me his wok was careful to watch and correct my hand movements and assess when each batch was adequately fired—all via sign language, as he spoke no English and I didn't speak Chinese. Batch after small batch, the repetitive movements were hypnotic. I was in a joyous blur pressing the leaves up along the walls of the hot wok, then scooping them out to cool. I got up from my wok at the end of the day, and the privilege of what I had just experienced suddenly hit me: I had transformed those tea leaves from the field to the finished product. I lost it then—I actually started to cry. The farmer was quite worried, thinking that perhaps I had burned my fingers on the wok (as a chef, I had long ago deadened my nerve endings, so that was no real risk). Our translator explained to him that I was simply overwhelmed by the beauty of the experience.

As clichéd as it sounds, at that moment my life changed, and tea literally became a part of my soul. It was no longer simply a commodity that I respected and loved, but something much more: I felt a personal connection to this place and plant. It is difficult to articulate, but I have never looked at tea the same way since.

—Cindy Gold

soup: good for whatever ails you—a cold, stress, bad news. The toasted brown rice buffers the sharpness of the sencha, yielding a nutty, earthy, and relaxing tea, almost brothy. Due to the space the rice takes up in a teaspoon, scoop a bit more (a heaping teaspoon) in cooler water than might be used for other green teas.

CULINARY PAIRINGS: Pairs well with seafood, rice, chicken, and light vegetables.

GUNPOWDER (CHINA)

This rich, full, assertive green tea typically from Zhejiang Province gets its name from the appearance of the tightly rolled leaves, which resemble gunpowder pellets. It was one of the first Chinese teas to be exported out of Asia, beginning in the early seventeenth century. It is used as the base tea for Moroccan mint tea and takes very well to sweeteners. Due to the tight roll of the leaf, Gunpowder holds its freshness very well for a green tea and, like all greens, is very vulnerable to oversteeping.

CULINARY PAIRINGS: Pairs well with fish, lemon, mint, basil, and vinegar. Due to its pungency, it pairs more effectively with smoked and barbecued meats than many other green teas. Use it when you want a pungent result: in a vinaigrette or powdered for a green tea salt.

GYOKURO (JAPAN)

This fine tea is shade-grown and steamed. The striking dark green needle-like leaves steep into a sweet and delicate liquor. This tea should be steeped at a much cooler temperature, around 140°F/60°C, for about $1\frac{1}{2}$ minutes.

CULINARY PAIRINGS: With its delicate flavor, gyokuro is best enjoyed as a beverage, rather than used in cooking. It pairs well with seafood, rice, egg dishes, and raw or lightly cooked vegetables.

JASMINE (CHINA)

Jasmine is a scented tea most commonly made with green or *pouchong* teas (although you can occasionally find jasmine-scented white, oolong, and even black teas). Traditionally Chinese, this tea is now made all over the world, with a range of quality differences—from clean, sweet, and subtle to overpoweringly perfumed. The finest jasmines are scented by layering tea leaves with fresh jasmine petals, which are removed when they wilt and replaced with fresh petals up to seven times. Jasmine teas can be found in traditional leaf form, in pearls formed by tightly rolling the buds, and in flowering display teas which blossom when steeped.

CULINARY PAIRINGS: Pair jasmine tea with fresh fruits and curried dishes. Better jasmines are superb for infusing into custards and other dairy, or for steaming or curing fish. Moderate grades are good to use for smoking.

MATCHA (JAPAN)

This green tea is ground to a fine, vibrantly colored powder that can be whisked into hot water to be consumed as a frothy beverage, or used in cooking. Traditionally prepared Matcha is full bodied, starting off astringent and vegetal on the palate but with a lingering sweetness. It is typically finely ground from *tencha*, a shade-grown green tea which has first had all stems and even veins removed from the carefully harvested, steamed, and dried leaves. The finest-grade matcha is used in *chanoyu*, the Japanese tea ceremony; an affordable culinary grade, is recommended for cooking.

CULINARY PAIRINGS: Matcha works well with white chocolate, cheese, rich dairy, lightly cooked vegetables, most seafood, and with tea salts.

SENCHA (JAPAN)

The most readily available Japanese green tea is sungrown and steamed. The first spring harvest, called *ichiban-cha*, is considered the finest. Good-quality sencha offers a delicate sweetness, mild astringency, and herbaceous character. Watch the steeping time and temperature carefully as it is very prone to oversteeping.

CULINARY PAIRINGS: Sencha pairs very well with seafood, rice, egg dishes, and raw or lightly cooked vegetables. It infuses nicely into vodka or sake; adding fruits, herbs, or flower petals to the infusions can result in marvelous tea cocktails.

◯ OOLONG TEAS ◯

All oolongs make ideal food pairings, both within and alongside, as their lingering finishes will meld with and support the flavors of properly chosen accompaniments. That sweet lingering finish can serve to tame the fire of particularly hot, spicy dishes, allowing you to taste the dish more clearly and enjoy it without palate burnout.

TI KUAN YIN, ANXI-STYLE OOLONG (CHINA)

All true Ti Kuan Yin teas use the specific Ti Kuan Yin cultivar, but there are several styles of Ti Kuan Yin processing, resulting in a fascinating amount of variation within the style. All demonstrate sweet and floral aromatics. The teas can be developed as greener and more herbaceous or dark and rich, or anywhere in between.

CULINARY PAIRINGS: Ti Kuan Yin pairs especially well with pork and with spicy or smoky foods, fruits, caramel, and chocolate.

WUYI SHAN OOLONGS
(FUJIAN PROVINCE, CHINA)

The Wuyi Mountains must truly be one of the most beautiful places on earth.

The "rock oolongs" produced in this region, so called because they grow among the cliffs and crumbling rocks of the Wuyi Mountains, have distinct flavor profiles attributed to the unique climate, conditions, and mineral content offered by the mountains. There is a limited supply of these teas, but they are worth finding. Da Hong Pao ("Big Red Robe") is one of the more heavily oxidized examples. It is a legendary tea exhibiting a hint of smokiness and a warm roasted flavor that develops into a sweet, creamy, complex fruity finish. Rou Gui, another rock oolong, is more readily available than Da Hong Pao and is a touch smokier with complex fruit and cinnamon tones.

CULINARY PAIRINGS: These oolongs are ideal with pork or spiced chicken or fruity, earthy desserts, spiced tea breads, basil, and stone fruits. As with all oolongs, they work well to tame fiery dishes.

Tasting Notes

Donna Fellman, the Director of the Tea Education Alliance, teaches certification classes with the Specialty Tea Institute. During a discussion of the method of teasing out the layers of flavors and aromatics from an oolong tea using the Gong Fu method of multiple steepings, she jokingly coined the descriptive phrase, "Time-lapse Tasteography!"

POUCHONG (TAIWAN AND CHINA)

Pouchong is actually a general style, not a specific tea, and refers to very lightly oxidized teas. Technically, pouchong is an oolong, but because the oxidation is so subtle it's sometimes given its own category. It is closer to a green tea than the more heavily oxidized oolongs, and therefore is steeped at cooler temperatures, around 180°F/82°C. Superb examples of this style are produced in both China (in Fujian Province) and Taiwan. The light oxidation and complex manufacture result in a beautiful smooth, sweet, complex cup with distinct floral aromatics, a touch of earthiness, and a fruity finish.

CULINARY PAIRINGS: This tea pairs beautifully with lightly spicy or curried foods, smoked foods, shellfish, buttery desserts, and fresh fruit.

BLACK TEAS

Black, or fully oxidized, teas tend to be full-bodied and rich. In general, they stand up to meats and heartier foods because of their assertive flavor and their tannin levels. There is an unexpectedly broad range of characteristics found in different black teas, however, so it is best to consider the specific tea before pairing.

ASSAM (INDIA)

Assam, from northeast India, is valued for its pungency, rich red color, full-bodied flavor and mouth feel, and its characteristic maltiness. It is often the base of Irish Breakfast blends, and is an exceptional breakfast choice because it has good levels of caffeine and adequate tannins to pair with sausages, buttery pastries, and other traditional breakfast foods. It also makes an excellent base for a masala-style tea (chai), as it works well with a variety of spices and can hold its own with large quantities of milk. It can be found processed as a CTC for that extra body and assertiveness that is craved by those who like plenty of milk in their cuppa, or in a more complex and a bit less assertive Orthodox Style. (Recently, the Assam region has also begun to produce other styles of tea including green teas; the above description is for the flavor profile of the classic Assam teas.)

CULINARY PAIRINGS: Assam pairs very well with dark chocolate, sharp cheeses, mushrooms, smoked fish and meats, eggs, spiced desserts such as carrot cake and gingerbread, or anything with cinnamon, nutmeg, brown sugar, or caramel. It also works nicely with Mexican food and chilies. It adds a nutty depth of flavor to shortbread and pastry crusts.

CEYLON (SRI LANKA)

Ceylon is the historic name of the island of Sri Lanka, which is just off the southern tip of India. The teas from Sri Lanka are still typically called Ceylon teas. The different growing regions in Sri Lanka are differentiated largely by elevation, with what some people consider the finest teas produced at the higher elevations. Low-grown teas, produced at elevations up to 1,800 or 2,000 feet, are often used in blending, giving good strength and color with a full, thick mouthfeel. Mid-grown teas, between 2,000 and 3,500 feet (4,000 feet by some standards) are richer and complex in flavor. High-grown teas, above 3,500 (or 4,000) feet, are smoother, brighter, more delicate, and have more pronounced aromatics. Sri Lanka has many exceptional estates; some of our favorites include New Vithanakande, Kirkoswald, and Lumbini.

CULINARY PAIRINGS: Ceylons pair well with a wide variety of meats (beef, ham, lamb, chicken) and spicy foods. They are very good breakfast teas: they stand up to milk and work nicely with eggs and cured meats, while their tannin levels allow them to balance out rich, creamy foods like cream cheese or breakfast pastries. Ceylon teas also take well to both pairing and flavoring with fruits.

CONGOU (CHINA)

This is simply a general name for Chinese black (called "red" in China, see page 25) fully oxidized teas. You will often find them further differentiated as Keemun, Yunnan, etc. But there are many very nice, sometimes value-priced teas simply referred to as congou. They tend to be full-bodied and rich, sometimes sweet, and can be enjoyed with or without milk. Look to individual black styles given for more details.

DARJEELING (INDIA)

Teas from the northern Indian region of Darjeeling are

known for their complex, delicate flavors and aromas. "Single Estate" teas have long been available, when a particular estate and often a sub-harvest within that estate is too noteworthy to blend with other teas, but it is a newer trend in tea marketing to identify teas with the specific farm (also called estates and plantations) that grew them as a mark of distinction. The distinctive differences that lead to Single Estate designations are seen more often in Darjeelings than in other teas. Darjeelings make excellent teas for pairing, as they work with a wide range of foods. There are many exceptional estates in this region; some of our favorites include Arya, Castleton, Makaibari, and Namring.

First Flush: The spring harvest Darjeeling is delicate, perfumed, and relatively astringent, sometimes with a hint of muscatel. It should be enjoyed without milk as an afternoon tea.

CULINARY PAIRINGS: Pairs well with fresh fruits, especially strawberries, apples, raspberries, apricots, grapes, lemony items, and currants. Due to its astringency, it is very nice with soft cheeses, custards, and eggs. Salmon, grilled fish, polenta, and curries are also nice combinations.

Second Flush: The second flush (summer harvest) has a rounder flavor with a bit more muscatel and possibly a hint of nuttiness. It too is best enjoyed without milk and makes a lovely afternoon tea.

CULINARY PAIRINGS: Pairs well with fruit and soft cheeses. With its nuttiness and muscatel flavors, it can combine well with warmer spices like nutmeg, and with wild mushrooms, such as morels.

Autumnal Flush: The Autumnal Darjeeling is fuller still, sweeter with more pronounced muscatel, fruit, and nut flavors.

CULINARY PAIRINGS: Try this with milk chocolate, cinnamon, custards and other dairy dishes, fruits, nutty dishes, and with both softer cheeses and semi-soft cheeses like Gouda and Edam. It also goes well with sweeter vegetables such as carrots, squash, and sweet potatoes.

EARL GREY

This scented black tea has become one of the most popular and commonly available teas in the West. Although at one time there was a very specific proprietary blend, today there are as many (if not more) Earl Grey blends available as there are breakfast blends. What defines an Earl Grey is oil of bergamot, from the skin of a citrus plant with inedible fruit that resembles a tangerine. It is typically found in a medium-bodied black tea blend, but there are now bergamot-scented teas of all styles, including assertive black tea blends and green tea blends. Earl Grey blends vary by the quantity and quality of the bergamot oil used and the strength, balance, and quality of the base teas.

CULINARY PAIRINGS: Pairs well with a wide variety of baked goods, dairy, eggs, spices, bourbon, and chocolate.

KEEMUN (CHINA)

Keemun black teas from northern China can be rich and earthy, with hints of cocoa and spice, or softer, rounded, and sweet, with a distinct fruity and Burgundy-like character. They exhibit superb, rich aromatics and have a full, "thick" mouthfeel.

CULINARY PAIRINGS: The earthier top-grade Keemuns go well with vanilla, chocolate, spicy foods, cheeses, and eggs. The everyday Keemuns are wonderful for smoked tea recipes, and go well with eggs and vanilla. They both go well with breakfast foods.

KENYA (AFRICA)

Midway down the east coast of Africa, Kenya is better known for its coffee, but it also produces some lovely teas. Most commonly produced are CTC blends with a robust, full, rich, fruity, well-balanced flavor and distinctive reddish liquor. It's an excellent breakfast or afternoon tea, best when enjoyed with milk.

CULINARY PAIRINGS: Pairs well with chocolate desserts, eggs, and hamburgers.

LAPSANG SOUCHONG (CHINA)

This earthy tea is smoked with pine needles, giving it a distinctive smoky, tarry flavor that is sometimes an acquired taste. It is very well suited to cooking and will impart its characteristic smokiness into a dish—without needing to actually smoke the food.

CULINARY PAIRINGS: Pairs beautifully with savories, especially pork and lamb, and is ideal with cheese.

LYCHEE CONGOU (CHINA)

This traditional Chinese scented tea is a rounded, full-bodied black tea that has been scented with lychee fruit. It is sweet, aromatic, and floral.

CULINARY PAIRINGS: Its sweetness can work well to balance against salt or heat. Try it with a medium- to full-bodied blue cheese like a Shropshire Blue. It also works very well with smoked foods, or, because of its sweet, aromatic nature, as the tea used when smoking.

MASALA CHAI
(ORIGINALLY INDIA, NOW UBIQUITOUS)

Masala is a spice blend and *chai* literally means tea, so masala chai means spiced tea. The various spice blends seen in chai can be mixed within a variety of teas, although the most traditional base is northern Indian Assam, or a full-bodied aromatic southern Indian Nilgiri. In the United States, chai on its own has come to mean Indian masala chai. There are numerous variations. The best masala chai teas are made by slowly steeping the spices in water separately from the tea or sometimes directly in milk to unleash the fat soluble components of the spices more effectively (see our recipe for Masala Chai on page 235). Many tea makers sell their own masala chais, but you can create your own using your choice of spices.

Masala chai is typically enjoyed sweetened at the end

of a meal, or as an afternoon pick-me-up. Although much less common today, traditionally, *chai-wallas* (tea sellers) would hawk their wares to passengers on trains in India, selling their slow-simmered chai in disposable clay cups which customers would just throw out the window of the train when they finished drinking from them.

CULINARY PAIRINGS: Use it in custards and ice creams. Try with bread pudding or French toast, a wide variety of baked goods, or infused rum. It also goes well with grains such as rice and oatmeal, and with chocolate.

NILGIRI (INDIA)

This beautiful region in southwest India produces bright, flavorful, and aromatic teas, which can be enjoyed with or without milk. They are excellent choices for iced teas as they hold their clarity when chilled better than many other teas. Black teas are the classic Nilgiris, but more recently they have produced some mid-level oxidation oolongs as well. These have the bright flavors of their black cousins but with even higher levels of aromatics and a nice dose of fruitiness.

CULINARY PAIRINGS: Nilgiri pairs well with vanilla, mushrooms, beef, chocolate, and raw vegetables. The oolong Nilgiri is also very nice with fruits, nuts, and milk chocolate.

SIKKIM (INDIA)

This lovely tea is in short supply because it is grown on just one estate—Temi Estate—in this small Indian state just north of Darjeeling. It is a wonderful tea similar to a high-end second flush Darjeeling but with less of a flowery nature and more fruitiness and body. It is best enjoyed without milk and makes a lovely afternoon tea. This tea can be used interchangeably with a Darjeeling.

CULINARY PAIRINGS: It goes well with fruity baked goods, delicate shortbread, fresh fruit, vanilla, ginger, lemon, smoked fish, and eggs.

YUNNAN (CHINA)

Yunnan is known for its superb aged Pu-erh (see below) but it also produces some excellent black teas as well. Yunnan black teas exhibit golden buds and steep up full-bodied, creamy, and aromatic, with a hint of pepper and spice.

CULINARY PAIRINGS: Yunnan blacks pair well with turkey, lamb, and beef, and are terrific in chili. They also go very well with chocolate. Try it in tea breads with cinnamon, nutmeg, or pepper.

PU-ERH (YUNNAN, CHINA)

This earthy aged tea from the Yunnan Province (sometimes nicknamed "dirt tea") is not to everyone's palate, but it is worth acquiring a taste. It is one of our favorite culinary teas, because of the earthy richness it imparts to a dish, especially meats and poultry.

The slow-aged or "raw" sheng cha Pu-erh can take

twenty to thirty years to come into its peak, and is consequently scarce and expensive. More recently, shou cha, an artificially aged or "cooked" (sometimes also called "ripe") Pu-erh has been developed as a substitute. This cooked style of Pu-erh is more readily available and wonderful for everyday drinking, or to use in cooking. A well-aged raw Pu-erh should be saved for special occasions and savored on its own. Its aroma often reminds us of freshly tilled soil, or moist leaves on a forest floor. A guest once said of a particular Pu-erh that we shared with her that it smelled just like the inside of an Etruscan tomb. (We've never been in an Etruscan tomb, but that poetic description will always stick with us.) Traditionally, it would be served after a meal as a digestive. It makes a non-traditional but very nice breakfast tea as well, especially with rich breakfast foods.

CULINARY PAIRINGS: Pair Pu-erh with wild mushrooms or chocolate. It is an excellent accompaniment to Chinese dim sum, and it also pairs well with most meats, poultry, and with soy sauce. A well-aged Pu-erh is the ideal way to end a very rich or heavy meal or pair against virtually any high fat or greasy dish.

Nineteenth century photographs from the Kandy tea growing region in Sri Lanka

Home Blending

CREATING HOME BLENDS OF TEA IS ANOTHER aspect of culinary tea. You can combine a variety of teas, as well as non-tea ingredients such as spices, flowers, herbs, and dried fruits to create personal signature tea blends that you can use both for sipping and for cooking. Familiarize yourself with the ingredients you plan to use and decide what kind of flavor profile you want to create. This can be the fun part—and it's a good way to get to know teas to use for cooking as well, as you sip and savor different teas and get to know their characteristics.

Steep a wide variety of different teas and taste them. Ask yourself what you particularly like—or dislike—about that tea. Take notes. Do you want to create something full-bodied and rich? Light and bright? Medium-bodied? Is your goal a spiced blend, a floral blend, or a fruity blend?

Keep in mind that really special teas should probably be savored on their own. But don't make the mistake of trying to cover up an inferior tea with heavy flavors. Blending is used to create new experiences in teas, or a consistent flavor profile of a tea that changes with the seasons or growing years.

Refer to the list of Flavor Profiles of Tea for teas that might inspire your own blending. Some common teas to use for blending:

DARJEELINGS: Offer brightness and complexity. Vary by flush; can be delicate and floral, nutty, or have hints of muscatel. Nice in an afternoon blend. Takes floral notes well when used sparingly.

LAPSANG SOUCHONG: Has smokiness; good for a relaxing evening tea or smaller amounts blended into a breakfast or afternoon tea.

YUNNAN: For richness, body, earthiness. Smooth and complex with a peppery tone.

KEEMUN: Rich, full-bodied, well-rounded character; fruity and sweet, sometimes earthy as well. Some smokiness.

ASSAM: For bold character, strong flavor, with a touch of maltiness. Good with milk and takes well to the addition of spices.

CEYLON: For briskness and body. Varies by region and elevation. Takes very well to fruit.

AFRICAN: Rich, robust, flavorful, and brisk, sometimes sweet. Good with milk.

CHINESE CONGOU: Smooth, full-bodied, blends well with fruit or floral notes.

You can also use an almost endless variety of non-tea components. For example:

SPICES (WHOLE, CRACKED, OR GROUND): Cinnamon sticks, cardamom pods, allspice berries, cloves, coriander seeds, peppercorns

DRIED OR FRESH FLOWER PETALS: Lavender, rose petals, chrysanthemum, chamomile, hibiscus, elderflower, jasmine

WELL-DRIED FRUITS: Raisins, cranberries, blueberries, cherries, apples, pears

DRIED CITRUS PEEL: Lemon, orange, lime, grapefruit

MISCELLANEOUS: Cocoa nibs, vanilla beans, dried herbs

How do you determine how much of each tea to use? Experiment and taste, but as you get started, keep these general guidelines in mind:

- Remember that each blend will be steeped at one temperature for the same length of time, so all the components have to add something positive to the blend at the same temperature and time. This can make it challenging to blend, say, a black and a green together, but not always; tasting is the final deciding factor.
- Try to use ingredients that are similar in size and weight. This will ensure that each scoop of tea has well-balanced flavors.
- Avoid adding moisture, which can cause mold. If you want to blend in bits of dried fruit, make sure that they are very well dried, or use freeze-dried fruit.
- Use only food-grade ingredients. This includes dried flowers and aromatic or essential oils. When in doubt, read packaging carefully and ask the vendor.

Say you are considering creating your own rich full-bodied breakfast blend, and you've chosen Keemun for roundness and body with a touch of sweetness, Assam for additional body and strength and a hint of maltiness, and a Kenyan tea for added rich sweetness and briskness. You can blend varying amounts of each leaf and test steep, or you can consider a first quick pass look by steeping up a pot of each (at identical time and temperatures) and then blending the steeped liquid in varying quantities in your cup to find your favorite ratio. Then, following the chosen ratios, blend a small quantity of the dry leaves and do another steep and taste test.

After the base is determined, think about how to add the secondary ingredients, or non-tea components. For instance, if a hint of vanilla is desired, consider mixing in finely chopped vanilla bean. The time-honored way of introducing a floral scent is to layer the leaves with fresh flower petals as they slowly release their volatile oils, then remove the petals, replacing them with a fresh set if further scenting is desired. You can easily follow that approach at home. Lay out a thin layer of your chosen tea or teas, sprinkle a layer of fresh petals and then cover with a thin layer of additional tea. When the petals start to discolor, remove and replace them. If you plan to leave the petals in the tea, use fully dried petals to avoid introducing any moisture.

When blending in small quantities, there is no shame in taking short cuts! If, for instance, you want a touch of jasmine scent in your blend, you don't necessarily need to find fresh food-grade jasmine petals—just blend in a quantity of your favorite jasmine tea. If you want a hint of smoke, blend in Lapsang Souchong. You can blend with scented or blended teas just as easily as with straight unblended teas. All that matters is that it is a fun and creative experience and that you are happy with the end result.

Left: Chai walla making tea at the Coonoor train station, Tamil Nadu, India;
Right: Tasting room in the award winning Delmar Estate, Sri Lanka

CHAPTER 4:

STEEPING & KEEPING TEA

How to Properly Steep Tea

LOOSE-LEAF TEAS CAN PRODUCE WONDER-ful, aromatic, complex infusions. But how you brew tea matters. Tea for drinking consists of four basic components: water, tea leaves, temperature, and time. While you can easily steep an acceptable cuppa, why not steep an extraordinary one, with a little attention to detail? You'll be surprised by the difference that temperature, for example, can make. Try an experiment: Pour boiling water on green tea, then try a cup with barely steaming water. Green tea often has a reputation for being dull, muddy, and bitter, when in reality a green tea should be clean and lightly sweet. Boiling water burns the leaves, dulling the flavor, and oversteeping it makes it bitter. When teas steep at their optimum temperature, for the length of time best suited to that tea, the results are well worth the attention.

∽ WATER ☙

SINCE STEEPED TEA IS MOSTLY WATER, WATER quality will have a distinct effect on its flavor. Teas are very sensitive to water tastes and mineral content. If your tap water has a chlorinated, chemical, or off-taste, use bottled water (avoid distilled water, which gives tea a flat taste) or use a good-quality home water filter, such as a Brita, for your tap water.

Always start with freshly drawn water. Water that has been sitting in your teakettle, especially if it has previously been boiled, should not be used again for making tea. When water has boiled for too long or multiple times, it becomes de-oxygenated. Using de-oxygenated water can result in flat-tasting tea (similar to the flat taste that would result from using distilled water).

Bring fresh water into play when working with a water heating and holding system such as a water tower or for water pulled off of coffee-making equipment. Drain some water through the system to avoid water that has sat too long in the boiler or holding tank.

WATER TEMPERATURE

CORRECT WATER TEMPERATURE IS CRITICAL TO steeping a good pot of tea. Each type of tea needs a different temperature for best results. For a black tea, fully boiling water (about 212°F/100°C) is ideal. For a more delicate green or white tea, cooler water is preferable, water that is steaming rather than boiling, around 175°F/180°C. While an instant-read thermometer is useful, the eye test works fine (see chart, below).

Water that is too hot can produce a muddy tasting green tea. Some very delicate Japanese green teas do best at water as cool as 145°F/63°C. Partially oxidized oolongs and pouchongs, which are between blacks and greens in oxidation levels, require water temperatures that are also in between. Because there's such a range in oxidation levels, the optimal steeping temperature can range as well, with the most lightly oxidized pouchongs responding like green teas, and requiring cooler water. A light- to medium-oxidized oolong should use slightly hotter water, around 185°F/85°C, and a medium- to heavily oxidized oolong does best with lightly boiling water, around 190°F to 195°F/90°C.

The following table indicates the optimal steeping temperatures, with visual cues, for different types of teas, as well as steeping times.

TEA TYPE	WATER APPEARANCE	WATER TEMPERATURE	STEEP TIME
Black and *shou cha* Pu-erh*	Full, rolling boil (fully bubbling)	212°F	4 minutes +
Delicate Black (ie. Darjeeling)	Full, rolling boil (fully bubbling)	212°F	2 to 3 minutes
Oolong	Light boil (light bubbling action)	185°F to 195°F	2 to 3 minutes
Pouchong	Steaming to light boil (light steam, tiny bubbles)	180°F to 185°F	3 minutes
Green	Steaming or cooler (light steam, no hint of bubbles)	145°F to 175°F (usually 175°F)	1½ to 3 minutes
Yellow	Steaming or cooler (light steam, no hint of bubbles)	175°F	1½ to 3 minutes
White	Steaming or cooler (light steam, no hint of bubbles)	175°F	1½ to 3 minutes

*Steeping times/temperatures may vary depending on the age of the Pu-erh for a *sheng cha*.

MAINTAINING TEMPERATURE

Not only is it important to start with the correct temperature water, it is best to maintain that proper temperature throughout the steeping process. To begin with, rinse and preheat the teapot by pouring some boiling or steaming water into it, letting it sit a few moments, then pouring it out. Depending on how cool the pot was to begin with, and how thick its walls are, the amount of time it will take to warm will vary.

When the pot is warm, measure in the correct amount of tea, add the correct temperature water and begin timing. If the teapot has thin, delicate walls (like glass) that were quick to warm up, then it will be quick to cool as well. Place the teapot on a hot pad, potholder, or folded towel to insulate it. For thick-walled teapots (like terra-cotta) this is not necessary.

When the tea has steeped close to the recommended time, taste it; if it tastes ready, strain the tea (or remove the infuser, ball, or bag) into pre-warmed mugs, cups, or a serving teapot. To help maintain the heat in a serving teapot for an extended time, keep it on a hot pad, covered with a tea cozy (they really do work!) or on a base with a tealight candle; the gentle heat will help keep the tea warm.

You can use a little trick to help tea stay warmer longer. Steep the tea with about one-third less water than needed. After the correct time has gone by, add that last third of freshly heated water. This will boost the temperature, and give you time to enjoy the whole pot.

TEA QUANTITY

You've got a nice selection of loose-leaf teas, ready for brewing, and the water is heating up. But what's the ideal water-to-tea ratio?

The general rule for typical European-style steeping is one slightly heaped measuring teaspoon of tea per $3/4$ cup water. (Standard instructions say 1 cup, but the "cup" referred to is based on a teacup; one teacup's worth of water is about 6 ounces, or $3/4$ cup.) However, 1 teaspoon is given as an equivalent to a weight designation (around 1.75 grams) so the size of the tea leaf is going to have a significant effect on the volume of tea you use. If the leaf is a very small leaf or is broken into fine pieces, it will pack more densely into the teaspoon and will take less than a heaped teaspoon to equal 1.75 grams. If the tea is a particularly large-leaf style (such as a large-leaf white tea) it will not pack into the teaspoon well, and will require more than a slightly heaped teaspoon to equal 1.75 grams. Consult this chart for brewing individual cups of tea.

TEA LEAF SHAPE	TEA TO USE PER $3/4$ CUP WATER
Oversized (bold) style leaf	1 tablespoon
Tightly rolled leaf	1 scant teaspoon
Medium leaf	1 teaspoon
CTC, broken or fine leaf	1 scant teaspoon

STEEPING TIMES

THERE ARE GENERAL RULES THAT CAN BE FOL- lowed, but these rules can vary according to the specific style of tea, the way it is steeped, and individual taste. A more tightly rolled leaf will take longer to steep, and in general, the smaller the leaf size (more exposed surface area) the shorter the steep time. The best way to prepare tea is to steep it loose in a pot or measuring cup, then strain it into a separate warmed pot for serving. If you prefer not to steep loose, use a pot with a built-in infuser, a tea sack (a make-your-own tea bag) or an infuser ball (less desirable). The better the water flow, the better the resulting tea. If the tea is constrained in a tea infuser, this will slow down the steeping process. Keep this in mind when timing the tea. If an infuser ball is overfilled (halfway full is the maximum) and the tea

can't expand freely in the water, the result may be weaker tea. The times listed in the table on page 44 are based on steeping tea loose in a pot.

The final deciding factor is personal taste. Start tasting the tea a little earlier than the full steeping time, and continue until it is to your liking. This is not simply a question of strength. Under-steeped teas can be bland and lack complexity, and oversteeped teas can be bitter. With some teas it may be possible to taste more of the subtle notes at a shorter steep time; this is often the case with Darjeelings. Sometimes catching the tea at just the right time can take practice. Some green teas can go from crisp, complex perfection to bitterness in 15 seconds.

HOW TO BOIL (OR STEAM) WATER

A STOVETOP KETTLE—OR EVEN A POT—IS ALL YOU really need to prepare water for tea. To heat water to anything other than a full boil (212°F/100°C), you can either stop the water on its way up towards boiling, bring the water to a boil and let it cool to the correct temperature, or bring the water to a boil and actively cool it by adding a small amount of room temperature water. But we are big fans of electric kettles. There are models, such as the dispensing hot pot made by Zojirushi, which may be set to various standard temperatures for steeping tea, from 145°F/63°C for very high-end delicate green teas to 212°F/100°C for fully oxidized teas.

Steeping Culinary Tea

W E'VE DISCUSSED STEEPING TEA TO enjoy as a beverage. What about when you are steeping tea for use in a recipe? In water-steeped tea recipes, typically the only difference is the ratio of leaf to water; in certain cases the temperature and timing can be altered. The basic concept is still the same. Within the recipes we typically call for steeping tea leaves in a bowl, but you can of course still use your favorite teapot. Using a Pyrex measuring cup is often a good way to check quantities and begin steeping at the same time. Just be sure that you follow the guidelines in the recipe for tea quantities and that your water is of good quality and freshly drawn (not previously boiled). If using an open bowl or measuring cup, cover it with a plate while the tea steeps to avoid excessive heat loss.

TEAPOTS

THERE ARE ENDLESS TEAPOTS AND VARIATIONS ON tea steeping equipment on the market today. Teapots are made of ceramic, glass, and metal, as well as many other non-standard materials, and each has its pros and cons.

Consider your needs in choosing the best one for you:

• Which types of teas will you be making?

• Will you steep the teas loose in a pot or in an infuser or bag?

• How much tea will you be making at a time?

• Will the tea be served from the pot directly, or transferred to another vessel?

• Are you adding to a collection of pots? Will this be an everyday teapot or a special occasion teapot?

• Is all the tea to be served from the pot immediately, or will you be lingering over the pot, slowly consuming it cup by cup?

CLASSIC GLAZED TERRA-COTTA TEAPOTS

The classic six-cup English teapot, such as the Brown Betty, is always a good choice. It makes enough for two generous mugs of tea, or six dainty teacups worth. Its round shape allows the tea leaves to swirl around in the pot when the hot water is poured over. The Brown Betty has been made the same way for generations by the same English company using the same clay. The glaze on the teapot is based on a manganese brown glaze developed by the Marquis of Rockingham on his estate in England in the late 1700s. This Rockingham brown glaze and the Betty shape were eventually shortened to the affectionate term "Brown Betty" which is used today. The teapot was made for the general public as a very utilitarian piece for daily use. It needed to be durable and cheap and so was made from a good terracotta clay which would hold the heat nicely.

If you want more color choice than the traditional brown, there are many companies offering similarly well-made pots. The teapots from the English company Chatsford are very solid, based on a classic English style, and come in a variety of sizes, from a two-cup pot on up. They have the added convenience of a wide and deep built-in infuser basket which enables the leaves to be exposed for maximum water flow. Made of a very fine nonreactive mesh, the infuser basket can be used with any size tea leaf without becoming clogged or allowing leaves to escape. It nests neatly into the pot and has a handle that makes it easy to remove, even when the tea is hot.

The Chatsford infuser basket is an ideal model; if buying an infuser separately, look for similar characteristics. Infusers should always be made of non-reactive materials that can be easily and thoroughly cleaned.

These ceramic pots take well to a tea cozy, if you are pouring and drinking from it gradually.

YIXING AND POROUS CLAY TEAPOTS

Porous teapots are unglazed ceramic teapots. Because they are unglazed, they absorb the flavors of tea over time, and therefore are best dedicated to brewing only one style of tea. They're particularly nice for brewing earthy Pu-erh and aromatic and complex oolong teas.

The most notable example of a porous teapot is the Chinese Yixing (pronounced *yee-shing*) clay teapot, which comes in all shapes, colors, and sizes, the most common of which is small and reddish brown. Since they are fired at lower temperatures than porcelain teapots, Yixing teapots have the ability to withstand sudden extreme temperature changes.

What is so special about these pots is how the clay reacts to the tea over time; the pots season and develop, similar to a cast-iron skillet. The flavors will continue to develop with use, and provided there is no change of teas (which would muddy the taste) the resulting steep will continue to be finer and more complex over time.

You should pre-season the pot by steeping your tea of choice and discarding the tea, ideally several times. When curing a new Yixing pot, these steeps should be considerably longer than when you're brewing tea for drinking. After using, rinse with warm water and invert the pot to dry. Don't use soap, and don't even use a towel to dry it. It is said that with a well-aged Yixing teapot so much flavor is released from the walls that you can periodically steep a pot of tea without adding any tea!

GAIWANS

In China, during the Ming Dynasty (1368—1644 C.E.), the *gaiwan,* or covered bowl, was introduced. This is the successor to the *chawan* (tea bowl) preferred by Lu Yu. These charming little vessels are elegant and practical and are still in use throughout much of China today. Although gaiwan literally translates to "lidded bowl," it actually consists of three parts: the cup (or bowl) in which the tea is steeped; a lid which is used to stir, cover, and strain the tea; and a dish to catch drips and to insulate so that the bowl may be handled when hot. To use a gaiwan, pour hot water into the bowl to warm it, then pour out the water. Place the loose-leaf tea in the bowl, then pour in the correct temperature water for that tea. You can use the edge of the lid to stir the leaves, then place it on the bowl where it fits snug inside to keep the heat in while steeping. When the tea is ready, use the lid to hold back the leaves while decanting the tea into tasting cups, or while drinking directly from the gaiwan. The leaves remain in the bowl, and can be resteeped as desired.

> ### Gong Fu Steeping
>
> Both Yixing pots and Gaiwans are traditionally used for the repetitive short steeps of the Gong Fu Chinese Tea Ceremony. In Gong Fu steeping, a higher ratio of tea leaves to water are used than in European style steeping, and a series of short steeps allow you to tease the complex layers of flavors and aromatics from a well-made oolong tea.

THIN-WALLED TEAPOTS (GLASS AND PORCELAIN)

Thin-walled, delicate pots are lovely to use, but do not hold heat well. A solution is to use the two-pot method of steeping: Steep the tea in a thick-walled workhorse pot that will hold the heat well, and then strain the tea into the more delicate pot for serving. Alternatively, many porcelain and glass teapots come with a base that holds a tealight candle underneath the pot to maintain heat. This flame is small enough not to scorch the tea, but offers enough heat to delay the rapid cooling of the tea that can happen with thin-walled teapots. Glass teapots are aesthetically pleasing in that they enable you to enjoy the color of the tea;

they are also crucial to enjoying the beauty of blooming display teas, which include closed flower buds that opens as the tea steeps.

TEA BAGS

TRADITIONALLY, THERE HAVE BEEN TWO PROBLEMS with tea bags: they often contained low-quality tea, and the design of the bag itself did not allow for optimal water flow and expansion of the tea leaves. The flat tea bag was invented in 1908, and tea bags remained virtually unchanged for almost a century. But a few years ago, alternate styles, such as the larger pyramid-shaped tea bags were introduced. This new generation of tea bags are made of higher quality materials, are engineered to allow for better water flow, and are being filled with better and better teas. They are roomy enough to contain whole-leaf teas, with room for the leaves to more fully unfurl as they steep.

An alternative is to make your own tea bags. Disposable tea bags, such as those sold under the label T-Sac, can be filled with your tea of choice. Keep in mind that it's just as easy to use a reusable tea infuser basket. Since room for unfettered leaf expansion and good water flow are so important for steeping tea, consider purchasing and using a larger-size disposable tea bag than the man-

ufacturer recommends. For instance, if the manufacturer offers 1-cup, 6-cup, and 12-cup sizes, use the 6-cup for steeping even a single cup or mug of tea and use the 12-cup size to steep a 6-cup pot of tea. If steeping for an oversized pot, divide the leaves between several of the largest bags available. These disposable filter bags are especially useful when making test infusions for tea cocktails (see page 231).

OTHER INFUSING OPTIONS

DESIGNED FOR MAKING A SINGLE MUG OF TEA, THE Utilitea pot from Adagio Teas is an example of the new breed of modern convenience. It is made of heat-resistant plastic and shaped like a lidded mug, with a fine-mesh strainer at the bottom. After the leaves steep, you place the Utilitea pot atop your cup or mug; the lip of the mug will release a catch at the base of the pot, allowing the tea to stream into the mug.

Other companies offer a wide range of products designed for convenience and style. There are many variations on coffee presses as well. In fact, a good coffee press that is clean of any coffee residue will work very well for brewing tea.

Buying and Storing Tea

FRESHNESS IS CRUCIAL FOR VIRTUALLY ALL teas, except for aged teas such as Pu-erh. While it's tempting to collect a cabinet full of different varieties, tea will go stale. It's better to purchase small quantities that will be consumed relatively quickly.

The ideal way to purchase tea is in person, where you can see the leaves, smell them, and possibly even taste the infusion. When looking at the leaves, look for clean, glossy, even-sized leaves without twigs or stray particles. The tea should not look dusty, crushed, or powdery. When steeped, the infusion should be clear, never muddy looking. The aroma and taste should be fresh. The specifics of the taste and aroma will vary by the style of tea, but dull, musty, or strong off flavors or aromas should be a red flag of improper handling. If the freshness or quality of the teas is questionable, purchase from another source.

Realistically, few of us live near a perfect tea source, and many teas are available only to certain vendors. The Internet has made mail-order purchasing of tea easier and more reliable. Most good online vendors offer sample sizes for purchase—a good way to experiment with new styles. Better vendors have pictures of what the teas should look like; you can compare your purchase to those pictures. Once you find vendors with the desired quality, price, and selection, you can purchase larger quantities.

When storing teas, be sure to keep them away from air, light, moisture, and heat. This means you should *not* store teas in that cabinet above the stove that is so convenient to the kettle! The variability of temperature within that cabinet will shorten the lifespan of the tea considerably. Tea should be stored in airtight and moisture-proof containers. Clear containers should be stored inside a dark cupboard. Never put a damp teaspoon back into the container to scoop more tea!

Historically, tea caddies had locks on them, but these days we're more worried about moisture and air than theft.

While you may not be collecting tea, you may still want to have a few different varieties available at a given time—it's good to have a selection of blacks, greens, oolongs, scented teas, and Pu-erhs, both for sipping and for supping. If you do buy larger quantities of tea, transfer a smaller amount to the container you'll be using every day, so that the bulk of the tea is not exposed to air on a regular basis. Ideally, well-stored tea should be used within six months of purchasing.

PART II:
TECHNIQUES OF COOKING WITH TEA

SINCE WE STARTED USING CULINARY TEA IN OUR KITCHENS, JUST ABOUT EVERY TIME WE DEVELOP a new recipe, we consider whether tea would enhance it. Incorporating tea into food doesn't mean that food should taste like tea— often there's no easily identifiable tea flavor from the tea used—but the tea adds an extra element that helps bring out the best a dish has to offer.

There are several different ways you can cook with tea. Specific methods can yield different results, and we offer recipes that exemplify the different techniques we've employed.

Cooking with Water-Steeped Tea

ONE OF THE EASIEST WAYS TO USE TEA IN COOKING IS TO MAKE A CUP OF TEA—HEAT WATER TO THE optimum temperature for the type of tea, steep the leaves, strain, and use the resulting tea in your recipe. Often, in order to obtain the maximum flavor, the tea may need to be steeped at higher concentrations than would be typical for straight sipping. By higher concentrations, we mean the tea-to-water ratio, *not* the steeping time; an increased steeping time in water yields tea that is bitter, rather than more concentrated.

Often, the steeped tea needs to be fully cooled before you can use it—for instance, to add to a marinade for raw meat. It is best to let tea cool gradually, but in a pinch, there are a number of ways to rush-cool your infusion, although this is not ideal (rush-cooling can subtly affect the flavor, clarity, and aromatics of certain teas). You can make the infusion with a reduced amount of hot water, then add cold water or ice cubes once the tea is strained, as a way to quick-cool the tea. Be sure to use fresh ice that has not picked up odors from the freezer. Alternatively, you can make a regular infusion and put the ice into a resealable plastic bag or other container, and then immerse that in the infusion, or you can place the tea infusion in an ice bath to speed up cooling.

Another approach is to steep the tea in cooler water (room temperature or chilled) whether for cooking or drinking. This takes advance planning, as the tea needs to steep for several hours or overnight, but can give a very smooth, clean, crystal clear, slightly sweeter infusion. This is sometimes referred to as the "refrigerator method" and can be particularly nice when the steeped tea is the base of a subtle recipe where the tea is dominant. This method is especially good for infusions used for sorbets or granitas, or if there will be extensive cooking afterward with the infused tea.

Using Tea in Everyday Cooking

Try using a strong tea infusion to deglaze pans instead of wine, or to thin down a soup or sauce instead of additional stock. Tea can be the liquid you use when cooking couscous, rice, or other grains.

Poaching and Braising with Tea

WATER-STEEPED TEA IS ONE OF THE most common techniques we use when cooking with tea; poaching and braising are subsets of this method of culinary tea. Braising and poaching are both classified as "wet" cooking techniques, as water-based liquids are used to cook the ingredients. In braising, the item to be cooked—usually meat—is typically seared in fat, then slowly simmered in a flavorful liquid which tenderizes and flavors the meat as it cooks. At the end of the braising, the cooking liquid can then be reduced into a sauce. The base liquid is traditionally stock, but using part or all tea brings the flavor and aromatics of the chosen tea into the food. With poaching, the meat or other food is not usually seared first. The food is similarly simmered in a liquid, but usually it is a more delicate item that requires a shorter period of cooking time.

When braising or poaching with tea, the tea you use can either be highly concentrated or relatively standard. For a brief poach, you can even leave the tea leaves in the poaching liquid, as in the Lapsang Souchong Scallops Ceviche (page 94). For a slow braise, such as the Tea-Rubbed Short Ribs with Smoky Barbecue Sauce (page 152), it's best to steep and fully strain the tea before using, ideally in cooler water and at a lower concentration, to avoid overdevelopment of the tannins during the extended cooking. This is less necessary if the tea being used is not prone to oversteeping, such as Pu-erh tea.

For poaching or braising, in general use green tea or light oolongs for fruit, fish, seafood, or chicken. Use darker oolongs for pork or chicken, and black or Pu-erh tea for pork, chicken, beef, or lamb.

When choosing the best tea for your recipe, pay

attention to the secondary ingredients—sometimes they are more important than the protein element. For example, for the Slow-Cooked Chinese Pork (page 160), we chose Pu-erh to support the earthiness of the Chinese black mushrooms and to meld with the richness of the soy, molasses, and star anise.

The chosen tea infusion may also be used as a marinade to develop the flavors more slowly, as in the Clay-Cooked Asian Chicken (page 135). If the tea is used as a supplemental liquid, and not the main braising liquid, the infused concentration should be high.

Cooking with Tea Steeped in Other Liquids

WHEN A RECIPE INCLUDES LIQUID AS one of its components, you don't always want to dilute it with more liquid, such as water-steeped tea. In such cases, you can steep the tea leaves directly in the cooking liquid. This works well with dairy products, especially those higher in fat, such as whole milk or cream. Milk or cream used in ice cream, custard, ganache, or cream soup holds the flavor of tea very well. Typically, a recipe will call for adding tea leaves to scalded milk or cream and steeping until the desired strength is achieved. This technique works well with most styles of tea except for the most subtle.

The steeping time for heated dairy products is often much longer than when steeping in hot water, because the dairy buffers the tannin development that can make tea bitter when oversteeped in water. The tea can steep in cream for as long as 30 to 90 minutes or more if desired; the best way to determine when the infusion is ready is by tasting it. Similarly, you can infuse tea leaves into melted butter, and then use as is, or chilled to firm up again to be used in a recipe in solid form. You can infuse tea into heated oil as well, as with the Silver Tip Tea Oil used to garnish the Beef Tenderloin with Ceylon Tea Béarnaise (page 148). The lower the moisture content of the oil or fat, the longer it will take to infuse; some infusions are best steeped overnight. Similarly, the higher the viscosity of the liquid, the longer the infusion time.

Vinegars absorb the flavors of tea very well, and are usually heated before steeping. You can bring your chosen vinegar to a boil, remove it from the heat, and add the tea leaves. Let cool to room temperature and then strain. Consider keeping a variety of tea-infused vinegars on hand for quick vinaigrettes, finishing sauces, deglazing pans, etc. We offer several recipes, as well as suggested tea-and-vinegar combinations, such as Darjeeling Tea Vinaigrette (page 75). When complementing the teas with spices and herbs, you will typically add the spices with the tea, right off the boil. Fresh herbs should be added later, once the vinegar has cooled.

Cold-steeping is necessary when infusing a liquid that will be damaged by heat. Alcohol and fruit juices, for example, shouldn't be heated, as they will lose some of their characteristics (such as the alcohol!). You should steep tea in these liquids at room temperature, or even chilled, to prevent any damage to the flavor, aromatics, or alcohol content (see chapter 8: Tea Beverages, page 230). Tea-infused alcohols are not just for drinking—try a tea-steeped wine in a béarnaise sauce, or brush a tea-infused rum between layers of cake. We offer specific timing guidelines in each recipe, but for playing with different teas and different liquids, steeping to taste is often the best approach.

Straight Tea: Adding the Tea Leaves Directly

THIS TECHNIQUE REFERS TO ANY RECIPE in which the processed tea leaf itself, whole or in part, remains in the final cooked dish. Adding tea leaves directly is a technique to use when the addition of extra liquids won't work with the recipe. Cookies, for example, rarely have much liquid added to them; in order to obtain the desired tea flavor, adding straight tea may be the best approach. Straight tea adds not only flavor, but also texture, as in the Assam Shortbread Diamonds (page 186). Further textures, aromas,

and flavors develop when the leaves are baked.

Often you'll need to crumble, chop, or grind the tea leaves before adding them. Some recipes, such as Breakfast Tea Scones (page 196) and Oolong Mayonnaise (page 77), call for the leaves to be steeped first, then chopped. But most call for coarsely or finely ground dry tea leaves. Japanese matcha is green tea ground to a fine powder, and there are some companies starting to offer other teas in a powdered form as well, but most teas you will need to grind yourself to use in recipes. To grind tea, you can use a mortar and pestle, spice or coffee grinder, or blender. There is also a terrific Japanese dedicated tea grinder (see Sources, page 280) that can grind tea to a fine powder. Keep in mind that if tea is used in a recipe in a ground form, it will require more loose tea leaves by volume to produce. The exact change in size will depend on the leaf size and shape before grinding, but in general, 1 tablespoon of loose-leaf tea will yield 2 teaspoons of standard ground tea. If the tea leaves are to be ground all the way down to a powder, it will take more.

When grinding teas, make sure that the grinding equipment is completely clean and dry before adding the leaves. Remaining particles of a strong spice or coffee could overwhelm a delicate tea.

Another use for straight tea is in tea rubs, such as the Eleven-Spice Tea Rub (page 83). Dry rubs can be a wonderful initial flavoring for meats, left to develop overnight and then cooked, as in the Tea and Spice

Rubbed Pork Tenderloin with Mango Chutney (page 163). They can also be used immediately, when coating and then searing meats or seafood, as in the Seared Tuna with Tea-and-Peppercorn Crust (page 129).

Curing or Brining with Tea

BOTH CURING AND BRINING INVOLVE SALT. Historically, salt was used purely as preservation; today we have the luxury of using these techniques to add variation and flavor complexity to our foods, as well as to retain or eliminate moisture. Curing is a dry method, defined as preserving a food by salting; for brining or pickling, the salt is dissolved in water or in water plus an acid such as vinegar.

Benefits of Tea-Brining

Teas can be added to the cure or brine mix giving variability to the flavors and aromatics. Green and oolong teas impart sweetness and complexity, while black teas add richness and depth.

For curing, tea leaves are simply mixed in or layered with the salt, as in the Jasmine Tea-Cured Gravlax (page 93). For brining, tea leaves can be added directly to the brining liquid, or used to make a concentrated steeped tea. Tea brines are an especially good way to prep pork or poultry for smoking or grilling; they keep the meat moist during cooking and add flavor and richness, as in the Grilled Tea-Brined Pork Chops with Onions (page 167). With the addition of tea to brines, the ratio of salt to water may be reduced slightly. When brining or marinating meat or seafood using water-steeped tea, it is crucial to cool the infusion completely before adding the meats to prevent them from cooking or being pushed into the temperature danger zone.

Smoking with Tea

SMOKING IS AN ANCIENT FOOD PRESERVATION technique, but today we use it more for the unique flavor it imparts. There are two styles of smoking: hot and cold. With a hot-smoke process, the food is cooked by heat at the same time it is permeated with smoke, as with smoked ribs. With a cold-smoke process, the heat is kept to a minimum while the smoke permeates the food, preserving and flavoring it, but not cooking it, such as with traditional smoked salmon or smoked cheese. Either way, the wood used in the smoking imparts its own unique flavor to the food.

Smoking with tea leaves is not that different from imparting flavor with wood smoke. Tea leaves can be the main medium for producing the smoke, or you can use a combination of wood and tea leaves blended with un-cooked rice to buffer the heat. Other secondary flavor components (whole spices, nut shells, sugar) may be blended with the tea leaves to add more complexity to the smoke and the resulting flavor.

Larger-leaf aromatic teas work particularly well for smoking. We like smoking with Keemun, Yunnan, Nilgiri, lychee, and jasmine. There are several different approaches to smoking with tea leaves. You can use a commercial smoker, following the manufacturer's instructions for using wood chips. Similarly, if an outdoor grill comes with a smoker box, follow those instructions. In this book, we use three approaches to smoking: traditional, packet, and direct. An alternative to the wok method described in recipes such as Keemun Smoked Quail (page 147) and Tea Smoked Salt (page 81) is to use a hotel or roasting pan stretched over two burners. You should split the rice mixture and place it in the pan over each burner. A perforated pan over this makes an ideal rack for the items to be smoked, then foil and a sheet pan completes the "smoker."

Cooking with Fresh Tea

IT WAS ON A SMALL TEA FARM IN HANZHOU, China, where Cindy first tasted dishes made with tender, fresh tea leaves lightly wok-cooked or tossed in raw, and it has been her personal quest to see fresh tea leaves available in America ever since. Transportation is an issue. Most of the regions where tea is grown are not set up to handle the packing, refrigeration, and rapid shipment requirements needed to treat tea leaves as a fresh herb rather than a dried, processed product. There are a few options for growing tea in the United States, notably in Hawaii. There are also some West Coast chefs growing tea plants themselves. Things are beginning to progress on this front however, so the handful of sources for mail-order fresh tea leaves (see Sources, page 277) will continue to grow with demand. Eventually, we expect that fresh tea leaves will be easily available seasonally, wherever you buy fresh herbs.

Fresh tea offers different culinary possibilities than the processed leaf, with a subtly sweet, complex tang. The aromatics when fresh leaves are first cooked are incredible, as in the Salmon en Papillote with Fresh Tea Leaves (page 119).

The tender young buds and leaves are best suited for most recipes. They can be tossed into salads, lightly sautéed, steamed, blanched, or prepared using other techniques calling for minimal cooking. Older, larger leaves tend to be too tough and bitter for most uses, although they can undergo more extensive cooking, such as blanching and candying (similar to citrus peel) or blanching and then deep-frying, as with tempura. They also look beautiful as a garnish to a dish that contains tea. We include a few fresh tea recipes, with alternate suggestions using loose-leaf tea leaves.

Sides, Sauces, & Condiments

MATCHA SALT ...79

TEA-SMOKED SALT ...81

EARL GREY DRIED CHERRY MUSTARD ...82

ELEVEN-SPICE TEA RUB ...83

LYCHEE TEA SPICE RUB ...84

DARJEELING BEURRE BLANC ...85

SMOKY TEA-SPICED PECANS ...86

DARJEELING ROASTED SWEET POTATOES ...87

BALSAMIC AND TEA CARAMELIZED ONIONS ...88

TOASTED PEPPER SALT ...92

Appetizers

TEMPURA-FRIED FRESH TEA LEAVES ...89

TEA-MARBLED EGGS ...91

JASMINE TEA-CURED GRAVLAX ...93

LAPSANG SOUCHONG SCALLOPS CEVICHE ...94

SHRIMP IN LEMON-TEA ASPIC WITH BASIL-TEA JELLY ...95

TUNG TING SHRIMP ...97

FRESH SPRING ROLLS ...98

TEA-GRILLED WINGS WITH HOT GREEN DIPPING SAUCE ...100

JASMINE DUMPLINGS ...103

MEXICAN BLACK BEAN SOUP

SMOKY LAPSANG SOUCHONG ENHANCES THE SUBTLE FLAVOR OF BLACK BEANS. THIS MEATLESS SOUP *is healthy, delicious, hearty, and satisfying. Meat eaters can add chunks of Tea-Smoked Chicken Breast (page 137), Clay-Cooked Pu-erh Marinated Chicken (page 135), or Tea-Brined Pork (page 164), if you happen to have leftovers on hand. Warm tortillas on the side and a green salad make it a meal. Serving Tea-Smoked Salt (page 81) on the side is also a nice touch.*

Serves 6

1 pound/455 grams dried black beans, rinsed

12 cups/2.8 liters water, divided

2 medium yellow onions, divided

8 garlic cloves, divided

½ teaspoon dried marjoram, plus more for garnish

½ teaspoon dried oregano

¼ cup/10 grams loose-leaf Lapsang Souchong tea leaves

2 tablespoons olive oil

4 tomatoes, peeled, seeded, and chopped in ¼-inch pieces

½ teaspoon fine sea salt or Tea-Smoked Salt (see page 81), or more to taste

Crumbled fresh goat cheese (optional) for garnish

1 jalapeño, membranes and seeds removed and thinly sliced (optional) for garnish

Place the beans in a large pot and cover with at least 4 inches of tap water. Soak at least 6 hours or overnight.

Drain and rinse the beans, return them to the pot, and add 9 cups/2.1 liters of the water. Cut 1 of the onions in half and add both halves, along with 5 of the garlic cloves, marjoram, and oregano. Bring to a boil and immediately reduce to a simmer. Partially cover and let simmer until the beans are tender, 2½ to 3 hours. Add more water during cooking if the water level gets low.

Bring the remaining 3 cups/720 milliliters of water to a boil. Put the tea leaves in a medium bowl or measuring cup; pour boiling water over the tea leaves and steep, covered, for 6 minutes. Strain, discarding the leaves.

When the beans are tender, remove from heat. Transfer half the beans, along with the cooked onion and garlic, to a blender or food processor. Add the steeped tea and purée, in batches if necessary. Return the puréed mixture to the remaining cooked beans.

In a large skillet, heat the oil. Chop the remaining onion and mince the remaining 3 garlic cloves and add to the skillet, along with the tomatoes. Sauté for 5 minutes, until the onion begins to soften. Add to the soup mixture and season with salt to taste. Stir to distribute the seasonings.

Serve warm, garnished with crumbled goat cheese, a few thin slices of jalapeño, if using, and a sprinkle of marjoram.

GENMAI CHA VEGETABLE SOUP

CHEF LAURIE BELL, OWNER OF GREAT FALLS TEA GARDEN IN GREAT FALLS, VIRGINIA, LIKES TO USE *brewed tea as a base for soup. She calls it the perfect answer for vegetarians looking for a tasty but meat-free stock. Bell loves this as a simple vegetarian soup, but also "soups" it up with added rice or pasta and beans to turn it into a filling, complete meal. You can also add cooked shrimp, chicken, beef, or pork.*

Serves 4

3 tablespoons loose-leaf genmai cha tea leaves

6 cups/1.4 liters steaming water (about 175°F/80°C)

8 ounces/225 grams mushrooms, cleaned and sliced

1¼ cups/225 grams fresh or frozen corn kernels

1 (5- to 7-ounce/140- to 200-gram) bag baby spinach

1 to 2 tablespoons soy sauce

1 to 2 teaspoons rice or cider vinegar

⅛ teaspoon freshly ground black pepper, preferably Szechuan

Salt to taste

Put the tea leaves in a large bowl; pour the steaming water over the tea leaves and steep, covered, for 2½ minutes. Strain the tea into a large stockpot. Reserve the leaves.

Heat the tea over medium heat and add the mushrooms, corn, and spinach. Add 1 tablespoon of the soy sauce and 1 teaspoon of the vinegar; taste and add more if needed. Taste and add salt if needed. Ladle into bowls. If desired, top each serving with a pinch of the steeped tea leaves. Serve hot.

❧ JASMINE TEA CHICKEN SOUP ❧

ROSALIND CHAN CREATED THIS ELEGANT RENDERING OF CHICKEN SOUP WHILE SHE WAS A STUDENT *at the Bunker Hill Community College Culinary Arts program in Boston, Massachusetts. Her serving presentation of the vegetables, floated on a crisp, browned rice raft, is as original as her use of fragrant jasmine tea.*

Enoki mushrooms are elegant thin tiny white mushrooms with long stems. If you can't find them, use finely diced white button mushrooms.

Serves 4

¼ cup/30 grams finely diced carrots

¼ cup/30 grams fresh or frozen green peas or thinly sliced snow pea pods

2 tablespoons finely diced celery

1 cup/240 milliliters water

1 ounce enoki mushroom stems trimmed to 1 inch from the head

8 ounces/225 grams cooked chicken breast, diced (about 2 cups)

Salt to taste

Freshly ground white pepper to taste

4 cups/960 milliliters chicken stock

2 tablespoons loose-leaf jasmine tea leaves

1 cup/215 grams cooked short-grain rice

1 tablespoon vegetable oil

In a small saucepan, combine the carrots, peas, and celery. Add the water and bring to a boil over high heat. Lower heat to maintain a simmer and cook until vegetables are tender, about 20 minutes. Drain.

Heat the chicken stock in a medium saucepan until just steaming. Put the tea leaves in a medium bowl; pour over the chicken stock and steep, covered, for 2 minutes. Strain, discarding the leaves and returning the stock to the pan. Keep warm over low heat.

Take ¼ cup of rice at a time and squeeze to form 4 patties, each about 2 inches/5 centimeters in diameter. Heat the oil in a large nonstick skillet over medium-high heat. When the oil is hot, add the 4 patties and sear on both sides until golden brown. Remove and drain on a paper towel.

To serve, divide the hot stock among 4 bowls. Divide the chicken and the enoki mushrooms among the 4 bowls. Top each bowl with a rice patty, and divide the vegetable mix and place on top of each rice patty. Serve immediately.

LAPSANG SOUCHONG TEA and PARSNIP SOUP

MATTHEW J. MAUE, CHEF DE CUISINE AT TASTINGS WINE BAR & BISTRO IN FOXBORO, MASSACHUSETTS, *is a fan of tea, and has long been incorporating culinary tea into his menus. He says, "A good tea is like a good stock or broth. It can add that extra element to a recipe. I was inspired by how the subtle smokiness of the tea marries well with the sweetness of spring-dug parsnips, as well as the slight bitterness of the cocoa nibs." This delicious puréed soup will warm you right up on a chilly day.*

Serves 4

- 2 cups/480 milliliters boiling water (about 212°F/100°C)
- 2½ teaspoons loose-leaf Lapsang Souchong tea leaves
- 1 tablespoon extra-virgin olive oil
- 1 pound/455 grams parsnips, peeled and chopped
- 3 cups/720 milliliters chicken stock
- ⅛ teaspoon ground allspice
- ½ cup/120 milliliters cup heavy whipping cream
- ½ teaspoon fine sea salt, or more to taste
- ⅛ teaspoon white pepper
- 1 teaspoon cacao nibs for garnish (optional)

Put the tea leaves in a medium bowl; pour the boiling water over the tea leaves and steep, covered, for 4 minutes. Strain tea and discard the leaves.

Heat the oil in a large pot over medium-high heat. Add the parsnips, and cook for about 5 minutes. Add the tea, stock, and allspice and bring to a boil. Reduce the heat and simmer. Cook until the parsnips are cooked through, about 15 to 20 minutes.

Remove the soup from the heat and stir in the cream. Season with salt and pepper.

Purée the soup in a blender or food processor (or use an immersion blender) until completely smooth.

To serve, divide soup among 4 bowls. Garnish each bowl with ¼ teaspoon cacao nibs, if desired. Serve hot.

NOTE: Cacao nibs are crushed bits of roasted cocoa beans. They can be found in natural food stores and online, and add a subtle, bitter-chocolate flavor and crunch that goes well with the smoky tea.

JASMINE WATERMELON GAZPACHO *with* CRAB

THIS RECIPE WAS CREATED BY CHEF ROBERT BEAN WHEN HE WAS THE EXECUTIVE CHEF OF TODD
English's Bonfire Steakhouse in Boston. A more complex version was served at the restaurant, but the flavors were so lovely that we asked him to create a simplified variation for home cooks. This is the result: a light and refreshing starter, perfect for a summer evening. The crabmeat here is almost a garnish, and can be omitted if you prefer a vegetarian dish. The jalapeño adds an appealing heat balanced by the sweetness of the watermelon. Add more or less jalapeño, depending on how much heat you like.

Serves 8

2 tablespoons loose-leaf jasmine tea leaves

3 cups steaming water (about 175°F/80°C)

1 small watermelon peeled, seeded, and chopped, about 4 to 5 cups

1 red onion, coarsely chopped

1 garlic clove

1 or 2 jalapeños, deveined and seeded, quartered

¼ cup/10 grams chopped fresh mint leaves

¼ cup/10 grams chopped fresh cilantro leaves

¼ cup/10 grams chopped fresh basil leaves

½ cup/70 grams lump crab meat

4 teaspoons extra-virgin olive oil

Put the tea leaves in a medium bowl; pour the steaming water over the tea leaves and steep, covered, for 2 minutes. Strain the tea, discarding the leaves.

In a blender or food processor, combine the watermelon, onion, garlic, jalapeño, mint, cilantro, and basil. Blend on high until thoroughly puréed. Transfer to an airtight container and stir in the jasmine tea. Refrigerate at least 6 hours or overnight, to allow the flavors to meld.

To serve, divide the chilled soup among 8 bowls. Top each bowl with 1 tablespoon crabmeat and drizzle with ½ teaspoon olive oil.

NOTE: The soup needs to chill several hours or overnight, so plan accordingly.

LAPHET THOTE
(Burmese Tea Salad)

THIS TEA SALAD IS AN EXAMPLE OF CLASSIC, HISTORIC CULINARY TEA. EACH BITE IS A BALANCE OF *sour, bitter, salty, and sweet that is positively addictive.* Laphet *refers to fresh tea leaves that have been pickled or fermented. In Myanmar (formerly Burma)* laphet *is used as a spread, often with cabbage slices, but is most commonly finished into a salad,* laphet thote. *It is a special Burmese dish served as a snack at formal gatherings as well as social get-togethers. Special thanks to Oomay Tan for introducing us to her family's version of this classic.*

The dish is often presented as a composed salad; diners help themselves to the ingredients to mix together on their own plate. Additional ingredients include assorted fried beans, fresh sprouts, and diced green tomatoes.

Serves 6

⅓ cup/15 grams loose-leaf green tea leaves, such as Dragonwell

½ cup/120 milliliters steaming water (about 175°F/80°C)

6 tablespoons/90 milliliters peanut oil, divided

7 garlic cloves, divided

1 fresh Thai chile, seeded and finely diced, divided

1 lime, cut in half

1 teaspoon fish sauce, such as nam pla, or more to taste (optional)

Matcha Salt (page 79) or fine sea salt to taste

2 tablespoons dried shrimp

⅛ head cabbage, thinly sliced

1 medium tomato, seeded and diced (optional)

2 tablespoons roasted, salted peanuts, coarsely chopped

1 tablespoon toasted sesame seeds

To make the "pickled" tea leaves: Put the tea leaves in a small bowl; pour the steaming water over the leaves. After 15 seconds, pour off any unabsorbed water, pressing out as much water as you can from the tea leaves. This is just to soften the leaves, not to steep them.

In a medium skillet, heat ¼ cup/60 milliliters of the peanut oil until hot but not uncomfortable to the touch. Pour over the softened tea leaves. Knead the oil into the leaves and set aside at room temperature until the leaves are very soft, at least 1 hour, but depending on the size and freshness of the green tea leaves, this may take substantially longer. You can leave the leaves to soften in the oil overnight.

When the leaves are sufficiently softened, drain off and discard any excess oil, but do not squeeze oil from the mixture. Mince 1 of the garlic cloves and add it to the tea with half of the diced Thai chile. Squeeze over the juice from half of the lime, add the fish sauce (if using), and sprinkle with salt to taste. Stir and set aside. The resulting seasoned tea leaves will take on a paste-like texture. They can be stored in a airtight container, refrigerated, for several weeks; stir well before using.

Heat the remaining 2 tablespoons oil in the skillet over medium-high heat. Thinly slice the remaining 6 garlic cloves and add to the oil. Fry the sliced garlic until it turns golden, 1 to 2 minutes. Remove and drain on a paper towel.

To serve, place the prepared tea leaves in the center of a serving platter. Place the fried garlic in a small mound next to it, and do the same with the dried shrimp, cabbage, diced tomatoes (if using), and peanuts. Cut the remaining lime half into wedges and place on the platter. Sprinkle the toasted sesame seeds and remaining chili pepper over the platter. Alternatively, the ingredients may be tossed together. Serve at room temperature or chilled.

NOTES: Finding laphet in the United States can be challenging but is well worth it. Some Asian markets carry it, it's sometimes available online, and if there's a Burmese restaurant in your neighborhood, you might be able to bargain with the owners. We've offered a technique to create a similar flavor using standard dried green tea leaves. Dried shrimp are sold at Asian markets.

Left: Glenmorgan Tea Estate in India; *Right:* Bruised tea leaves in Fujian Province prepared to begin oxidation for oolong tea.

FRESH TEA LEAF SALAD *with* GREEN TEA-ROASTED PEACHES *and* BLUE CHEESE

FRESH TEA LEAVES ARE JUST BEING INTRODUCED IN THE UNITED STATES. IF YOU CAN FIND THEM, *they add a complex, lightly bitter, sharp-yet-sweet touch to various dishes. The fresh tea leaves are not cooked in this recipe, so make the salad with the smallest tender leaves and buds. (Larger or older leaves are best when cooked or used as garnish.) If unavailable, make the salad with an extra cup of mixed greens.*

We like Great Hill Blue Cheese, an artisan cheese made in New England with raw milk and aged several months, but any good, well-developed blue cheese will balance nicely with the sweetness of the fruit and the sharpness of the vinaigrette.

Serves 4

2 teaspoons loose-leaf green tea leaves, such as Gunpowder

1 cup/240 milliliters steaming water (about 175°F/80°C)

2 peaches, halved and pitted

2 tablespoons (packed) light brown sugar

6 cups/90 grams mixed baby salad greens

1 cup/30 grams tender new fresh tea leaves and buds

½ cup/120 milliliters Fresh Tea Vinaigrette (page 76) or the green tea variation of the Darjeeling Tea Vinaigrette (page 75)

4 ounces/115 grams blue cheese

8 thin baguette slices, lightly toasted

Preheat the oven to 400°F/200°C/gas 6. Have a small roasting pan ready.

Put the dry green tea leaves in a small bowl; pour the steaming water over them and steep, covered, for 3 minutes. Strain the tea, discarding the leaves.

In a medium bowl, toss the peach halves with the brown sugar and 1 to 2 tablespoons of the steeped tea. Place the peaches cut-side up in the roasting pan and pour the remaining tea around them. Roast until the peaches are tender and beginning to gain a caramelized color, about 15 minutes. Remove the peaches from the oven and cool in the pan on a cooling rack. When the peaches are cool enough to handle, slip off the skins and discard.

In a large bowl, toss together the baby greens, fresh tea leaves, and vinaigrette. Divide the greens among four plates. Thinly slice each peach half and fan the slices on top of the greens or present them uncut. Cut the blue cheese into wedges and place a wedge and 2 toasted baguette slices on each plate. Serve immediately.

GREEN TEA-POACHED CHICKEN SALAD

POACHING CHICKEN IN TEA CAN GIVE IT NEW DIMENSIONS OF FLAVOR; DIFFERENT TEAS PRODUCE *different flavor profiles. This salad uses lighter ingredients and rice vinegar, which complement green tea. A richer chicken salad would work well with black tea or a heavily oxidized oolong. If the dressing is fruity or sweet, then a Ceylon, light to medium oolong, or Darjeeling can work very nicely. A version of this recipe originally appeared in Hannaford Supermarkets'* fresh *magazine.*

Serves 8

3½ quarts/3.4 liters water

½ cup/20 grams loose-leaf green tea leaves, such as Dragonwell

8 (4-ounce/115 grams) boneless skinless chicken breasts

1 tablespoon olive oil

1½ teaspoons toasted sesame oil

1 medium red onion, chopped medium-fine

2 ribs celery, chopped medium-fine

⅓ cup/75 milliliters rice vinegar

⅔ cup/165 milliliters mayonnaise, preferably homemade

1 tablespoon finely chopped fresh tarragon, or more to taste

1 tablespoon finely chopped fresh sage, or more to taste

Salt to taste

Freshly ground black pepper to taste

Salad greens or sliced baguette, for serving

Bring the water to a simmer in a large pot over medium-high heat. Lower the heat so that the water is just barely simmering and add the tea leaves. Add the chicken and continue to adjust the temperature to barely simmering (if the tea mixture gets too hot the chicken will be tough). Cook until the chicken is just cooked through, about 10 to 15 minutes, depending on the size of the chicken breasts. Remove the chicken when just done. Strain the tea leaves from the liquid and reserve about 2 tablespoons of the leaves. Discard the liquid and finely chop reserved leaves. Set the chicken aside to cool completely. The breasts may be poached and refrigerated up to 2 days in advance.

While the chicken cools, heat the olive and sesame oils in a medium skillet, over medium heat. Add the onion and celery and sauté until they just begin to soften. Remove from the heat, draining any extra oil, and cool completely.

In a large bowl, whisk together the vinegar, mayonnaise, tarragon, and sage.

When the chicken is completely cool, chop or shred it. Add the chicken to the dressing in the bowl, along with the cooled onions and celery and 1 tablespoon of the reserved steeped tea leaves. Season with salt and pepper to taste, and add additional steeped tea leaves, if desired.

Serve mounded over salad greens, or use as a filling for open-faced tea sandwiches.

VARIATIONS

CHICKEN SALAD WITH PARSLEY AND CHIVES: Replace the tarragon and sage with 2 tablespoons chopped fresh Italian parsley and 1 tablespoon chopped chives. If using in a sandwich, top with thinly sliced pears and a sprig of watercress.

BLACK TEA-POACHED CHICKEN SALAD: Replace the green tea with Darjeeling or other black tea and red wine or malt vinegar for the rice vinegar.

⌒ CURRIED GREEN TEA EGG SALAD *with* LAVENDER ⌒

MATCHA IS A HIGH-QUALITY JAPANESE GREEN TEA THAT HAS BEEN GROUND TO A VERY FINE POWDER. *It is easy to use, and goes very well with eggs. Egg salad is a classic filling for afternoon tea sandwiches, but this can also be served in full-sized sandwiches, or on a bed of greens. Make sure the lavender you use is food-grade, and not one sold for potpourri.*

Makes 12 tea sandwiches

8 eggs

⅓ cup/75 milliliters mayonnaise

¼ cup/60 milliliters sour cream or crème fraîche

2 teaspoons dried lavender

1 teaspoon Dijon mustard

½ teaspoon curry powder

½ teaspoon matcha green tea powder, or more to taste

1 scallion, finely chopped

⅛ teaspoon fine sea salt, or more to taste

⅛ teaspoon freshly ground black pepper, or more to taste

1 cup/15 grams mixed baby salad greens, for serving

12 thin baguette slices, for serving

Place the eggs in a large saucepan and cover with cold water. Bring to a boil over high heat. Turn off the heat, cover the pot, and let sit for 14 minutes. Drain and run cold water over the eggs until water stays cold. Let the eggs sit in the cold water while you prepare the dressing.

In a large bowl, whisk together the mayonnaise and sour cream until smooth. Add the lavender, dijon mustard, curry powder, matcha, scallion, salt, and pepper. Stir until blended. Drain the eggs, peel, and chop coarsely. Add the chopped eggs to the dressing and stir until combined. Taste and adjust seasonings as desired. The egg salad may be made 1 day in advance and stored, refrigerated, in an airtight container. Use chilled.

To make tea sandwiches, place a few leaves of baby greens on each baguette slice. Divide egg salad among the 12 slices and serve immediately. For a nice contrast in textures, brush the baguette slices with olive oil and toast briefly right before using. Garnishes could include a slice of olive or pimento with a couple fresh chive sprigs.

WILD RICE and CHICKEN SALAD

THIS IS NICE TO MAKE FOR A CROWD, AND THE RECIPE CAN BE EASILY DOUBLED. THAI CHILI SAUCE *and Chinese chili-garlic sauce are available at Asian markets and at many grocery stores. If you can find only one, double the quantity; if you can't find either, substitute chopped fresh garlic and your favorite hot sauce.*

Serves 6

6 quarts/5.7 liters water, divided

½ cup/20 grams full-bodied loose-leaf black tea, such as Assam, Chinese congou, or Keemun, divided

4 teaspoons fine sea salt, or more to taste, divided

1½ cups/315 grams wild rice

1 cup/215 grams long grain white rice

4 (4 ounces/115 grams) boneless, skinless chicken breasts

1 tablespoon Asian chili sauce, such as Sriracha, or more to taste

1 tablespoon Chinese chili-garlic sauce, or more to taste

½ cup/120 milliliters rice vinegar

½ cup/120 milliliters olive oil

Freshly ground black pepper to taste

1 medium white onion, chopped

1 bunch chives, chopped (about ⅔ cup/10 grams)

⅓ cup/5 grams coarsely chopped fresh basil leaves, plus additional for garnish (if desired)

7 ounces/200 grams baby greens, optional, for serving

Bring 3 cups/720 milliliters of the water to a boil in a large saucepan and add 5 tablespoons of the tea leaves. Add the chicken and lower the heat to maintain a gentle simmer until just cooked through, about 10 to 15 minutes, depending on the size of the chicken breasts. Remove chicken when just done. Strain the tea leaves from the liquid, reserving the leaves. Discard the liquid. Set the chicken aside to cool completely, then dice or shred it. Finely chop the reserved tea leaves and set aside.

Bring 1 gallon/4 liters of the water to a boil in a large pot over high heat. Add 1 tablespoon of the salt and the wild rice. Cook for 10 minutes uncovered, then drain in a sieve, discarding the salted water.

Heat the remaining 5 cups/1.2 liters water to lightly steaming (about 175°F/80°C) and pour over the remaining 3 tablespoons of tea in a medium bowl. Steep, covered, for 4 minutes. (You steep the black tea in cooler water here because there is extensive cooking to follow; this reduces the chance of the liquid becoming bitter.) Strain and pour the tea into the pot used for the wild rice. Discard the leaves. Bring the tea to a boil and add the drained wild rice; cover tightly. Reduce the heat to low and simmer for 10 minutes. After 10 minutes, add the white rice. Stir, cover, and simmer for 20 more minutes until tea is absorbed.

In a large bowl, whisk together the chili sauces, vinegar, olive oil, remaining 1 teaspoon salt, pepper, onion, and chives. Add the chopped or shredded chicken and the warm rice mixture, stir in the basil and adjust the seasonings, adding some of the reserved chopped tea leaves to taste. Serve hot, room temperature, or cold. If desired, for a beautiful presentation, place greens on a platter, top with salad, and garnish with additional chopped basil.

Variations

WILD RICE AND SHRIMP SALAD: Substitute 1 pound/455 grams of shrimp for the chicken. Poach the shrimp in the tea for 3 minutes or until just cooked through and opaque. (Timing will vary by size of the shrimp.)

WILD RICE AND BEAN SALAD: For a vegetarian version, substitute 2 (15-ounce/425-gram) cans chickpeas and 1 (15-ounce/425-gram) can red kidney beans for the chicken. Drain and rinse the beans, then heat in the hot tea until warmed through.

⟳ GREEN TEA-LEMON BASIL DRESSING ⟲

THIS DEEP GREEN DRESSING IS A DELICIOUS BLEND OF BRIGHT FLAVORS: GREEN TEA, FRESH BASIL, *tangy lemon zest and chili sauce. We like the clean flavor of Sriracha; for an earthier flavor that goes well with seafood, try a smokier chili sauce. This dressing works well on a green salad, as a dip for raw vegetables, or as a cold sauce for poached salmon, shrimp, or other seafood.*

Makes 2½ cups/600 milliliters

1 cup steaming water (about 175°F/80°C)

1 tablespoon loose-leaf green tea leaves

1 tablespoon grated lemon zest

2 tablespoons fresh lemon juice

¼ cup/60 milliliters olive oil

1 tablespoon Asian chili sauce, such as Sriracha

1 cup/15 grams chopped fresh basil

4 garlic cloves, chopped

¼ teaspoon fine sea salt, or more to taste

¼ teaspoon freshly ground black pepper, or more to taste

½ teaspoon honey, or more to taste

Pour steaming water over the tea leaves in a small bowl. Steep, covered, for 2 minutes, then strain, discarding the leaves. Let cool to room temperature, about 15 to 20 minutes.

In a blender or food processor, combine the tea with the remaining ingredients; purée until smooth. Store in an airtight container, refrigerated, for up to 1 week. If dressing separates, whisk or blend again briefly.

SESAME-GINGER GARLIC DRESSING

TOASTING TEA LEAVES IN OIL BRINGS OUT A DIFFERENT FLAVOR; THEY ALSO CRISP UP NICELY. THIS
dressing for green salads or salads with seafood also works very nicely as a dipping sauce for Jasmine Dumplings (page 103).

Makes 2 cups / 480 milliliters

½ cup/120 milliliters steaming water
   (about 175°F/80°C)

2 tablespoons plus 1 teaspoon
   loose-leaf green tea, divided

2 tablespoons sesame seeds

¾ cup/180 milliliters canola oil, divided

6 garlic cloves, finely chopped

2 tablespoons finely chopped fresh ginger

½ cup/120 milliliters soy sauce

½ cup/120 milliliters rice vinegar

3 tablespoons toasted sesame oil

2 scallions, finely chopped

In a small bowl, pour the steaming water over 1 teaspoon of the tea. Steep, covered, for 2 minutes, then strain, discarding the leaves. Set aside to cool to room temperature, 15 to 20 minutes.

Heat a large, nonstick skillet over medium heat. Add the sesame seeds and heat, shaking the pan, until toasted, about 3 to 5 minutes. Watch carefully—the sesame seeds can go from barely toasted to burnt very quickly. Transfer seeds to a small bowl or plate.

Return skillet to heat and heat 1 tablespoon of the canola oil over medium-high heat. Add the remaining 2 tablespoons of tea leaves and toast the tea leaves in the oil until crisp and very fragrant, about 1 to 2 minutes. Remove to paper towels to drain any excess oil.

Combine the steeped tea with the garlic, ginger, soy sauce, and vinegar. Pour in the remaining canola oil and sesame oil, whisking constantly. Add the scallions, toasted sesame seeds, and the fried tea leaves with a last whisk or two to distribute evenly. This dressing is best the day it's made, but it may be stored, refrigerated, in an airtight container for up to 5 days.

DARJEELING TEA VINAIGRETTE

THIS VINAIGRETTE IS NICE WITH A SALAD FEATURING FRUIT, SUCH AS PEARS OR FRESH FIGS, AND *blue cheese on baby greens. You can easily customize it to harmonize with other flavors—see the variations. Garlic adds a pleasing sharpness, but if you want a milder salad, omit it and use shallot only.*

Makes 1½ cups/ 360 milliliters

½ cup/120 milliliters rice vinegar

1 teaspoon loose-leaf Darjeeling tea leaves

2 teaspoons honey

1 teaspoon minced shallot

1 garlic clove, chopped (optional)

1 tablespoon chopped fresh herbs, such as a blend of thyme, sage, and tarragon, or more to taste

¼ teaspoon fine sea salt, or more to taste

¼ teaspoon freshly ground black pepper, or more to taste

1 cup/240 milliliters vegetable oil

In a small saucepan, bring vinegar to a boil over high heat. Add tea leaves and remove from heat. Let steep until cool, about 15 to 20 minutes, then strain into a large bowl, discarding the leaves.

Add the honey, shallots, garlic (if using), herbs, salt, and pepper, and whisk well. Drizzle in oil while continuing to whisk. Alternately, combine the tea-vinegar with all remaining ingredients in a blender and blend to emulsify. Use immediately, or store, refrigerated, in an airtight container for up to 5 days.

Variations

REPLACE THE RICE VINEGAR and the Darjeeling tea leaves with any of the following pairings:

- **WHITE BALSAMIC** vinegar and oolong tea leaves
- **MALT VINEGAR** with Assam or other full-bodied black tea leaves
- **RICE VINEGAR** and green tea leaves
- **RED WINE VINEGAR** and Keemun tea leaves
- **APPLE CIDER VINEGAR** and Darjeeling, Ceylon, or oolong tea leaves

FRESH TEA VINAIGRETTE

FRESH TEA LEAVES ARE JUST BEING INTRODUCED IN THIS COUNTRY. IF YOU CAN FIND THEM, THEY *add a unique fresh, spicy tang to this dressing, which is also good made with fresh thyme or sorrel if fresh tea leaves are unavailable. This multipurpose vinaigrette works well with a wide variety of vegetable salads or can be used as a dipping sauce or drizzle for seared scallops or tuna. If fresh tea leaves are available, use small, tender leaves and buds.*

Makes 1½ cups/360 milliliters

1 teaspoon loose-leaf green tea leaves, such as Gunpowder, Dragonwell, or sencha

½ cup/120 milliliters rice vinegar or white wine vinegar

1 teaspoon honey, or more to taste

1 teaspoon minced shallots

2 teaspoons chopped fresh tea leaves or sorrel or 1 teaspoon fresh thyme leaves

¼ teaspoon fine sea salt, or more to taste

¼ teaspoon freshly ground black pepper, or more to taste

1 cup/240 milliliters canola or other neutral-tasting vegetable oil

Combine the loose-leaf tea and vinegar in a small saucepan and bring to a simmer over medium heat. Simmer for 1 minute. Remove from heat and let cool to room temperature, about 20 minutes. Strain and discard the tea leaves. Transfer the vinegar to a nonreactive bowl. Whisk in the honey, shallots, fresh tea leaves or thyme, salt, and pepper. Slowly drizzle in oil and whisk well. Refrigerate for several hours in an airtight container to allow flavors to blend. This dressing will keep well, refrigerated, for 3 to 4 days.

❧ OOLONG MAYONNAISE ❧

Chefs Jon Riley and Emma Roberts of Capers Catering Company in Stoneham, Massachusetts, *shared this recipe with us. They use it with their Oolong-Brined Turkey Breast (page 146) to make a flavorful and unique tea sandwich. They created these recipes using Six Summits oolong tea, a cranberry-scented oolong, but we've added dried cranberries so that you can use any good-quality oolong. This particular recipe uses whole eggs, not all yolks, so it is a bit lighter than a classic mayo.*

Makes 2½ cups/600 milliliters

2 tablespoons loose-leaf oolong tea leaves

1 tablespoon chopped dried cranberries

1 cup/240 milliliters steaming water (about 185°F/85°C)

2 eggs

1 egg yolk

2 teaspoons grated fresh ginger

2 teaspoons rice vinegar

2 cups/480 milliliters canola oil

Fine sea salt or Tea-Smoked Salt (page 81) to taste

Freshly ground black pepper to taste

Combine tea and cranberries in a medium bowl. Pour over the steaming water and steep, covered, for 3 minutes. Strain the tea. Discard the liquid and reserve the leaves and berries and let cool, about 15 minutes. When cool, coarsely chop the tea leaves and berries.

In the bowl of a food processor or blender, combine the eggs, yolk, ginger, and rice vinegar. Process or blend to combine. With processor running, slowly add the oil in a steady stream through the feed tube over the course of about 2 minutes. When all the oil has been emulsified stop the processor and scrape the sides and bottom of the bowl. Add the cooled, chopped tea leaves and berries to the mixture in the food processor and continue processing for another minute. Scrape the bowl, then season with salt and pepper to taste. Continue processing for 30 seconds more. The chopped tea leaves will produce a mayo that looks like tartar sauce—but it will taste infinitely more interesting.

Store in an airtight container in the refrigerator for up to 3 days.

Note: Homemade mayonnaise has a wonderful flavor, quite different from commercial mayonnaise. It does, however, call for raw eggs. Because of the slight risk of salmonella, raw eggs should not be served to the very young, the ill or elderly, or to pregnant women. If this is a concern, or if you're short on time, follow this alternate method; Blend the steeped, chopped tea leaves and cranberries with the grated ginger and 2 cups/455 grams store-bought mayonnaise.

⚬⚬ MATCHA MAYO ⚬⚬

THIS QUICK AND EASY RECIPE MAKES A NICE SPREAD FOR VEGETABLE- OR SEAFOOD-BASED SANDWICHES.
Try it with the Tea-Cured Gravlax (page 93). It also works well as a dip for raw vegetables, broiled scallops, steamed mussels, shrimp, or other seafood.

Makes 1 cup / 240 milliliters

1 cup/240 milliliters mayonnaise

2 teaspoons matcha green tea powder

2 teaspoons finely minced fresh ginger
(or 1 teaspoon ground ginger)

1 tablespoon finely chopped chives

1 teaspoon grated orange zest

Combine all ingredients in a medium bowl; whisk to blend. Cover and chill at least 1 hour before using, to give flavors a chance to meld.

Left: Matcha Powder; *Right:* View of the beautiful Nilgiri Blue Mountains from the Glendale Estate in Southern India.

MATCHA SALT

USING A FEW SIMPLE PULSES OF A SPICE GRINDER, A TEA-SMOKED OR PLAIN SEA SALT CAN BE LIGHTLY *coated with matcha green tea powder or other finely ground teas and spices. Depending on the size of your spice grinder, the amount you can make at a time will vary, but it is so quick and easy that multiple batches are not a problem. You can substitute other finely ground teas for the matcha.*

Makes ¼ cup / 40 grams

¼ cup/40 grams coarse sea salt or kosher salt

¼ teaspoon matcha green tea powder

Place salt and matcha in a clean coffee or spice grinder. Pulse once or twice to completely distribute the powder. Store at room temperature in an airtight container. It will keep for several months.

Variations

KEEMUN-CINNAMON: Replace the matcha with finely powdered Keemun and the salt with Tea Smoked Salt (page 81). Add ⅛ teaspoon cinnamon and a pinch of mace.

JASMINE: Replace the matcha with jasmine tea ground to a fine powder. (Note: the Japanese tea grinder will not work on non-tea components, so remove any visible jasmine flowers before grinding the tea to a powder.)

KEEMUN-5 SPICE: Grind Keemun tea to a fine powder. Pulse sea salt briefly with a blend of ground Keemun tea and Chinese 5-spice powder (page 191).

PU-ERH COCOA: Grind Pu-erh tea to a fine powder. Pulse sea salt briefly with a blend of ground Pu-erh and cocoa powder.

MATCHA WITH A KICK: Add ⅛ teaspoon ground ginger and a pinch of wasabi powder or white pepper to the matcha before pulsing.

NOTE: A tea grinder, like the Japanese Green Tea Grinder (see Sources, page 280) will grind tea more finely than a regular spice grinder.

TEA-SMOKED SALT

THIS IS A VERY FLEXIBLE TECHNIQUE THAT CAN BE ALTERED BY CHANGING THE SMOKING TIME, THE *types of tea, and any herbs, spices, and flavorings. You can also use it as a base salt to finish with an additional application of other teas or spices. Any kind of uncooked rice may be used, as it merely serves as a buffer for the tea leaves. The rice enables the tea leaves to smoke, rather than just burn off.*

Makes 2 cups/340 grams

¼ cup/5 grams loose-leaf Keemun tea leaves

2 tablespoons fine cherry wood chips

¼ cup/50 grams rice

2 cups/320 grams coarse sea salt or kosher salt

Line a wok with heavy-duty aluminum foil. Mix together the tea, wood chips, and rice in the bottom of the wok and top with a rack. Pour the salt onto a doubled sheet of heavy-duty foil and fold edges up to form a tray. The salt should be no deeper than ¼-inch/6 millimeters so the smoke can properly permeate it. Place the tray of salt on the rack making sure there is sufficient room all around for the smoke to circulate around it.

Turn the flame underneath the wok to high; make sure the exhaust fan or hood is on. After a few minutes, the tea mixture should begin to smoke. As soon as you see the first wisps, reduce the heat to low, and once it starts to smoke well, cover with a wok lid or a baking sheet. This is necessary to keep the smoke in. Smoke for 15 minutes. Taste the salt. Depending on the tea you have chosen, the secondary ingredients, and the size of the salt crystals, the color may range from light golden to fairly deep golden. (The smaller the salt crystals, the less the smoke can penetrate between the crystals.) Stir the salt in the tray and decide if you want more intensity of color and flavor. Continue smoking until it has reached a desirable level.

If you want a more a intense smoke flavor, have a second batch of tea and rice ready. Remove the tray of salt and the rack that is supporting it. Discard the smoked out tea-rice mixture and replace it with the new mix. Continue smoking for another 15 minutes. After the smoking is complete, stir again. The colors should be bolder and the smoke flavor and aroma more intense. Once it is fully cooled, store the smoked salt in an airtight container at room temperature. It will keep for several months.

If you are using a smoker, follow the instruction provided for wood chips and replace the wood chips with the rice-tea mixture. If you are using a home covered grill like a Weber to smoke with, you can put the rice-tea mixture into a sealed foil packet and poke holes in the top to release the smoke. Place the packet on top of the heated, ashed coals. Alternatively, you can sprinkle well-moistened tea leaves and wood chips right onto the coals. (Use moistened tea leaves since the intense heat of the coals would cause dry leaves to burn away immediately.)

Variations

USE DIFFERENT WOOD CHIPS AND TEAS, and add herbs and spices to the smoking mixture. Try

• **APPLEWOOD CHIPS** and Darjeeling tea and cinnamon sticks
• **KEEMUN OR LYCHEE** tea with whole star anise

ᴇᴀʀʟ ɢʀᴇʏ ᴅʀɪᴇᴅ ᴄʜᴇʀʀʏ ᴍᴜsᴛᴀʀᴅ

STEPHEN BRAND, EXECUTIVE CHEF OF UPSTAIRS ON THE SQUARE IN CAMBRIDGE, MASSACHUSETTS, *created this versatile condiment. He likes it with steak and pork chops; it's also great as a spread with foie gras, on a charcuterie or cheese plate, or in a turkey sandwich (try it with the Tea-Brined Turkey on page 146). Dried cranberries may be substituted for dried cherries.*

Makes 2 cups / 480 milliliters

2 tablespoons loose-leaf Earl Grey tea leaves

2 cups/480 milliliters boiling water (about 212°F/100°C)

2 cups/340 grams dried sour cherries

½ cup/120 milliliters Dijon mustard

¼ cup/29 grams dry mustard powder, preferably Colman's

Place the tea leaves in a medium bowl. Pour the boiling water over them and steep, covered, for 5 minutes. Strain the tea into a blender, discarding the leaves. Add the dried cherries and let them rest for 5 to 10 minutes to soften.

Add the Dijon mustard and the mustard powder. Blend until thoroughly puréed. Use warm, at room temperature, or cold. Store in an airtight container, refrigerated, for several weeks.

⟋ ELEVEN-SPICE TEA RUB ⟍

THIS IS A WONDERFULLY VERSATILE COMBINATION OF FLAVORFUL BLACK TEA AND SPICES. TRY IT
rubbed on chicken, pork, beef, and game for grilling or roasting. It can also be added to braising liquids, soups, chutneys, or even ketchup for an easy burger sauce.

Grind the tea using a spice grinder or a mortar and pestle, or tea grinder, if you have one (see Sources, page 280). The spice blend will retain its flavor for up to two months, kept at room temperature in an airtight container.

Makes ³⁄₄ cup / 30 grams

5 tablespoons finely ground full-bodied
   black tea leaves (Chinese congou,
   low-grown Ceylon, and Nilgiri teas
   all work very well)

¼ cup/50 grams (packed)
   light brown sugar

2 teaspoons ground cinnamon

1 teaspoon curry powder

1 teaspoon ground cumin

1 teaspoon ground red pepper flakes
   or ground Szechuan peppercorns

½ teaspoon cayenne pepper

1 teaspoon freshly ground black pepper

½ teaspoon ground star anise or
   anise seed

½ teaspoon ground cloves

½ teaspoon ground fennel seed

½ teaspoon ground ginger

½ teaspoon ground mace

Combine all ingredients in a medium bowl, mixing well until thoroughly combined. Store in a tightly sealed jar or tin at room temperature for up to 2 months.

LYCHEE TEA SPICE RUB

LYCHEE TEA HAS A SWEET AROMA THAT GOES ESPECIALLY WELL WITH DUCK (AS IN THE LYCHEE-
Smoked Duck Breasts; page 145), as well as with other poultry. Freshly ground whole peppercorns, coriander, and allspice add a more intense kick of flavor to the rub, but ground versions may also be used. This is great as a dry rub on pork or chicken before roasting or grilling, or to season a couscous salad. Try using a small amount of the extra rub to make a lychee tea salt (page 79), or roll a log of fresh goat cheese in the rub and serve it with roasted fruit.

Makes about ½ cup/20 grams

¼ cup/10 grams loose-leaf lychee
   black tea leaves

1 tablespoon whole black peppercorns

1 teaspoon whole coriander seeds

½ teaspoon anise seeds

1 teaspoon allspice berries

1 tablespoon ground cardamom

1 tablespoon ground ginger

1 teaspoon ground cumin

½ teaspoon ground cinnamon

½ teaspoon ground cloves

Grind the tea, peppercorns, coriander seeds, anise seeds, and allspice in a spice grinder until fine and even in consistency. Blend with the cardamom, cumin, cinnamon, and cloves until thoroughly combined. Store in an airtight container at room temperature.

DARJEELING BEURRE BLANC

BEURRE BLANC, THE CLASSIC FRENCH BUTTER SAUCE, DEPENDS ON A CONCENTRATION OF ACIDS TO *keep the butter in suspension. For this reason, the wine and vinegar can't be replaced by steeped tea, but you can develop a complex, alternative flavor profile by infusing the tea leaves in the wine or vinegar first. A slow infusion overnight gives a cleaner flavor, but if you're short on time, bring the wine and vinegar to a boil, infuse the tea leaves for 4 minutes, strain, and continue. Serve this with Salmon en Papillote with Fresh Tea Leaves (page 119).*

Makes 1½ cups/360 milliliters

- ¼ cup/60 milliliters plus 1 teaspoon white wine vinegar
- ¼ cup/60 milliliters dry white wine
- 3 teaspoons loose-leaf Darjeeling tea leaves, divided
- ½ cup/120 milliliters boiling water (about 212°F/100°C)
- 1 tablespoon finely minced shallots
- ¼ teaspoon fine sea salt, or more to taste
- ⅛ teaspoon freshly ground white pepper
- 12 ounces/345 grams (3 sticks) unsalted butter, chilled, cut into 24 pieces

Combine the vinegar, wine, and 1 teaspoon of the tea leaves in a nonreactive container. Cover and set aside overnight or longer to infuse. When ready to continue, strain the wine-vinegar mixture, pressing as much liquid out of the leaves as possible. Discard the leaves.

Put the remaining 2 teaspoons tea leaves in a glass measuring cup. Pour over the boiling water and steep, covered, for 3 minutes. Strain, discarding the leaves and set the steeped tea aside.

Place the infused wine-vinegar mixture, shallots, salt, and pepper into a small saucepan. Bring to a boil over medium-high heat and reduce to about 1½ tablespoons, 2 to 3 minutes. Remove from the heat and immediately whisk in 2 or 3 pieces of the chilled butter. When incorporated smoothly, place the saucepan over low heat and, whisking constantly, continue to add the chilled butter, one piece at a time. The sauce will be thick and light gold in color. As soon as the last piece of butter is incorporated, remove from the heat. Whisk in 1 tablespoon of the reserved steeped tea. Taste and add additional tea and salt if needed. Serve immediately.

NOTE: For a tea concentrate, steep leaves in at least ½ cup boiling water, even if it's more than needed, so the tea won't cool as it steeps. Use chilled beurre blanc to enrich sauces or serve with grilled fish.

Variation

GREEN TEA AND CITRUS BEURRE BLANC: Substitute green tea for the Darjeeling and finish with a splash of fresh lemon and orange juices. A touch of citrus zest may also be whisked in at the end.

SMOKY TEA-SPICED PECANS

THIS RECIPE COMES FROM CHEF LAURIE BELL OF GREAT FALLS TEA GARDEN IN GREAT FALLS, VIRGINIA.

These nuts have an appealing salty-sweet flavor, which is complemented by the earthy smokiness of Lapsang Souchong tea. You can use the basic recipe and vary the tea and spices. Serve these with tea cocktails, as a snack, or sprinkled over salads. You could also stir them into melted dark chocolate to make an unusual chocolate bark candy (page 178).

Makes about 8 cups / 920 grams

2 tablespoons loose-leaf Lapsang Souchong tea leaves

6 tablespoons granulated sugar

½ teaspoon Tea-Smoked Salt (page 81) or smoked sea salt

¼ teaspoon ground cinnamon

¼ teaspoon ground allspice

¼ teaspoon cayenne pepper

1 egg white

1 tablespoon water

1 pound/455 grams pecan halves

Finely grind the tea leaves in a spice grinder. Once ground, the yield should be just over 1 tablespoon. In a small bowl, mix together the ground tea, sugar, salt, cinnamon, allspice, and cayenne.

In a large bowl, whisk the egg white until frothy. Add the water and whisk to incorporate. Add the tea mixture and whisk well. Let rest for 15 minutes to allow the sugar to dissolve and the flavors to blend together.

Preheat the oven to 300°F/150°C/gas 2. Line a baking sheet with parchment paper.

After 15 minutes (do not wait longer than that or the mixture can separate) whisk the mixture briefly, then add the pecans. Stir well to coat the nuts as evenly as possible. Spread the nuts on the prepared baking sheet. Transfer to the oven and immediately reduce the temperature to 250°F/120°C/gas 1/2. Bake for 45 to 60 minutes, until the nuts are crisp and toasted. Stir them midway through and rotate the pan. Test the nuts after 45 minutes: remove a few nuts from the oven, cool 3 to 4 minutes, then taste to see if the nuts are crisp. If not, test every 5 minutes until the desired texture is achieved. Remove from the oven and let the nuts cool completely in the pan, about 1 hour. When cool, break apart any big clumps of nuts. Store in an airtight container at room temperature or in the freezer.

Variation

BLACK SPICE: Use Assam or Nilgiri tea and fine sea salt. Replace the cinnamon and allspice with ½ teaspoon each crushed fennel and ground cardamom, and omit the cayenne.

DARJEELING ROASTED SWEET POTATOES

THESE INDIAN-INFLECTED SWEET POTATOES HAVE INTRIGUING, SAVORY FLAVORS THAT MAKE THEM *a hit for all ages—even kid-tasters came back for seconds. The Indian ingredients are available online or in Indian markets. Amchoor is dried, powdered green mango. If it's unavailable, substitute grated lime zest. Black salt, also called* kala namak, *is a powdery salt that's actually a pinkish tan color; regular salt or Smoked Tea Salt may be used instead.*

Serves 8

3 pounds/1.4 kilograms sweet potatoes, peeled, cut into ½-inch/12-millimeter pieces

1 tablespoon olive oil

½ teaspoon amchoor or grated lime zest

½ teaspoon black salt, fine sea salt, or Tea-Smoked Salt (page 81)

1½ teaspoons loose-leaf Darjeeling tea leaves

Preheat oven to 400°F/200°C/gas 6. Line a baking sheet with foil and spray with olive oil cooking spray.

In a large bowl, toss the sweet potatoes with the oil and stir to coat. Add the amchoor and black salt. Crumble the tea with your fingers, crushing it as you sprinkle it over the potatoes. Stir well to distribute the tea and spices.

Spread the potatoes in prepared pan in an even layer. Bake for 10 minutes, then stir. Bake for an additional 10 to 20 minutes, until the sweet potatoes are just slightly firm in the center. Serve warm or at room temperature.

Tea Salts

SALT INFUSED WITH TEA IS A TERRIFIC WAY TO FLAVOR FOODS. They're great served as a condiment with bread and olive oil. Lighter profile salts like the Matcha Salt (page 79) are wonderful with fish or pasta dishes, or sprinkle some lightly on a fresh mozzarella-and-tomato salad in the summer. Try smoked salt on caramels or chocolate (see Tea Toffee with Tea-Smoked Salt, page 177), corn on the cob, or just a touch on fresh fruit.

A good quality sea salt with the largest crystals you can find is ideal for tea-smoking, but kosher salt is less expensive and will also give very nice results. Once your kitchen is stocked with a selection of tea salts, you'll often find yourself reaching for one of them to finish a dish rather than using a traditional salt.

⸱ BALSAMIC *and* TEA-CARAMELIZED ONIONS ⸱

THIS EARTHY, TANGY CONDIMENT GOES WELL WITH PÂTÉ AND CHEESES AND A WIDE VARIETY OF *charcuterie. Try these tucked into a sandwich with shaved prosciutto, Dijon, and melted Brie, or with avocado, arugula, and hummus. The onions keep very well, so consider making a very large batch at a time.*

Makes 1 cup/240 milliliters

1 tablespoon loose-leaf full-bodied black tea leaves such as low-grown Ceylon, Nilgiri, or Assam

¾ cup/180 milliliters boiling water (about 212°F/100°C)

2 tablespoons olive oil

3 medium onions, halved and thinly sliced

¼ cup/50 grams (packed) light brown sugar

1 tablespoon balsamic vinegar

¼ teaspoon ground ginger (optional)

¼ teaspoon Chinese 5-spice powder, (page 191) (optional)

Salt to taste, preferably Tea-Smoked Salt (page 81)

Place the tea leaves in a medium bowl. Add the boiling water and steep, covered, for 5 minutes. Strain and set aside, discarding the leaves.

Heat the oil in a saucepan over low heat. Add the onions and cook, stirring frequently until translucent and soft, about 15 to 20 minutes. Increase the heat to medium and sprinkle in the brown sugar. Stir and cook until the onions begin to color. If desired, add the ginger and 5-spice powder. Add the balsamic vinegar and the steeped tea and continue cooking on medium-low several minutes longer, stirring constantly until any excess liquid is absorbed. The onions will be a deep reddish brown color and very tender. Season with salt to taste. Serve immediately, or cool to room temperature, then store, refrigerated, in an airtight container.

TEMPURA-FRIED FRESH TEA LEAVES

FRESH TEA LEAVES ARE JUST BEING INTRODUCED IN THE UNITED STATES. IF YOU CAN FIND THEM, *the tender, young buds and shoots are best for most applications, including this one, but for tempura, you can also make use of slightly older or larger leaves. To use larger leaves, first blanch them briefly in salted boiling water until they are tender to the bite. (The timing will vary depending on the age and size of the leaves.) Be sure to dry them off completely before dipping them into the batter for frying. These tempura leaves, especially when made with the young buds and shoots, are so subtle and wonderful they don't need a dipping sauce, just a light sprinkling of salt. They're especially nice with Matcha Salt (page 79) or Tea-Smoked Salt (page 81).*

Serves 4

Vegetable oil for frying

1 cup/130 grams all-purpose flour

1 tablespoon cornstarch

1½ cups/360 milliliters ice-cold seltzer water

2 cups/60 grams fresh tea leaves and buds

Matcha Salt (page 79), Smoked Tea Salt (page 81), or sea salt to taste

In a wok or large sauté pan, add the oil to a depth of 1 inch/2.5 centimeters. Heat the oil over medium-high heat to 340°F/170°C.

While oil is heating, sift together flour and cornstarch into a medium bowl. Add ice-cold seltzer and whisk until just combined. There will still be some lumps. Be very careful not to over-mix.

To check the temperature of the oil without a thermometer, drop a small amount of batter into the hot oil. It should sink halfway to the bottom and float to the top. If it sinks all the way to the bottom before returning, the oil is too hot. If it is too hot, turn off the heat for a moment to cool, and then return to medium-high. When oil is ready, dip tea leaves one at a time into batter while holding the stem, and fry in oil until pale golden and crisp. Do not fry too many at once (which will lower the temperature of the oil). Use chopsticks, a spider, or a mesh strainer to remove the tea leaves from the oil and place on a plate lined with paper towels. Sprinkle lightly with salt and serve immediately.

NOTE: Do not make the batter in advance. Make a fresh batch immediately before you are ready to use it.

⌒ TEA-MARBLED EGGS ⌒

THIS HISTORIC RECIPE IS AN EXAMPLE OF EARLY CHINESE CULINARY TEA. SMOKY LAPSANG SOUCHONG *is the traditional choice, but the beautiful marbled look can still be achieved without that earthy smokiness. Experiment with different kinds of full-bodied black teas to find the combination that you like best.*

Makes 12

12 eggs

¾ cup/180 milliliters soy sauce

2 tablespoons packed dark brown sugar

5 cups/1.2 liters water

3 tablespoons loose-leaf Lapsang Souchong tea leaves

4 whole star anise

1 cinnamon stick

Put the eggs in a saucepan large enough to hold them in a single layer. Cover the eggs with cold water and bring to a rolling boil over high heat, partially covered. As soon as the water boils, remove from the heat and let the eggs stand, covered, for 10 minutes. Transfer the eggs with a slotted spoon to a bowl of ice water and let cool enough so that you can handle them; discard the hot water. Gently tap the shells all over with the back of a spoon to lightly crack all over (do not peel). Do not tap too hard or tea liquid will seep into the shell instead of just staining the cracks.

In the same saucepan, bring the soy sauce, brown sugar, and the 5 cups/1.2 liters water to a boil over high heat, stirring until the sugar is dissolved; add the tea. Reduce the heat and add the eggs. If the eggs are not completely covered by liquid, add additional water until they are just covered. Simmer, covered, 10 minutes. Remove the pan from the heat and let the eggs stand in the liquid, uncovered, until cool, then chill in the liquid at least 2 hours or up to 2 days. When ready to serve, remove the eggs from the liquid and peel. The whites will be stained into a beautiful marbled pattern.

The eggs may be served as is, or can be deviled: slice each egg in half lengthwise and transfer the yolks to a medium bowl. Add ¼ cup/60 milliliters Oolong Mayonnaise (page 77), a touch of dry mustard powder, and the tea liquid to taste, and mix well. Mound or pipe a bit of the seasoned yolks in the hollow of each egg.

If you are not deviling the eggs, slice in half lengthwise and serve with any of the following accompaniments: Toasted Pepper Salt (page 92); Tea-Smoked Salt (page 81); Matcha Mayo (page 78).

NOTE: As pictured, these eggs display a soft, delicate marbling. For a more vibrant marbling and more depth of flavor, allow the eggs to chill in the liquid for longer, 1 to 2 days.

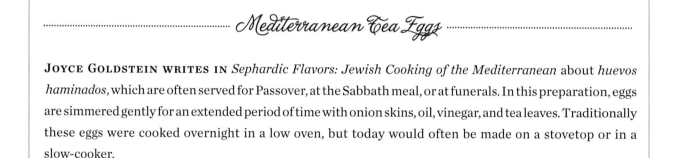

Mediterranean Tea Eggs

JOYCE GOLDSTEIN WRITES IN *Sephardic Flavors: Jewish Cooking of the Mediterranean* about *huevos haminados*, which are often served for Passover, at the Sabbath meal, or at funerals. In this preparation, eggs are simmered gently for an extended period of time with onion skins, oil, vinegar, and tea leaves. Traditionally these eggs were cooked overnight in a low oven, but today would often be made on a stovetop or in a slow-cooker.

TOASTED PEPPER SALT

SERVE THIS CONDIMENT WITH TEA-MARBLED EGGS (PAGE 91), OR USE AS A SEASONING FOR MEATS, *salads, and vegetables.*

Makes 3 tablespoons

2 tablespoons whole black or Chinese Szechuan peppercorns

2 tablespoons coarse sea salt or Tea-Smoked Salt (page 81)

Toast peppercorns in a small, dry skillet over medium heat until fragrant, about 5 minutes. Let cool and crush coarsely using a mortar and pestle or a spice grinder. Add the salt, and crush or pulse slightly further. Store at room temperature in an airtight container.

JASMINE TEA-CURED GRAVLAX

GRAVLAX IS A SCANDINAVIAN PREPARATION IN WHICH SALMON IS "COOKED" OR CURED BY SOAKING *it in a mixture of sugar and salt. With thanks to Mark Yedvabny who worked on an earlier version of this recipe while at Tea-Tray in the Sky. Use salmon with the skin on, which makes it much easier both to cure and to serve. Jasmine tea adds a heavenly perfume to the fish. You can serve it plated with lightly dressed mixed baby greens and a dollop of herbed crème fraîche. It's also terrific in a sandwich—on thin bread, on its own, spread with Boursin or goat cheese, or with thinly sliced onions and apple-smoked bacon—or on toast points with capers, or, of course, on a bagel with cream cheese. This is a very large quantity, great for a large cocktail party, paired with cocktails, dry white wine, sake, or vodka. If your gathering is more intimate, store any leftovers wrapped well in plastic and refrigerated for a week to 10 days.*

Serves 16

⅔ cup/130 grams (packed) light brown sugar

⅔ cup/115 grams kosher salt (non-iodized)

1 whole side salmon (3 to 4 pounds/1.4 to 1.8 kilograms) preferably with skin on

½ lemon

⅛ teaspoon freshly ground black pepper, or more to taste

1 teaspoon finely chopped garlic

2 tablespoons coarsely chopped fresh dill or cilantro

½ cup/20 grams loose-leaf jasmine green tea leaves

In a large bowl, combine the brown sugar and salt. Spread a large piece of plastic wrap on a work surface. Take one-third of the sugar-salt mixture and spread it out on the plastic wrap to be roughly the size and shape of the salmon side. Place the salmon on the sugar-salt mixture, skin-side down. Check that no bones remain in the salmon, squeeze the lemon over the skinless side, then spread black pepper and garlic over evenly. Sprinkle on the dill or cilantro and the tea. Spread the remaining two-thirds of the salt-sugar mixture over the tea leaves.

Bring plastic wrap up around the salmon to enclose it very well. Place the wrapped fish in a large pan that can hold the fish lying flat. Place a second pan on top so that it presses down on the fish. Place canned goods on the second pan to weigh it down. Refrigerate. Flip fish over every 12 hours. After 24 hours, unwrap and check for doneness—it should be firm and translucent, similar to smoked salmon. Depending on the thickness of the fillet, it should take between 24 and 48 hours to cure.

To serve, cut cured salmon thinly on the diagonal. When you reach the skin, curve the knife upward and the fish will release easily.

Variation: **SMOKY ORANGE**
Use Lapsang Souchong instead of Jasmine and substitute juice of ½ orange for lemon juice. Add 1 teaspoon orange zest when adding the garlic and pepper.

LAPSANG SOUCHONG SCALLOPS CEVICHE

A LIGHT POACHING IN CONCENTRATED SMOKY LAPSANG SOUCHONG TEA DOESN'T COOK THE SCALLOPS, *but imparts a different dimension to the final flavor profile. The hint of smokiness contrasts with the clean and sharp citrus and pepper flavors found in a classic ceviche. The scallops are "cooked" by the acids in the marinade, while preserving a fresh flavor and texture in the final dish. Orange is not traditional for a ceviche marinade, but we find that it works beautifully with the smoky flavors of the tea. Scotch bonnet chiles are very hot, but also add flavor. Use the smaller amount if you prefer less heat. The scallops need to chill and develop overnight before serving.*

Serves 4 to 6

¾ cup/180 milliliters fresh lime juice

½ cup/120 milliliters fresh orange juice

¼ cup/60 milliliters fresh lemon juice

1 teaspoon light brown sugar

½ cup/120 milliliters rice vinegar

½ to 1 Scotch bonnet or other hot chile, deveined, seeded, very finely chopped

1 red or yellow bell pepper, seeded and coarsely chopped

1 small red onion, coarsely chopped

1 tomato, seeded and coarsely chopped

2 garlic cloves, finely chopped

1 tablespoon minced fresh cilantro or flat-leaf parsley

⅛ teaspoon fine sea salt, or more to taste

⅛ teaspoon freshly ground black pepper, or more to taste

1 quart/960 milliliters water

¼ cup/10 grams loose-leaf Lapsang Souchong tea leaves

1 pound/455 grams scallops

Parsley or cilantro sprigs for garnish

In a large bowl, combine the lime, orange, and lemon juices with the brown sugar, vinegar, hot chile, bell pepper, onion, tomato, garlic, cilantro or parsley, salt, and pepper. Mix well and set aside.

Add the water to a large soup pot or sauté pan; the depth should be between 1 and 2 inches/2.5 and 5 centimeters. Add the tea leaves. If you need to add more water due to the diameter of your pan, add additional tea leaves as well. Heat over medium-high heat and let simmer 4 minutes. Gently add the scallops. Poach small bay scallops for 1 minute or less and poach larger sea scallops for up to 1½ minutes. The exterior should be a beautiful rich dark gold, with the interior still uncooked. Remove from the tea and rinse scallops in cold water to stop cooking.

Add the scallops to the prepared marinade and toss well to coat completely. Refrigerate overnight or for up to 3 days, stirring every 12 hours, and serve, garnished with the chopped vegetables from the marinade and fresh sprigs of cilantro or parsley.

SHRIMP IN LEMON-TEA ASPIC *with* BASIL-TEA JELLY

THIS ELEGANT APPETIZER HELPED ROHAN FERNANDOPULLE, THE EXECUTIVE CHEF AT THE COLOMBO
Hilton in Sri Lanka, win a culinary tea competition sponsored by Dilmah Tea company. The combination of shrimp with lemon aspic and creamy crème fraîche jelly mixed with fresh tea leaves is especially refreshing in the summer. If you can't find fresh tea leaves, a good substitute is barely steeped green tea leaves, as described in this recipe. This recipe was created using Dilmah Tangy Lemon Tea, a black tea flavored with lemon. For convenience, we use good-quality Ceylon tea and add a teaspoon of freshly grated lemon zest. If you use lemon tea, then omit the grated lemon zest used with the tea.

Serves 4

LEMON TEA ASPIC

1 cup/240 milliliters boiling water
(about 212°F/100°C)

¼ cup/10 grams loose-leaf Ceylon
tea leaves

½ teaspoon grated lemon zest

2 teaspoons granulated sugar

1 teaspoon gelatin powder

Pinch fine sea salt

SHRIMP

2 cups/480 milliliters boiling water
(about 212°F/100°C)

2 teaspoons loose-leaf Ceylon tea leaves

1 teaspoon finely grated lemon zest

8 jumbo shrimp

2 tablespoons diced mango

1 teaspoon finely chopped chives

(continued)

TO MAKE THE ASPIC: Pour the boiling water over the tea leaves and lemon zest in a medium bowl. Steep, covered, for 4 minutes, then strain, discarding the leaves. Add the sugar, gelatin, and salt and stir until the gelatin has fully dissolved and is clear. Divide aspic among 4 martini glasses and let cool at room temperature until no longer warm to the touch, but not beginning to solidify. It should be cool enough by the time you have finished preparing the shrimp.

TO MAKE THE SHRIMP: Pour the boiling water over the tea leaves and lemon zest in a medium bowl. Steep, covered, for 4 minutes, then strain, discarding the leaves. Pour the tea in a medium saucepan and set aside.

Fill a second medium saucepan with water and bring to a simmer over medium-high heat. Lightly poach the shrimp in simmering water until not quite cooked through. Remove from the water and dice 4 of the shrimp, leaving 4 whole for the garnish.

Reheat the reserved tea until just simmering. Remove from heat and pour over the shrimp, both diced and whole, and let sit for at least 20 minutes, until tea has cooled. The shrimp will finish cooking in the hot tea. Remove the shrimp from the tea, pat completely dry and divide the chopped shrimp evenly among the 4 glasses of aspic. Refrigerate the whole shrimp to be used for garnishing in a covered container until ready to serve.

Toss the mango with the chives and add to the glasses. Chill until aspic is set with the shrimp, about 1 hour. *(continued)*

BASIL-TEA JELLY

2 tablespoons chopped fresh tea leaves
(tender young leaves only) or

1 tablespoon loose-leaf green tea
leaves and 2 tablespoons steaming
water (about 175°F/80°C)

¼ cup/4 grams chopped fresh basil,
plus whole leaves for garnish

¼ cup/4 grams crème fraîche

2 teaspoons gelatin powder

1 teaspoon granulated sugar

Pinch fine sea salt

Lemon zest in long strips for garnish

MEANWHILE, PREPARE THE BASIL-TEA JELLY: If fresh tea leaves are not available, steep the loose-leaf green tea leaves in the steaming water for 30 seconds. Strain, discarding water. Chop the moistened tea leaves. Place the fresh tea or the moistened tea leaves in a blender. Add the basil and the crème fraîche and blend.

Strain the crème fraîche well. Add the gelatin, sugar, and salt to the strained crème fraîche and mix well. Pour on top of the set aspic. Chill until set, at least 1 hour, or up to 2 days in advance. Garnish with the reserved whole shrimp, fresh tea leaves (if available) or fresh basil leaves and a long twisted spiral of lemon zest. Serve chilled.

Wuyishan, China, Fujian Province, the birthplace of oolong tea

⟋⟋ TUNG TING SHRIMP ⟍⟍

TUNG TING IS A LIGHT AND EXTRAORDINARILY AROMATIC OOLONG. THE TEA BRINGS OUT THE CLEAN, *natural sweetness of the shrimp. Although we are particularly partial to using a lightly oxidized or "green" oolong, feel free to use other oolongs if desired for different but equally enjoyable results. Green tea may also be substituted. These shrimp are very nice in the Fresh Spring Rolls (page 98), chilled in salads, or served (chilled or at room temperature) as an appetizer.*

Serves 4

5 tablespoons loose-leaf Tung Ting oolong tea leaves, or other light oolong

4²/₃ cups/1.2 liters steaming water (about 185°F/90°C) divided

1 teaspoon kosher or fine sea salt

1½ pounds/680 grams medium or large shrimp

½ cup/120 milliliters Chinese rice wine, such as Shaoxing wine, or gin

½ cup/120 milliliters rice vinegar

4 garlic cloves, minced

3 tablespoons finely minced fresh ginger

2 scallions, thinly sliced

1½ tablespoons toasted sesame oil

1 tablespoon fish sauce, such as *nam pla*

4 cups/120 grams baby spinach, washed and dried

1 tablespoon toasted sesame seeds

Put 1 tablespoon of the tea leaves in a small bowl or measuring cup. Pour ²/₃ cup of the steaming water over the tea leaves and steep, covered, for 3 minutes. Strain, discarding the leaves, and set the tea aside to cool.

Place the remaining 4 tablespoons tea leaves in a large bowl with the salt. Add the remaining 4 cups/960 milliliters steaming water and stir to dissolve salt. Add the shrimp and let sit until the shrimp is just opaque; timing will vary by size of shrimp, 1 to 4 minutes. Remove the shrimp from the tea and rinse off the leaves in cold water to stop cooking. Discard the liquid.

Combine the reserved cooled tea with the rice wine, rice vinegar, ginger, scallions, sesame oil, and fish sauce. Stir well, then add the cooked shrimp and toss to coat.

To serve, divide the spinach among 4 plates and top with the shrimp, drizzling plenty of the tea dressing over the spinach leaves. Sprinkle with toasted sesame seeds.

❧ FRESH SPRING ROLLS ❧

SPRING ROLLS ARE BEST SERVED THE DAY THEY ARE ASSEMBLED. THE TWO RECOMMENDED FILLINGS, *Tung Ting Shrimp (page 97) and Clay-Cooked Asian Chicken (page 135), can both be made in advance. You could also use sliced tofu, or just the vegetables—spring rolls are flexible, and a good use for leftovers. The Tea Dipping Sauce can also be made 1 to 2 days in advance.*

Makes 12 spring rolls

SPRING ROLLS

8 ounces/225 grams dried thin bean thread or glass noodles

¼ cup/10 grams loose-leaf green or low-oxidation oolong tea leaves

5 cups/1.2 liters steaming water (about 175°F/80°C)

½ cup/50 grams grated carrots

1 cup/100 grams bean sprouts

½ cup/50 grams thinly sliced scallions

½ cup/2 grams chopped fresh mint leaves

¼ cup/4 grams chopped fresh cilantro

½ cup julienned cucumber

1 tablespoon toasted sesame oil

2 tablespoons Tea Dipping Sauce (recipe below)

¼ teaspoon fine sea salt, or more to taste

¼ teaspoon freshly ground black pepper, or more to taste

12 round dried rice paper wrappers

3 cups/510 grams Shredded Clay-Cooked Asian Chicken (page 135), or 24 Tung Ting Shrimp (page 97), sliced in half

TO MAKE THE NOODLES FOR THE SPRING ROLLS: Place the bean thread noodles in a large bowl.

Place the tea leaves in a large bowl. Add the steaming water and steep, covered, for 2 minutes, then strain, discarding the leaves. Pour 2 cups/480 milliliters of the tea over the bean thread noodles, reserving 3 cups/720 milliliters in the bowl; let cool. Soak the bean thread noodles until soft, about 15 minutes. Drain and discard tea. Coarsely cut noodles into shorter lengths and reserve.

TO MAKE THE DIPPING SAUCE: Transfer ½ cup/120 milliliters of the cooled reserved 3 cups/720 milliliters tea to a medium bowl. Whisk in the oil, garlic, honey, vinegar, and fish sauce. Add one-quarter of the minced chile and taste. Add additional chile and fish sauce as desired. Whisk well. If the dipping sauce will not be used within the next few hours, remove the 2 tablespoons needed for the spring rolls recipe and cover and chill the remainder until ready to serve. Whisk lightly before serving.

TO COMPLETE THE SPRING ROLLS: To the remaining 2½ cups/600 milliliters tea, add the carrots, bean sprouts, and scallions and soak them in the cold tea for 30 minutes. Drain, discarding the tea. Add the reserved noodles, mint, cilantro, cucumber, sesame oil, 2 tablespoons tea dipping sauce, salt, and pepper. Toss well.

Soak a sheet of rice paper in warm water until soft, about 1 minute. Transfer to a cutting board. Place 2 basil leaves along the bottom third of the sheet. Arrange 2 shrimp or ¼ cup shredded chicken over the basil

24 fresh basil leaves
(use Thai basil if available)

TEA DIPPING SAUCE

½ cup/120 milliliters steeped
green or oolong tea (reserved
from Spring Rolls)

1 teaspoon toasted sesame oil

3 garlic cloves, minced

1 tablespoon honey

¼ cup/60 milliliters rice vinegar

3 tablespoons Asian fish sauce,
such as *nam pla,* or more to taste

¼ to 1 small fresh Thai chile, deveined,
seeded, and minced

leaves, then top with some of the noodle and vegetable filling. Fold the sides over the filling and roll into a cigar-shaped cylinder. Repeat with the remaining rice paper wrappers and filling. To serve, cut each spring roll in half on the diagonal and serve immediately, with Tea Dipping Sauce on the side.

NOTE: Bean thread or glass noodles and rice paper wrappers are often available in supermarkets, and can be found in any Asian market.

TEA-GRILLED WINGS *with* HOT GREEN DIPPING SAUCE

THESE WINGS ARE BEST HOT OFF THE GRILL. SINCE THEY COOK QUICKLY, PLAN TO GRILL JUST BEFORE *serving and then keep the tea cocktails and iced tea flowing! These wings were quite popular in the Swans Bar at the Boston Park Plaza Hotel where João Barros, the executive sous chef, added this spicy fresh green sauce for dipping. The wings have deep, intense flavors, but are not particularly hot, so the crisp clean heat of the dipping sauce is the perfect foil. Use more or less jalapeño to taste. The wings can also be broiled. They need to marinate overnight before cooking, so plan accordingly.*

Serves 6

CHICKEN WINGS

5 tablespoons loose-leaf black
   tea leaves, divided

1½ cups/360 milliliters boiling water
   (about 212°F/100°C)

½ cup/120 milliliters soy sauce

3 tablespoons toasted sesame oil

3 tablespoons Asian fish sauce,
   such as *nam pla*

6 garlic cloves, finely chopped

3 tablespoons Asian chili sauce,
   such as Sriracha

Freshly ground black pepper to taste

18 chicken wings

HOT GREEN DIPPING SAUCE

2 cups/30 grams fresh basil leaves

¾ cup/4 grams cilantro leaves

2 to 4 jalapeño peppers, deveined
   and seeded

⅓ cup/75 milliliters rice vinegar

½ cup/120 milliliters extra-virgin olive oil

Fine sea salt to taste

Freshly ground black pepper to taste

TO MAKE THE WINGS: Place 3 tablespoons of the tea in a glass measuring cup or bowl. Add the boiling water and steep, covered, for 6 minutes. Strain and set aside to cool. Discard the tea leaves.

In a spice grinder or using a mortar and pestle, finely grind the remaining 2 tablespoons tea. Transfer to a medium bowl and add the soy sauce, sesame oil, fish sauce, garlic, chili sauce, and black pepper to taste. Add the cooled steeped tea and stir to combine.

Trim the wing tips and set aside for another use (they are great for making stock). Cut the remaining wings at the joint to separate. Place wings in a resealable plastic bag, then pour in the marinade. Seal bag and make sure wings are coated with the marinade. Refrigerate overnight or for up to 3 days, turning every 12 hours.

TO MAKE THE SAUCE: In the bowl of a food processor or in a blender, combine the basil, cilantro, jalapeño, and vinegar. Process for 30 seconds, then, with the processor running, slowly add the oil through the feed tube. Scrape down the sides, add the salt and pepper to taste, then process again until smooth. Transfer to an airtight container and refrigerate until ready to cook the wings.

When ready to cook, preheat grill to medium and remove the wings from the fridge to allow to come to room temperature. Remove wings from marinade (discard marinade) and grill (if using an outdoor grill, cover-cook with the vents open) until cooked through and juices are clear, about 6 to 8 minutes per side. Serve with the sauce on the side.

JASMINE DUMPLINGS

ON A TRIP TO CHINA, CINDY ATTENDED A TEA CEREMONY PERFORMANCE, WHERE SHE SAMPLED *delectable dumplings infused with jasmine tea, ginger, and sesame oil. When she returned, she recreated the recipe. A steamer, preferably bamboo, is the preferred gadget for preparing these dumplings, which are best the day they are made; the filling may be prepared up to one day in advance, and the dumplings may be assembled and kept refrigerated several hours before steaming. These are great to serve at a larger party. If you like a little heat, use toasted sesame oil with chiles.*

Makes 60 dumplings

FILLING

¾ pound/340 grams napa cabbage, shredded

2¼ teaspoons kosher salt, divided

2 tablespoons coarsely ground loose-leaf jasmine tea leaves

1 bunch scallions (about 6 to 8) both white and green parts, chopped

1 teaspoon finely chopped fresh ginger

3 garlic cloves, finely chopped

2 tablespoons soy sauce

2 teaspoons toasted sesame oil, (with hot chile if desired)

1 pound/455 grams ground pork

60 wonton wrappers (preferably round, but any shape will work)

JASMINE DIPPING SAUCE

1 cup/240 milliliters steaming water (about 175°F/80°C)

1 tablespoon loose-leaf jasmine tea leaves

2 tablespoons soy sauce

2 tablespoons rice vinegar

(*continued*)

TO MAKE THE FILLING: Toss the shredded cabbage with 2 teaspoons of the salt. Let sit for 30 minutes at room temperature (the salt will extract excess moisture from the cabbage). Drain, squeezing the cabbage well to get rid of any extra moisture. Don't worry about rinsing the salt off, most of it will flow off and be discarded with the excess moisture you've removed from the cabbage. In a large bowl, combine the remaining ¼ teaspoon salt, ground tea, scallions, ginger, garlic, soy sauce, and sesame oil. Mix to combine, then add drained cabbage and ground pork. Mix thoroughly. Filling may be stored up to 1 day in advance, covered tightly and refrigerated.

TO MAKE THE DIPPING SAUCE: Pour the steaming water over the tea leaves in a small bowl. Steep, covered, for 2 to 3 minutes, discard the leaves, and return the liquid to the bowl. Add the soy sauce, vinegar, sesame oil if using, garlic, and ginger, mixing well. Set aside. May be prepared 1 day in advance, covered tightly and refrigerated.

TO MAKE THE DUMPLINGS: Line a baking sheet with parchment paper or spray with vegetable cooking spray. Keep wonton wrappers covered with plastic or a damp cloth to prevent them from drying out. Place 1 wrapper on a work surface. Place a scant teaspoon of filling in the center, then lightly brush water around the edges of half the wrapper. Fold the edges to meet, pushing air pockets out, and press to seal. Continue until all the filling has been used.

Once all the dumplings are assembled, oil the steamer basket and prepare the steaming liquid. Add the water to a wok or large saucepan and

1 dash toasted sesame oil, with hot chile if desired (optional)

1 clove garlic, finely chopped

½ teaspoon finely chopped fresh ginger

STEAMING LIQUID

2 cups/480 milliliters room-temperature water

2 tablespoons loose-leaf jasmine tea leaves

Whole cabbage or lettuce leaves

heat over medium-high heat just until steaming. Add the tea to the steaming water, then place the oiled steamer basket over the lightly steaming tea. Place the cabbage or lettuce leaves in the steamer basket, then add as many dumplings as will fit comfortably in the basket without touching. (The leaves keep the dumplings from sticking.) Steam the dumplings until they are translucent and the filling is fully cooked, about 8 to 12 minutes. Test a random dumpling with an instant-read thermometer to be sure the filling has reached 165°F/75°C. If you are using a multi-level steamer basket, the levels farther away from the water may cook more slowly, so test on each level before removing.

Transfer the steamed dumplings to a serving platter. Serve warm, with dipping sauce on the side.

NOTE: Wonton wrappers come in a 1-pound/455-gram package, which will give you extra wrappers; the unused wrappers freeze well. Wrap them very well in plastic, pushing all the air out, before freezing.

Variation: **JASMINE POT STICKERS**

You can optionally finish these dumplings as pot stickers rather than steaming them. After the dumplings are formed, heat a nonstick sauté pan over medium heat and add 1 teaspoon vegetable oil. Place 8 to 12 (depending on the size of your pan; dumplings should not touch) dumplings in the pan and fill pan with just under ¼ inch of jasmine steaming liquid. Cover the pan and cook for 6 to 7 minutes, letting the liquid steam and evaporate out. Continue cooking without turning the dumplings until liquid has evaporated completely and the dumplings are lightly golden on the bottom. Remove to an ovenproof platter and place in warm oven. Clean the pan and repeat until all dumplings are cooked.

Tea-Steamed Dumplings

WHILE IN CHINA FOR THE INTERNATIONAL TEA CONVENTION IN CHANGSHA, Cindy took a side trip to Beijing and visited the Gengxiang Tea Company. The owners staged the most extraordinary stage show, with dancers pantomiming the Chinese tea ceremony as well as other dances, including one that involved pouring hot tea from pots with spouts that were several feet long while other dancers did acrobatic moves and became human tea tables. Not a drop was spilled!

During the show, guests were also served an exquisite meal that included unusual dumplings infused with jasmine tea, ginger, and sesame oil. It was impossible to decide which was more wonderful—the show or the food.

ENTRÉES

Meat

DARJEELING "DRY" MUNG BEANS

MUNG BEANS ARE A STAPLE OF INDIAN COOKING. WHOLE MUNG BEANS ARE DARK OLIVE GREEN IN *color, while the split version are golden yellow. Like lentils, mung beans cook relatively quickly and do not need to be soaked; usually a soup-like* dal *is made from them. This recipe, however, uses a technique of pre-soaking the beans for a few hours, which enables them to cook in less liquid and retain their shape. We adapted this "dry" technique from one described by Madhur Jaffrey in* World of the East Vegetarian Cooking. *Darjeeling tea nicely brings out the subtle flavor of the bean for this vegetarian entrée. Serve with basmati rice and plain yogurt or raita.*

Serves 8

- 2 cups/400 grams split yellow mung beans, picked over
- 6 cups/1.4 liters water, divided
- 1 tablespoon loose-leaf Darjeeling tea leaves
- 1 tablespoon safflower or canola oil
- 1½ teaspoons cumin seeds
- 1 teaspoon turmeric
- ¼ teaspoon salt

Place the mung beans in a sieve and rinse thoroughly several times, until the rinsing water is almost clear. Place the beans in a large bowl and cover with 4 cups/960 milliliters of the water. Soak for 3 to 5 hours.

Bring the remaining 2 cups/480 milliliters water to a boil and pour over the tea in a medium bowl. Steep, covered, for 4 minutes, then strain and discard the leaves. Set the tea aside to cool.

Drain and rinse the soaked beans. In a large pot, heat the oil. Add the cumin seeds and sauté until the color changes slightly, about 30 to 60 seconds. Immediately add the drained beans. Add the turmeric and salt and stir well. Add the reserved tea. Bring to a simmer, then reduce the heat to low and cook until all the liquid is absorbed, about 10 minutes. Check beans for doneness. They should be slightly tender, but just firm in the center. Remove from heat and serve warm or at room temperature.

TEA-ROASTED TOFU *with* PEANUT SAUCE

THIS RECIPE WAS INSPIRED BY A ROASTED TOFU IN NAVA ATLAS'S *VEGETARIAN EXPRESS* COOKBOOK.
Soy sauce has an earthy quality to it, which is enhanced with steeped Pu-erh or Keemun tea. Tofu "steaks" are dipped in the tea-steeped soy or tamari sauce, which infuses the bean curd with flavor as it roasts. The recipe takes minutes to prepare, adding to its appeal. Plus, it's kid friendly, thanks to the rich peanut sauce. Fresh mint adds an unexpected burst of flavor. Fresh cilantro may also be used.

Serves 6

¼ cup/60 milliliters reduced-sodium soy sauce

1 tablespoon loose-leaf Pu-erh or Keemun tea leaves, divided

3 (14- to 16-ounce/400- to 455-gram) packages extra-firm tofu

½ cup/130 grams unsalted natural peanut butter

¼ cup/60 milliliters fresh lemon juice

1 teaspoon honey

⅛ to ¼ teaspoon Tabasco, or more to taste

½ cup/120 milliliters boiling water (about 212°F/100°C)

3 tablespoons chopped fresh mint leaves

Preheat the oven to 425°F/220°C/gas 7. Line a baking sheet with foil and spray with vegetable cooking spray.

Place the soy sauce and 2 teaspoons of the tea in a medium microwave-safe bowl. Microwave on high for 25 seconds, then let steep, covered, for 5 minutes. Strain and discard the leaves.

Cut each block of tofu into 6 slices. Dip each slice in the soy-tea sauce, coating all sides. Reserve any leftover sauce. Place the tofu on the prepared baking sheet, about ¼ to ½ inch/6 to 12 milliliters apart. Make 2 shallow slashes on each piece of tofu. Bake for 15 minutes, until the surface of the tofu appears browned and dry. Flip each piece over and bake an additional 10 to 15 minutes, until the second side is browned.

Meanwhile, prepare the peanut sauce. In a small bowl, pour the boiling water over the remaining 1 teaspoon tea and steep, covered, for 5 minutes, then strain and discard the leaves. Reserve.

Add the peanut butter to the remaining soy sauce from the tofu and mix well. The mixture will thicken and be pasty. Stir in the lemon juice, honey, and Tabasco sauce. Add the tea, 1 tablespoon at a time; the mixture should be thin enough to pour, but not too watery.

To serve, place 3 pieces of tofu on each plate. Spoon a teaspoon of sauce over each piece and sprinkle with chopped mint. Serve warm with additional sauce and mint in bowls on the side.

❧ SMOKY BLACK LENTILS ❧

BLACK LENTILS ARE ALSO CALLED BELUGA LENTILS BECAUSE THEY RESEMBLE A LARGE VERSION OF THE *caviar. They hold their shape very well and don't tend to get mushy when overcooked. Smoky Lapsang Souchong goes well with them, and highlights the dark color of the legume. These lentils are also delicious served cold as a salad.*

Serves 8

4 cups/960 milliliters boiling water
(about 212°F)

4½ teaspoons loose-leaf Lapsang
Souchong tea leaves

2 cups/400 grams black lentils, picked
over and rinsed

1 (28-ounce/794-gram) can diced
tomatoes, preferably fire-roasted

¼ teaspoon fine sea salt, or more to taste

½ teaspoon freshly ground black pepper,
or more to taste

2 tablespoons minced fresh cilantro
or parsley, plus sprigs for garnish

Pour boiling water over tea leaves in a medium bowl. Steep, covered, for 4 minutes, then strain into a large saucepan and discard tea leaves. Add the lentils and tomatoes and bring to a boil over high heat. Lower the heat and simmer, uncovered, until most of the liquid is absorbed and the lentils are firm but tender, about 30 to 40 minutes. Let rest, covered, about 10 minutes. All the liquid should be absorbed. Stir in the salt, pepper, and cilantro or parsley and serve warm or at room temperature.

FRESH MATCHA PASTA

FRESH PASTA MADE WITH MATCHA POWDER IS DELICIOUS, WITH A SUBTLE FLAVOR AND A LOVELY, *pale green color. Use this pasta in the Spinach Rotollo on page 124, or toss with any light herb, vegetable, or cream-based sauce. You will need a pasta machine. The pasta is used fresh, and does not need to be dried. You could also use teas such as Assam, Keemun, Pu-erh, or Yunnan ground to a fine powder to create distinctly different but equally wonderful pastas.*

Serves 4

2 cups/260 grams all-purpose flour, plus additional, as needed

2 teaspoons matcha green tea powder

½ teaspoon fine sea salt (optional)

3 eggs, beaten

Water as needed

In the bowl of a food processor, pulse together the flour, matcha, and salt. Add the beaten egg and pulse to a rough ball. If it sticks to the sides, add a little more flour. If the dough doesn't pull together into a ball, add a little water. As soon as the dough starts to form a ball, remove it from the food processor and knead it on a lightly floured surface for 1 to 2 minutes. Form the dough into a ball and let it rest, covered, at room temperature for 15 minutes.

Cut the dough in half and flatten each half into a disk. Run one disk of dough at a time through a pasta machine with the rollers set to their widest. Fold into thirds and re-roll. Continue to run through until smooth, dusting lightly with flour if sticky. When smooth, start reducing the settings and continue running the pasta disk through the pasta machine until the dough is satiny and you can see your hand through it. As different pasta machines and even the weather can affect the pasta dough significantly, pay close attention to the texture and translucency of the dough to determine when it is ready.

Allow the finished pasta to rest about 10 minutes before cutting. To use for the Rotollo recipe, cut into sheets roughly 6 x 10 inches/15 x 25 centimeters. To use for lasagna, cut the dough into strips roughly 6 x 3 inches/15 x 7.5 centimeters. To make fettuccini, fold each sheet in thirds and cut into ¼ inch strands. Cook in boiling salted water for 1 to 2 minutes. Cool in a cold-water bath, then place on plastic wrap and cover until ready to use. The pasta is best cooked the day it is made but can be wrapped and refrigerated for 3 to 4 days.

GREEN TEA GNOCCHI *with* TOMATOES *and* GREENS

GNOCCHI ARE ITALIAN DUMPLINGS—A KIND OF PASTA, BUT THICKER, DOUGHY OVALS, USUALLY MADE *with potatoes or ricotta cheese and flour. Powdery matcha tea gives the gnocchi a subtle character that goes well with just about any pasta sauce, but especially well with lighter herb or vegetable sauces. Other teas, finely ground to a powder, give an equally delicious result. Consider a full-bodied black tea and pair these gnocchi with the Chicken and Mushroom Paprikash (page 130).*

Serves 4

GNOCCHI

2 cups/490 grams ricotta cheese

2 teaspoons matcha green tea powder

2 eggs, lightly beaten

Fine sea salt to taste

Freshly ground black pepper to taste

2 cups/260 grams all-purpose flour

SAUCE

2 tablespoons olive oil

2 garlic cloves, minced

2 cups/60 grams baby spinach leaves or baby arugula

1 cup/140 grams cherry tomatoes, halved

½ cup/60 grams freshly grated Parmesan or Asiago cheese, or more to taste

Freshly ground black pepper to taste

Matcha Salt (page 79) to taste (optional)

TO MAKE THE GNOCCHI: In a large bowl, stir together the ricotta, matcha, eggs, salt, and pepper until blended. Add the flour and stir until dough forms a large ball. This may also be done in a food processor.

Transfer the dough to a floured surface and knead slightly, adding more flour if mixture is too sticky. Divide the dough into several pieces and roll each one into cigar shapes about ⅓-inch/8 millimeters wide. Cut each "cigar" into 1 inch/2.5 centimeter segments. Lightly press your knuckle or the back of a fork into each segment to make slight indentations.

Fill a large pot with water and bring to a boil over high heat. When the water boils, sprinkle in 1 tablespoon salt. Drop the gnocchi into the boiling water in small batches. Cook until they float to the surface, about 3 minutes. Use a slotted spoon to transfer the cooked gnocchi to a colander. The gnocchi will have expanded slightly in size to tender pillowy dumplings.

WHILE THE GNOCCHI COOK, MAKE THE SAUCE: Heat the olive oil in a large skillet or sauté pan over medium heat. Add the garlic and cook 1 minute until it just begins to turn golden. Add the spinach or arugula and stir until the color just begins to brighten, then add the tomatoes. Stir to coat well with the garlic and oil, then add the cooked gnocchi. Toss well and transfer to a warmed serving platter. Garnish with grated cheese, pepper, and Matcha Salt, if desired.

Variation

GREEN TEA GNOCCHI WITH FRESH TEA LEAVES: Replace the baby spinach leaves or arugula with ½ cup/15 grams fresh young whole tea leaves and buds. Use 3 tablespoons cheese instead of ½ cup/60 grams, and garnish with 1 teaspoon grated orange zest.

VEGETABLE TART *with* FRESH TEA LEAVES

THIS RECIPE, AS WITH MOST RECIPES CALLING FOR FRESH TEA LEAVES, IS BEST MADE WITH YOUNGER *leaves, which have a subtle, delicate sweetness with a hint of tang. Older, larger leaves should be left for more intense cooking methods or for a garnish. Any kind of mushroom works in this tart, but we like portobello. Serve with a mixed green salad tossed with a tea vinaigrette. If fresh tea leaves are not available, fresh sorrel or basil may be used instead.*

Serves 8

ASSAM TEA CRUST

1¼ cups/160 grams all-purpose flour

½ teaspoon fine sea salt

1 teaspoon coarsely ground loose-leaf Assam tea leaves

6 tablespoons/85 grams unsalted butter, chilled and cut into pieces

2 to 3 tablespoons ice water

1 egg

1 tablespoon water

FILLING

1 cup/30 grams loosely packed fresh young tea leaves, fresh sorrel, or basil leaves

1 tablespoon unsalted butter

1 tablespoon olive oil

½ medium onion, coarsely chopped

1 garlic clove, minced

⅔ cup/45 grams sliced mushrooms

1 medium sweet potato, cut into ¼-inch/6-millimeter dice (about ⅔ cup/90 grams)

(continued)

TO MAKE THE CRUST: Add the flour, salt, and tea to the bowl of a food processor and pulse to combine. Add the butter and pulse until the mixture resembles pea-sized pebbles. Add 2 tablespoons of the ice water and pulse just until dough begins to pull together. If too dry, add additional water 1 teaspoon at a time. Avoid overworking, which can toughen the dough. Transfer the dough to a work surface and knead minimally, then form into a disk, wrap in plastic, and chill at least 30 minutes or up to 3 days. (You can also freeze the dough, double-wrapped in plastic, then thaw completely before using.)

When ready to bake, preheat the oven to 375°F/190°C/gas 5. Lightly grease a 10-inch/25-centimeter tart or pie pan.

On a lightly floured surface, roll out the chilled dough into a ⅛ inch/3-millimeter thick round. Fit into the prepared pan. Trim to a 1 inch/2.5 centimeter overhang and fold back in to strengthen the tart sides. (The tart shell may be wrapped in plastic and frozen at this point.) Prick the shell with a fork several times, then line with foil or parchment paper and fill with pastry weights or dried beans. Bake for 15 to 18 minutes, removing the foil and weights midway through. The shell should look dry with the beginnings of color.

Prepare an egg wash by mixing the egg with the water. Remove the crust from the oven, brush the bottom lightly with the egg wash and return to the oven for 2 minutes to set. The crust should be fully dry and slightly shiny. Remove from the oven and set aside.

Pinch sea salt, or more to taste

Pinch freshly ground black pepper,
   or more to taste

2 ounces/55 grams fresh goat cheese

3 eggs

1 cup/240 milliliters half-and-half

TO MAKE THE FILLING: Line the pre-baked shell with an even layer of tea leaves, reserving any extras. Set aside. Line a large baking sheet with parchment paper or foil.

In a large saucepan or skillet, heat the butter and oil over medium heat. When the butter has melted, add the onion and garlic and cook until they begin to soften, about 5 minutes. Add the mushrooms and sweet potato and continue to cook for a few minutes. The sweet potato and mushrooms should still be quite firm. Add salt and pepper to taste. Remove from the heat and toss in any remaining tea leaves. Stir well and spread the vegetables over the tea leaves in the tart shell. Crumble the goat cheese over the vegetables.

In a medium bowl, whisk together the eggs and half-and-half and pour over the vegetables in the tart. Place the tart on the prepared baking sheet and bake until the custard is just set and the edges of the crust are golden, about 25 minutes. If the crust is coloring too quickly, cover the rim with foil and continue to bake until the filling is just set. Transfer to a cooling rack. Cool for 10 minutes before slicing. Serve the tart warm or at room temperature.

Left: The classic Orange Pekoe, or "two leaves and a bud";
Right: Entering the low-elevation award-winning Sri Lankan tea estate New Vithanakande

OCEAN TROUT *with* GREEN TEA NOODLES

THIS RECIPE WAS CREATED BY PAUL FOREMAN, THE EXECUTIVE CHEF AT THE MARQUE IV IN TASMANIA, *as part of the Dilmah Tea 21st Anniversary event. He developed this recipe using a Sri Lankan green tea from Dilmah, but any good-quality green tea will work. Ocean trout are versatile to work with, rich but with a clean, fresh taste. They are not commonly available in this country, but salmon is a good substitute. Begin preparing this dish a day before you plan to serve it.*

Dried bonito flakes are made from a kind of tuna and are a staple of Japanese cooking. They are available at Asian supermarkets, and in the Asian food aisle of many supermarkets. If baby leeks are not available, scallions may be substituted.

Serves 4

FISH

4 cups/960 milliliters lightly steaming water (175°F/80°C)

2 dried lemon myrtle leaves or 1 tablespoon chopped fresh lemon grass

4½ tablespoons loose-leaf green tea leaves, divided

½ cup/30 grams bonito flakes

½ cup/50 grams scallions, green part only, sliced

1 teaspoon Matcha Salt (page 79) or coarse sea salt

Pinch white pepper

Pinch granulated sugar

4 (5- to 6-ounce/140- to 170-gram) ocean trout or salmon fillets, boned with skin on

2 tablespoons clarified butter, ghee, or light olive oil

12 baby leeks or scallions, cleaned and trimmed

4 shiitake mushrooms, stems removed, sliced

2 quarter-size slices fresh ginger, chopped

1 cup/65 grams enoki mushrooms

(continued)

TO MAKE THE TROUT: Pour the steaming water over the lemon myrtle or lemon grass and 3 tablespoons of the tea leaves. Steep, covered, for 4 minutes. Strain and let cool. Discard the leaves.

Combine the remaining 1½ tablespoons tea leaves with the bonito flakes, scallions, salt, pepper, and sugar and gently coat the skinless side of the fish. Wrap each piece of fish in multiple layers of cheese cloth and gently tie with cooking twine. Pour the cooled tea infusion into a shallow pan and place each fish skin-side up into the infusion. The skin should not be submerged. Cover and refrigerate 24 hours or up to 2 days.

TO MAKE THE GREEN TEA NOODLES: Place the flour, salt, and ground green tea in the bowl of a food processor and pulse several times to mix. Add the egg, yolk, and water and pulse until mixture forms a rough ball. Add more flour if it sticks to the bowl; add more water if it doesn't come together into a ball. Remove and knead on a lightly floured surface until smooth. Cover and set aside to rest for 15 minutes.

Fill a large stockpot with water and bring to a boil over high heat.

While the water comes to a boil, divide the dough into 6 portions and flatten each into a disk. You will need to roll the dough as thin as possible; this is most easily done using a manual pasta machine that has two rollers. Working with one disk of dough at a time, run the dough through the pasta maker with the rollers set to their widest. Fold into thirds and re-roll. Continue to run through until smooth, dusting lightly with flour if sticky. Repeat with each disk of dough. *(continued)*

GREEN TEA NOODLES

2 cups/255 grams all-purpose flour

4 teaspoons loose-leaf green tea leaves, coarsely ground to yield 2 teaspoons

¼ teaspoon Matcha Salt (page 79) or coarse sea salt

1 egg, lightly beaten

1 egg yolk

4 teaspoons water

NOTE: The ground green tea leaves result in a beautifully speckled pasta with some texture from the leaves. If you prefer a smoother look and mouthfeel, matcha green tea powder may be substituted. You will need a pasta machine to make the Green Tea Noodles.

When one disk is extremely smooth to the touch, fold it in thirds and set aside, repeating with remaining disks of dough. Once they are all smooth, start reducing the settings of the rollers. Continue to feed the dough through the rollers, folding and rerolling each piece of dough until smooth, then reduce the settings further. Continue rolling until the dough is satiny and you can see your hand through it, then run each strip through the spaghetti attachment.

When water comes to a boil, sprinkle in 1 tablespoon of salt, then add the noodles and cook for 1 minute, until just al dente. Because the pasta is fresh and not dried, it will cook very quickly. The salt in the water will help keep the pasta from becoming gummy or sticky. Immediately drain the pasta using a colander, cool slightly, then divide into four portions. Use a large fork, such as a carving fork, to twirl into individual bundles of a size comfortable for you to handle. Place on a tray, and cover and refrigerate for up to 3 days.

When ready to cook the fish, remove the trout from the green tea infusion and unwrap. Pour the tea infusion into a medium saucepan and reserve. Gently wipe off the bonito and scallions. Pat dry and sprinkle a small amount of salt on the skin.

In a large skillet, heat the clarified butter or oil until very hot. Add the trout, skin-side down, and press the fish down with a spatula for about 15 seconds so that the skin cooks flat and crisp. Continue to cook at moderate heat 1 to 2 minutes more until cooked through. Turn the fish over and let rest in the pan in a warm area until ready to serve.

Bring the reserved tea infusion to a boil over high heat. Maintain the boil for a minute, then lower heat to maintain a simmer. Add the leeks, shiitake mushrooms, and ginger and cook for 2 minutes. If you are using scallions rather than baby leeks, simmer the mushrooms and ginger for 1 minute, then add the scallions and simmer for 1 more minute. Add the green tea noodle bundles to warm through. Divide the noodles and the tea mixture among 4 large warm soup bowls. Set the trout on the noodles and top with the enoki mushrooms. Serve immediately.

SALMON EN PAPILLOTE *with* FRESH TEA LEAVES

BAKING SALMON IN PARCHMENT OR FOIL MAKES IT ESPECIALLY MOIST, TENDER, AND DELICIOUS.
The fresh tea leaves infuse the fish with a bright flavor, enhanced by white wine. Each person should open their own parchment packet at the table so they can enjoy the rich, sweet, aromatic steam that is released. Serve with lentils and a crisp green salad. If fresh tea leaves are not available, you can substitute fresh sorrel or spinach leaves for a tasty alternative. Serve this salmon with a Darjeeling or Green Tea Citrus Beurre Blanc (page 85).

Serves 4

4 (6-ounce/170 gram) salmon fillets

1½ cups/45 grams fresh tea leaves and buds (tender young leaves only)

1 medium tomato, seeded and diced

1½ cups/100 grams sliced mushrooms

½ cup/120 milliliters dry white wine

2 tablespoons unsalted butter

4 sprigs fresh thyme

Fine sea salt to taste

Freshly ground black pepper to taste

Preheat the oven to 350°F/180°C/gas 4.

Cut 4 (18 inch/46 centimeter) pieces of parchment paper or foil. Place a salmon fillet in the middle of each piece. Place ¼ of the diced tomatoes and ¼ of the tea leaves on each piece of salmon. Arrange the sliced mushrooms over the tea leaves and drizzle each fillet with 2 tablespoons white wine. Cut the butter into 4 pieces and place one over each pile of mushrooms. Place a sprig of fresh thyme on each and finish with a sprinkle of salt and grind of pepper. Fold each packet over fish and fold under edges to seal securely.

Place the packets on a baking sheet and bake until salmon is just cooked through to your taste, about 15 to 25 minutes; the timing will vary by the thickness of the fillet.

To serve, place a packet on each of 4 plates. Serve immediately.

GREEN TEA-LACQUERED SALMON

THIS RECIPE WAS CREATED BY CHRISTOPH LEU, THE CORPORATE CHEF OF STARWOOD HOTELS, AND *Julia Tolstunova, also with Starwood. It is regularly served at several Starwood hotels and resorts around the world.*

Serves 4

½ cup/120 milliliters steaming water (about 175°F/80°C)

4 teaspoons loose-leaf green tea leaves, such as Dragonwell or sencha

4 teaspoons honey

4 (6-ounce/170-gram) salmon fillets, preferably with skin on

4 tablespoons extra virgin olive oil, divided

4 medium sweet potatoes, peeled and diced

1 tablespoon minced garlic

8 cups/240 grams baby spinach

1 medium shallot, minced

4 ounces/115 grams shiitake mushrooms, stems removed, halved

½ cup/120 milliliters dry white wine

2 tablespoons fresh lemon juice

1 cup/240 milliliters chicken or vegetable stock

Fresh or dried thyme to taste

Fine sea salt to taste

Freshly ground black pepper to taste

Pour the steaming water over the tea leaves in a small bowl and add honey. Steep, covered, for 2½ minutes, strain, and discard the leaves. Place salmon in a nonreactive pan. Brush with honey tea and pour any remaining tea around the fish. Let marinate in the refrigerator, covered, for at least 1 hour and up to 2 days.

When ready to cook, preheat the oven to broil or preheat the broiler. If you have a separate oven, preheat it to 350°F/180°C/gas 4. Line a broiler pan with foil and spray with vegetable cooking spray. Place the salmon fillets in the pan skin-side down and broil them to just golden; the interior will not yet be cooked. The exact timing will vary by the distance from the heat source, but it will not take long, so keep a careful eye on the salmon.

Lower the heat to 350°F/180°C/gas 4 or transfer the fish to the preheated oven and bake until the fish is cooked through, about 5 to 10 minutes.

While the fish cooks, heat 3 tablespoons of the oil in a large skillet over medium heat. Add the sweet potatoes and sauté until golden, 6 to 10 minutes. Transfer the sweet potatoes to a bowl and tent with foil to keep warm.

Add the garlic and spinach to the pan and sauté until the spinach is just wilted, less than a minute. Transfer to a shallow serving bowl.

Add the remaining 1 tablespoon oil to the skillet. Heat over medium heat and add the shallots and shiitakes. Sauté until the shallots are translucent and the mushrooms have begun to release some of their juices, about 3 or 4 minutes. Deglaze with the white wine and lemon juice, scraping any bits stuck to the pan. Reduce the liquid by half over medium-high heat, then add the chicken stock and simmer to reduce by half again, another few minutes. Add thyme, salt, and pepper to taste.

Pour the mushroom and shallot mixture over the spinach. Add the sweet potatoes and place the salmon on top. Serve immediately.

GREEN TEA-POACHED BLACK BASS *with* PORCINI CREAM SAUCE *and* WHITE BEAN PURÉE

THIS RECIPE WAS SHARED WITH US BY CHEF DARRELL LAZIER, WHO FIRST BEGAN EXPERIMENTING *with tea when he was a sous chef at the Boston Park Plaza Hotel and Towers. The use of green tea with the fish and Pu-erh with the porcini mushroom sauce gives the dish a wonderful contrast between clean and sweet, rich and earthy flavors. Serve this with baby spinach quickly sautéed with garlic and olive oil.*

Serves 4

WHITE BEAN PURÉE

1 teaspoon loose-leaf green tea leaves, such as Dragonwell or sencha

1/2 cup/120 milliliters steaming water (about 175°F/80°C)

1 head garlic

2 teaspoons olive oil

1/2 cup/120 milliliters vegetable or chicken stock

2 (15-ounce/425-gram) cans white cannellini beans, rinsed and drained, or 2 cups cooked white beans

1/4 teaspoon fine sea salt

1/4 teaspoon freshly ground black pepper

1/2 teaspoon ground cinnamon

Zest of 1 orange

FRESH PORCINI CREAM SAUCE

2 teaspoons loose-leaf Pu-erh tea leaves, or other full-bodied earthy black tea leaves

1/2 cup/120 milliliters boiling water (about 212°F/100°C)

1 tablespoon vegetable oil

1/2 cup/80 grams chopped white onion

TO MAKE THE WHITE BEAN PURÉE: Preheat the oven to 400°F/ 200°C/gas 6. Place the tea leaves in a small bowl. Add the steaming water and steep, covered, for 2 minutes. Strain and discard the leaves. Reserve.

Slice the top 1/4 inch/6 millimeters or so off the head of garlic to expose the tips of the individual cloves. Spray a small baking pan with vegetable cooking spray. Place the garlic in the pan and drizzle 2 teaspoons of the olive oil over the top of the cut side. Cover the pan with foil and bake for 25 to 30 minutes, until the garlic is light golden and the cloves are soft. Remove from the oven and let cool until cool enough to handle. Break apart the head and squeeze the individual soft roasted cloves into a large saucepan. Use the back of a spoon to mash it. Add the stock and the reserved tea slowly so that the garlic and liquids mix together smoothly.

Add the beans and stir in the salt, pepper, and cinnamon and cook until beans are hot and 3/4 of the liquid is gone. Transfer to a blender or food processor and purée until smooth. Stir in the orange zest.

WHILE THE GARLIC ROASTS, PREPARE THE PORCINI CREAM SAUCE: Place the Pu-erh tea leaves in a medium bowl. Pour the boiling water over them and steep, covered, for 5 minutes. Strain, discarding the leaves. Reserve.

In a medium saucepan heat the vegetable oil over medium-high heat. Add the onion and garlic and sauté till translucent. Add the thyme, reserved tea, and cream. Stir in the tomato paste and season with salt and pepper to taste. Bring to a boil over high heat, then immediately

2 tablespoons chopped garlic

2 teaspoons chopped fresh thyme

1 cup/240 milliliters heavy whipping cream

2 teaspoons tomato paste

Fine sea salt to taste

Freshly ground black pepper to taste

2/3 cup/20 grams dried porcini mushrooms

POACHED BLACK BASS

3 cups/720 milliliters water

1 cup/240 milliliters white wine

2 teaspoons fine sea salt

1 teaspoon freshly ground black pepper

2 whole star anise

1/2 cup/20 grams loose-leaf green tea
    leaves, such as Dragonwell or sencha

Grated zest and juice of 1 lemon

4 (6- to 8-ounce/170- to 225-gram)
    boneless black bass fillets

reduce the heat to maintain a low simmer. Reduce the liquid by half, about 6 to 8 minutes. Strain and return to the pan, discarding the solids. Simmer and add the mushrooms. Cook until the mushrooms are tender and the sauce is the consistency of heavy whipping cream, about 4 or 5 minutes. Set aside. (The sauce may be prepared up to 3 days in advance. Refrigerate, covered, then reheat gently over low heat when ready to serve.)

TO MAKE THE POACHED BLACK BASS: In a large wide pan combine the water, wine, salt, pepper, star anise, tea, and lemon zest and juice. Bring to a simmer over medium-low heat. Add the bass. If the fish is not fully submerged, add additional hot water. Poach gently for 10 to 15 minutes or until the fish is fork-tender and cooked through.

To serve, place hot bean purée in the center of 4 plates. Top with the poached fish. Drizzle cream sauce over the fish and around each plate.

NOTE: When roasting the garlic for the White Bean Purée, you can use the same technique to roast several heads at once, and keep the extra on hand. Roasted garlic makes a flavorful addition to sauces and is great on its own as a spread.

SPINACH and RICOTTA SCALLOP ROTOLLO with CEYLON BEURRE BLANC

THIS DISH WAS CREATED BY CHEF PAUL BROWN OF THE MANTRA ERSKINE BEACH RESORT IN AUSTRALIA, *where he uses the local Tasmanian scallops, but any good-quality fresh sea scallop will work. Rotollo are sheets of fresh pasta that are rolled up with a filling (traditionally spinach, but it can vary) and sliced into pinwheels. We use homemade Matcha Pasta (page 112) but you can also use regular pasta sheets, as Chef Brown did.*

Serves 6

1 tablespoon loose-leaf Ceylon tea leaves (like Ceylon Pekoe)

1 cup/240 milliliters dry white wine

13 tablespoons/180 grams unsalted butter, divided

1 medium onion, finely chopped

1 garlic clove, minced

1 teaspoon grated lemon zest

¼ cup/4 grams chopped mixed fresh herbs (basil, parsley, sage, tarragon, or any combination)

9 cups/270 grams baby spinach

¾ cup/185 grams ricotta cheese

2 sheets plain fresh pasta or Matcha Pasta, roughly 6 x 10 inches/15 x 25 centimeters (page 112)

1 teaspoon fresh lemon juice

2 tablespoons vegetable oil

12 sage leaves

6 large sea scallops, cleaned

Place the tea leaves in a small bowl and pour the wine over them. Cover and steep overnight at room temperature.

In a large nonstick skillet, melt 1 tablespoon of the butter over medium-high heat. Add the onion and garlic and sauté until soft and translucent. Add the lemon zest and herbs and cook another 2 minutes. Remove from heat and let cool.

Fill a large pot with water and bring to a boil. Have a bowl of ice water nearby. Blanch the spinach by placing it in the boiling water, then immediately transfer it to the ice water to stop the cooking. Reserve the pot of boiling water. Place the blanched spinach in a sieve and gently press down to squeeze out as much liquid as possible from the spinach. Chop the cooked spinach and combine with the ricotta cheese. Mix well.

Make sure the pot of water is still boiling. Add 1 tablespoon salt to the water, then add the matcha pasta, boil for 2 minutes, then drain and run under cold water.

Spread the spinach-ricotta mixture evenly over the cooked pasta sheets with roughly a 1 inch/2.5 centimeter border at one of the short ends. Roll up as if you were making a jelly roll, starting from the other end. Moisten the end of the pasta sheet and continue to roll to close and seal. Cover the pasta roll with plastic wrap and refrigerate until ready to cook, up to 3 days. When ready to cook, cut each pasta roll into 3 slices (each slice should each be 2-inches/5 centimeters wide). Prepare a steamer basket by oiling it well and placing a 2½-inch/6-centimeter square of parchment paper in the basket for each rotollo to sit on, then place the rotollo upright, one cut-side down, and steam over an inch of boiling water until just heated through, about 10 minutes. The rotollo should not touch, so depending on the size of your steamer, you may need to steam them in 2 batches.

TO MAKE THE CEYLON BEURRE BLANC: Strain the tea leaves from the white wine and discard. Place the tea-infused wine in a medium saucepan and add lemon juice. Heat over medium-high heat and bring to a simmer. Cook until the wine is reduced by $3/4$—there should be about $1/4$ cup/60 milliliters. Gradually whisk in remaining 12 tablespoons butter, 1 tablespoon at a time: add a tablespoon, whisk until melted and incorporated, then add the next tablespoon of butter. The sauce should be smooth and velvety. Remove from the heat.

In a large nonstick skillet, heat the oil over medium-high heat. Add the sage leaves and fry until they are crisp, 1 to 2 minutes. Transfer to a paper towel to drain and add the scallops to the pan. Sear the scallops for 1 minute on each side. To serve, transfer each spinach rotollo to a plate. Place scallops and sage leaves on top and spoon the Ceylon beurre blanc around. Serve immediately.

NOTE: The tea needs to steep overnight, so plan accordingly. The dish was created with Dilmah Exceptional Valley of Kings Ceylon Pekoe tea but any good quality Ceylon may be used.

Left: Havakul Tea Estate, Nilgiri region in southern India; *Right:* A water buffalo greets our jeep while traveling in India.

SALMON in BLACK TEA-COCONUT SAUCE

CHEF SHARONE ARTSI WHO IS CURRENTLY LIVING AND COOKING IN JERUSALEM, WAS INSPIRED BY *Indian flavors and the use of Indian tea to create this dish for the 2009 New England Culinary Tea Competition. It has several components which can be made in advance. The tea infuses a coconut milk-based sauce, adding another dimension to the dish. Curry leaves can be found at Indian markets.*

Serves 6

CURRY TEA SPICE

10 tablespoons loose-leaf Darjeeling tea leaves

1 tablespoon turmeric

1 teaspoon ground ginger

4 teaspoons paprika

4 teaspoons ground coriander

1 teaspoon freshly ground black pepper

CILANTRO OIL

¼ cup/5 grams chopped fresh cilantro leaves

2 tablespoons chopped fresh basil leaves

⅓ cup/75 milliliters canola oil

COCONUT RICE

2 tablespoons olive oil

1 medium onion, chopped

2 cups/430 grams brown rice

4 cups/960 milliliters water

1 cup/130 grams chopped unsalted roasted cashews

2 cups/190 grams sweetened shredded coconut

Pinch fine sea salt

TO MAKE THE CURRY TEA SPICE: Combine the tea, turmeric, ginger, paprika, coriander, and pepper in a spice grinder or mortar and pestle and grind to a fine powder. Reserve 7 tablespoons for the salmon, and store any leftover in an airtight container in a dark cupboard.

TO MAKE THE CILANTRO OIL: Place the cilantro and basil leaves in a blender or food processor. Pulse to mince, then, with machine running, pour in the oil, slowly. Continue processing until the mixture forms a fine purée. Use immediately or store, refrigerated, in an airtight container, for up to 3 days.

TO MAKE THE COCONUT RICE: In a large pot, heat the oil over medium heat. Add the onion, stir, and cook until translucent, about 5 to 7 minutes. Add the rice, stir, and heat for 2 minutes, then add the water. Bring to a boil over high heat, stir, and reduce the heat to low. Cover and cook 40 minutes, until rice is almost tender yet still holding its shape well. Stir in cashews, coconut, and salt. Remove from heat, cover, and reserve.

TO MAKE THE SALMON: Rub the fillets on all sides with 3 tablespoons of the oil, then coat with the Curry Tea Spice. In a large, wide pan, heat the remaining 3 tablespoons oil over medium-high until hot. Add the salmon and quickly sear on both sides; this should take less than a minute per side and the center should stay rare. Transfer the salmon to a plate and set aside.

TO MAKE THE BLACK TEA-COCONUT SAUCE: In the same pan, add additional oil if needed and cook the onions over medium-high heat until translucent, stirring constantly. Add the garlic and ginger and mix

SALMON

6 (6-ounce/170-gram) salmon fillets

6 tablespoons olive oil, divided

3 tablespoons Curry Tea Spice

BLACK TEA-COCONUT SAUCE

2 medium onions, sliced

3 garlic cloves, finely chopped

1 (1-inch/2.5-centimeter) piece
fresh ginger

¼ cup Curry Tea Spice

1½ tablespoons tomato paste

2 (13½-ounce/400-milliliter) cans
coconut milk

1½ cups/360 milliliters water

1 tablespoon white vinegar

2 teaspoons fresh lemon juice

1 dried red chile (such as Thai), seeded,
or ½ teaspoon ground chile powder

5 tablespoons granulated sugar

5 curry leaves (optional)

2 russet potatoes, cut into ½-inch/
12-millimeter cubes

Fine sea salt to taste

½ red bell pepper, finely diced

½ yellow bell pepper, finely diced

½ orange bell pepper, finely diced

½ green bell pepper, finely diced

well. Add the Curry Tea Spice and cook for 3 more minutes.

Add the tomato paste, coconut milk, water, vinegar, lemon juice, chile, sugar, and curry leaves, if using. Increase heat to high and bring to a boil.

Reduce to low-medium heat, cover, and simmer for 25 minutes to meld flavors. The final sauce should be the thickness of heavy cream. Stir occasionally, adding additional water if mixture becomes too thick.

When the sauce thickens, add the potatoes and cook until partially cooked and still slightly firm, about 10 to 12 minutes. Add the salmon and cook for an additional 5 to 7 minutes, depending on the thickness of the salmon, until the salmon is cooked to your liking and the potatoes are tender when pierced with the tip of a knife. Taste and season with salt as needed.

To assemble, divide the rice among 6 plates. Surround it with a small amount of coconut sauce. Place a salmon fillet and potatoes on top of the rice. Drizzle about 1 tablespoon of the cilantro oil over each fillet, then garnish each plate with mixture of the diced peppers. Serve hot.

⊱ SEARED TUNA *with* TEA SPICE CRUST ⊰

A version of this recipe originally appeared in Hannaford Supermarkets' *fresh* magazine. *It's an adaptable dish, great served warm or chilled. Use a bright, aromatic black tea, such as a good Ceylon or Nilgiri. Serve with Darjeeling Vinaigrette (page 75), Fresh Tea Vinaigrette (page 76), or the Soy-Ginger sauce below.*

Serves 4

TUNA

6 tablespoons loose-leaf black tea leaves, such as Ceylon or Nilgiri

½ teaspoon whole coriander seeds

½ teaspoon whole black peppercorns

1 cinnamon stick or 2 teaspoons ground cinnamon

½ teaspoon anise seeds

½ teaspoon ground ginger

½ teaspoon kosher salt

1 tablespoon (packed) light brown sugar

1 (1½ pound/680-gram) tuna steak (1-inch/2.5 centimeters thick)

3 tablespoons safflower or canola oil

Salad greens or arugula, for serving

SOY-GINGER SAUCE

6 tablespoons/90 milliliters low-sodium soy sauce

¼ cup/60 milliliters vegetable stock or steeped jasmine tea

2 tablespoons rice vinegar

1 teaspoon minced fresh ginger or ½ teaspoon ground ginger

1 garlic clove, minced

¼ teaspoon toasted sesame oil

To make tea-spice crust: Combine the tea leaves, coriander, peppercorns, cinnamon, anise, ginger, and salt in a spice grinder or mortar and pestle and finely grind together. Transfer to a shallow plate and stir in the brown sugar. Mix well.

Cut the tuna steak into 1 inch/2.5 centimeter-thick by 1-inch-wide strips. Roll each strip in the safflower or canola oil, then roll in the tea-spice crust to coat well. Reserve the remaining oil. Let sit for 10 minutes for crust to set.

To make the soy-ginger sauce: In a small bowl, whisk together the soy sauce, stock (or tea), vinegar, ginger, garlic, and sesame oil. Set aside.

In a large nonstick skillet over medium-high heat, heat the reserved oil over medium-high heat until shimmering. Sear the tuna quickly on each side; it should still be very rare in the center. Keep a very careful eye; it should take only around 30 seconds per side. The tuna may be served immediately, or refrigerated until ready to serve.

When ready to serve, toss greens on a platter with ¼ cup/60 milliliters of the soy-ginger sauce. Slice each piece of tuna ⅓-inch/8 millimeters thick on a steep diagonal and arrange overlapping slices on top of the arugula. Drizzle tuna with remaining sauce or place in a small dish for dipping and serve immediately.

Note: Since the tuna should only be seared on the exterior and not cooked through, be sure to use only very fresh sushi-grade tuna.

CHICKEN and MUSHROOM PAPRIKASH

THIS SATISFYING CLASSIC HUNGARIAN ENTRÉE GAINS EVEN MORE DEPTH OF FLAVOR WHEN THE *chicken is marinated in a full-bodied, earthy black tea. We like the added smokiness imparted by Lapsang Souchong, but you will have equally wonderful (but different) results with an earthy Yunnan or Pu-erh, malty Assam, aromatic Nilgiri, or low-grown Ceylon.*

Since this dish depends on the quality of the tea and the paprika, make sure both are fresh. Vary the proportions of sweet and hot paprika used to suit your taste. The earthier the tea you choose, the more hot paprika the dish can support and balance nicely. If you have only sweet paprika, but want the kick, substitute additional sweet paprika plus half a teaspoon or more (depending on your taste) of cayenne pepper.

Serves 6

¼ cup/10 grams loose-leaf full-bodied black tea leaves, such as Lapsang Souchong or Pu-erh

1½ cups/360 milliliters boiling water (about 212°F/100°C)

4 pounds/1.8 kilograms bone-in chicken thighs, skin left on

Fresh sea salt, to taste

Freshly ground black pepper, to taste

2 tablespoons vegetable oil, divided

1 medium onion, thinly sliced

1 medium red bell pepper, cut into ¼-inch/6-millimeter slices

1 medium green bell pepper, cut into ¼-inch/6-millimeter slices

1½ cups/100 grams thinly sliced mushrooms

3 tablespoons sweet Hungarian paprika, divided

2 teaspoons hot Hungarian paprika

1 tablespoon all-purpose flour

Place the tea leaves in a glass measuring cup or bowl and add the boiling water. Steep, covered, for 5 minutes. Strain, discarding the leaves; cool.

Place the chicken thighs in a gallon-size resealable plastic bag. Pour the fully cooled tea over the chicken, seal bag, and refrigerate overnight or up to 2 days, turning the chicken over once. When ready to proceed, remove the chicken from the tea, pat dry, and reserve the liquid to use later. Season the chicken with the salt and pepper to taste.

In large pot or Dutch oven, heat 1 tablespoon of the oil over medium heat. Place half the thighs in the pot and brown each side, about 5 to 7 minutes per side. Transfer the browned thighs to a plate. Add the remaining 1 tablespoon oil to the pot and brown remaining chicken and transfer to the plate. Pour off any excess fat, keeping 1 tablespoon in the pan.

Add the onions and cook over medium heat 5 to 8 minutes until softened. Add the peppers and mushrooms and cook until the onions are browned, another several minutes. Add 2 tablespoons of the sweet paprika, the hot paprika, and the flour. Stir well and cook until you can smell the paprika. Add tomatoes, reserved tea from the marinated chicken, marjoram, and thyme. Stir well, scraping up any browned bits stuck to the bottom of the pot.

Return the browned chicken to the pot and cover with the tomato-vegetable mixture. Reduce the heat to medium-low, cover, and cook until the chicken is tender, about 1 hour.

1 (14.5-ounce/411-gram) can crushed tomatoes

¼ teaspoon dried marjoram

¼ teaspoon dried thyme

½ cup/120 milliliters sour cream

Fresh parsley sprigs, for garnish

Remove the pot from the heat and transfer the chicken to a warmed platter and tent with foil. Skim excess fat off the surface of the sauce in the pan and stir in the remaining 1 tablespoon sweet paprika. Temper the sour cream by stirring small amounts of the sauce into the sour cream until it is quite warm, then stirring all the sour cream into the sauce. Season to taste with additional salt and pepper, if needed.

To serve, spoon the sauce over the chicken on the platter, and garnish with parsley sprigs. Serve any extra sauce in a pitcher on the side.

NOTES: The chicken needs to marinate overnight, so plan accordingly. If desired, serve the chicken with egg noodles or with homemade Green Tea Noodles (page 118) or Fresh Matcha Pasta (page 112), cut as fettuccini, or Green Tea Gnocchi (page 113). Consider substituting finely ground black tea for the matcha in any of these accompaniments.

MURGH KALI MIRCH

(Peppered Chicken with Pomegranate-Darjeeling Jelly)

THIS INTENSELY FLAVORFUL DISH WAS CREATED BY CHEF ANIL CHABUKSWAR AT LE ROYAL MERIDIAN
Hotel in Mumbai, India. They cook it in a tandoor oven, but since few of us have that luxury, we finish it on the grill instead.

Serves 4

CHICKEN

2 pounds/910 grams boneless chicken (breast or thigh meat, but do not mix on the same skewer because the cooking times will vary)

½ cup/120 milliliters plus 2 tablespoons thick Greek-style yogurt

1 teaspoon minced fresh ginger

1 teaspoon minced garlic

¼ poblano chile, finely minced (about 2 teaspoons)

1 teaspoon freshly ground black pepper

1 teaspoon ground cumin

1 teaspoon ground coriander

2 teaspoons garam masala

2 tablespoons finely ground Darjeeling tea leaves

3 tablespoons crème fraîche

1 tablespoon mustard oil, or 1 tablespoon vegetable oil and ½ teaspoon mustard seeds, freshly ground

POMEGRANATE-DARJEELING JELLY

¾ cup/180 milliliters apple juice

1 tablespoon loose-leaf Darjeeling tea leaves

4½ teaspoons powdered gelatin

1 cup/240 milliliters pomegranate juice

TO MAKE THE CHICKEN: Cut chicken into cubes and thread onto 8 skewers. Set aside.

In a medium bowl, combine yogurt, ginger, garlic, poblano chile, black pepper, cumin, coriander, garam masala, ground tea, crème fraîche, and mustard oil. Whisk until smooth. Brush over the skewered chicken, being sure to coat all sides. Place the skewers in a 13 x 9-inch/33 x 23-centimeter pan; cover and refrigerate for at least 3 hours or up to 1 day.

TO MAKE THE JELLY: In a medium saucepan, bring the apple juice to a boil. Remove from the heat immediately and add the tea leaves. Let steep, covered, for 10 minutes—it should have a distinct Darjeeling taste but not a developed bitterness. When the juice has reached the desired infusion, strain, discarding the leaves. If the mixture has cooled to room temperature, warm it slightly over low heat. Turn off the heat, then add the gelatin powder. Stir in until clear, then add the pomegranate juice. Transfer to four small decorative glasses or bowls as desired. Refrigerate until set, about 4 hours. The Darjeeling jelly may be made ahead up to 3 days.

When ready to cook the chicken, remove from the fridge. Heat the grill to medium heat. Grill the chicken until cooked through, turning the skewers a quarter-turn every 2 minutes. The total cooking time will be about 8 to 9 minutes for dark meat, 6 to 7 minutes for white. Serve warm, with Pomegranate-Darjeeling Jelly on the side.

NOTES: The recipe calls for mustard oil, a staple in Indian cooking that is found in Indian markets. You can use vegetable oil combined with mustard seeds instead. If you use bamboo skewers be sure to presoak them in warm water for at least 10 minutes.

CHICKEN PESTO PIZZA *with* KUKICHA CRUST

ADAGIO TEAS, A WONDERFUL WEB SITE THAT IS A SOURCE FOR TEAS AS WELL AS A SOCIAL COMMUNITY, *periodically sponsors a cooking-with-tea contest. This recipe, by John Winter, is one of the winners. Kukicha is a toasty tasting green tea; a hojicha or Gunpowder green tea would work very nicely as well. The tea gives the dough a flavor that is simultaneously bright and earthy. Try experimenting using different teas for different flavors.*

Serves 4

CRUST

1 tablespoon loose-leaf kukicha tea leaves

1½ cups/360 milliliters steaming water (about 175°F/80°C)

1 (¼-ounce) package active dry yeast or 2 teaspoons instant yeast (also called rapid rise)

½ teaspoon light or dark brown sugar

1 teaspoon fine sea salt

2 tablespoons olive oil

3⅓ cups/430 grams all-purpose flour

TOPPINGS

¾ to 1 cup/180 to 240 milliliters prepared pesto sauce, as needed

1 green bell pepper, diced

1 small onion, diced

¾ cup/50 grams chopped white mushrooms

2 cups/280 grams diced cooked chicken

2 cups/225 grams shredded mozzarella cheese

1 cup/115 grams crumbled feta cheese

Put tea leaves in a bowl. Pour steaming water over them and steep, covered, for 3 minutes. Strain into a large bowl, discarding the leaves. Let cool to lukewarm (about 110 to 115°F/43 to 46°C; if the tea is too hot, it will kill the yeast).

If using active dry yeast, add the active dry yeast and sugar to the lukewarm tea. Let it sit for 10 minutes to proof and become foamy. Add the salt and oil to the liquid and mix to combine. Gradually mix in 2 cups of the flour. If using instant yeast, mix tea with sugar, salt, and oil, then add yeast and immediately start adding the flour. Place the dough on a floured surface and work in more flour until the dough is no longer sticky. Place the dough in an oiled bowl, cover, and let it rise until doubled or more in bulk, at least 1 hour and up to 3 hours.

When ready to bake, preheat the oven to 425°F/220°C/gas 7. Spray a round pizza pan or rectangular baking sheet with vegetable cooking spray. If you have a pizza stone, by all means use it!

Punch down the dough, then roll it out into a circle or rectangle to fit the prepared pan. Spread the pesto sauce over the surface, then distribute the green pepper, onion, mushrooms, and chicken evenly over the pesto. Top with the shredded mozzarella, followed by the crumbled feta cheese.

Bake at 425°F/220°C/gas 7 for 25 to 30 minutes, or until the dough is golden-brown. Cut into slices and serve hot.

NOTE: The dough may be made with either active dry yeast, which needs to be proofed, or instant yeast; note the different instructions. If using a bread machine, use instant yeast, which can be added directly to the flour.

CLAY-COOKED ASIAN CHICKEN

PU-ERH TEA, AN AGED BLACK TEA FROM SOUTHERN CHINA, WORKS WITH THE SOY SAUCE TO IMPART A *deep, musky earthiness to the chicken. Chicken cooked in a clay pot steams in the marinade and juices during the cooking, making it moist, tender, and extremely flavorful. The skin will not have the crispness of a traditionally roasted chicken. If you do not have a clay pot, you will also get excellent results cooking in a covered Dutch oven or other ovenproof heavy pot with a well-fitting lid. If the lid does not seal reasonably well, cover the top of the pot with a layer of foil before placing the lid on top. Serve this with Jasmine Dumplings (page 103) and blanched asparagus. You can also use this delectable chicken as a filling in Fresh Thai Spring Rolls (page 98), or the Chicken Pesto Pizza with Kukicha Crust (page 134).*

Serves 4

¼ cup/10 grams loose-leaf Pu-erh tea leaves

2 cups/480 millimeters boiling water (about 212°F/100°C)

½ cup/120 milliliters soy sauce

1 tablespoon Vietnamese chili-garlic sauce (or chili sauce and 1 pressed garlic clove)

2 garlic cloves, chopped

1 tablespoon chopped fresh ginger

2 tablespoons toasted sesame oil

1 (4- to 4½-pound/1.8-to 2-kilogram) whole chicken

Place the tea leaves in a medium bowl. Add the boiling water and steep, covered, for 6 minutes. Strain the tea, discarding the leaves, and let cool completely.

When the tea has cooled, add the soy sauce, chili-garlic sauce, garlic, ginger, and sesame oil and whisk until combined.

Rinse the chicken well, removing the neck and giblets from the cavity as well as any extra fat from the cavity entrance. Place the chicken in a gallon-size heavy-duty resealable plastic bag and pour in the marinade. Seal and turn to cover well. Place the bag in a large bowl or pan (to catch any leaks) and place in the refrigerator overnight or up to 3 days. Turn the bag periodically.

When ready to cook the chicken, fill the top and bottom of a clay cooking pot with cold water and let sit for at least 30 minutes. Pour out the water and place the chicken in the pot, pouring the marinade over it. Place the lid on the pot and place in a *cold* oven, immediately turning the temperature to 450°F/230°C/gas 8. Let roast undisturbed for 1 hour and 45 minutes. It is very important that the pot be placed in a cold oven or the shock of the sudden heat could cause the clay to crack. Test for doneness with an instant-read thermometer; the internal temperature should be 165°F/75°C. The chicken will be very tender and moist.

Carefully transfer the chicken to a cutting board and carve. Place the carved meat on a serving platter and tent with foil.

Pour the cooking liquid from the pot into a fat separator and discard the accumulated fat. Alternatively, if you are making this chicken to use shredded for Fresh Spring Rolls (page 98), simply chill the liquid and remove the solidified fat from the top.

Serve the skimmed juices along with the chicken for dipping or drizzling.

NOTES: The chicken needs to marinate overnight (or up to 3 days), so plan accordingly. If it marinates for longer than a day, the flavors will become more developed, richer, and earthier. If Vietnamese chili-garlic sauce is not available, substitute a chili sauce (such as Sriracha) and add another clove of garlic.

Clay Pots

Clay pots are always used from a wet, cold state, so as the oven heats the pot, the water evaporates, causing the contents to steam in a slightly pressurized environment. This ensures a moist product and helps to pull the full flavors of the marinade into the meat. Cooking in unglazed clay pots has a long history, stretching back to ancient Roman times, making this a very appropriate technique for cooking with such an ancient product as tea. Römertopf, a line of modern clay pots, literally translates to "Roman pot."

BLACK TEA-SMOKED CHICKEN *with* TEA-BLANCHED SHRIMP *and* UDON NOODLES

THIS IS A PARTICULARLY INTERESTING DISPLAY OF TEA CUISINE, AS THE SAME TEA (ASSAM OR NILGIRI) *is used three different ways in one dish: first to brine, then to smoke, and lastly as a blanching liquid, showing the true flexibility of tea in cooking. This recipe, developed by Jakob White representing Boston University's Culinary Arts program, won first prize for Best Use of Indian Tea at the 2009 New England Culinary Tea Competition.*

Serves 4

CHICKEN

1 gallon/3.8 liters plus 1 tablespoon water, divided

1 cup/170 grams kosher salt

½ cup/100 grams granulated sugar

1 teaspoon black peppercorns

2 bay leaves

1 lemon, sliced

7 tablespoons loose-leaf black tea leaves, such as Assam or Nilgiri, divided

4 bone-in chicken legs and thighs, skin left on

½ cup/100 grams rice

2 tablespoons canola oil

SHRIMP AND NOODLES

2 quarts/2 liters water

1 tablespoon kosher salt

2 tablespoons loose-leaf black tea leaves, such as Assam or Nilgiri

1 bay leaf

8 large shrimp

1 (8.8-ounce/250-gram) package udon noodles

(continued)

TO MAKE THE CHICKEN: In a large nonreactive saucepan, combine 1 gallon/3.8 liters of the water, salt, sugar, peppercorns, bay leaf, lemon slices, and 3 tablespoons of the tea. Bring the mixture to a boil over high heat, stirring to dissolve the salt and sugar. Remove from heat. Let cool to room temperature, about 30 minutes, then add the chicken. Cover and refrigerate for 2 hours.

PREPARE THE SMOKER: Line a wok with 2 layers of heavy-duty aluminum foil. Place the remaining ½ cup/10 grams of tea and the rice in the bottom and sprinkle with the remaining 1 tablespoon water. Place a round cooling rack in the wok.

Remove the chicken from the brine; rinse and pat dry. Make sure that the exhaust fan is on. Place chicken pieces on the cooling rack. Heat over high heat. When tea begins to smoke, decrease heat to medium-low and cover wok with foil or a wok lid. It is very important that the foil does not touch the chicken, so make sure that the rack is low enough in the wok that the chicken is fully inside. After 15 minutes, turn the heat off but leave covered for another 10 or 15 minutes for the chicken to absorb the smoke. The chicken will be smoked at this point, but not fully cooked. Remove and set aside.

Preheat the oven to 450°F/230°C/gas 8.

Heat a large, oven-safe skillet over medium-high heat until hot. Add the oil, then place the chicken skin-side down and brown 2 to 3 minutes on each side. Place the skillet with the chicken in the preheated oven and cook about 10 minutes (the cooking time will vary depending on

1½ teaspoons shrimp paste

2 tablespoons soy sauce

1 tablespoon honey

1 tablespoon toasted sesame oil

Pinch of cayenne pepper

1 onion, quartered and thinly sliced

2 garlic cloves, chopped

1 (1-inch/2.5-centimeter) piece fresh
   ginger, grated

8 ounces/225 grams shiitake
   mushrooms, sliced

10 ounces/280 grams snow peas,
   trimmed

½ napa cabbage, very thinly sliced

1 carrot, cut into julienne strips

2 tablespoons chopped fresh cilantro

4 scallions, diagonally sliced

size and cut of the chicken) until an instant-read thermometer inserted in the thickest part of the chicken reads between 165°F and 170°F/80°C.

TO MAKE THE SHRIMP AND UDON NOODLES: In a large pot, combine the 2 quarts/2 liters water, salt, tea, and bay leaf. Bring to a light boil over high heat. Add shrimp and noodles and blanch for about 3 minutes or until the shrimp are opaque throughout. Remove the shrimp and noodles and set aside. Discard the blanching liquid.

In a small bowl, combine the shrimp paste, soy sauce, honey, sesame oil, and cayenne. Whisk to blend and set aside.

Remove the chicken from the oven. Place it on a plate and tent with foil to keep warm. Discard excess oil from the skillet, leaving about 1 tablespoon.

In the same skillet, sauté the onion over medium heat until translucent but not colored, about 5 minutes. Add the garlic and ginger and sauté another 1 to 2 minutes. Add the mushrooms, snow peas, cabbage, and carrot, and cook until slightly softened, about 3 to 5 minutes. Add the reserved udon noodles and shrimp. Pour on the reserved shrimp-paste sauce and toss to coat and heat through.

To serve, divide the noodle-and-shrimp mixture among 4 plates. Rest the chicken thighs against noodle and shrimp mixture on each plate. Garnish with cilantro and scallions and serve immediately.

NOTE: Any kind of uncooked rice may be used, as it merely serves as a buffer for the tea leaves. The rice enables the tea leaves to smoke, rather than just burn off (see "Smoking with Tea," page 56).

ROASTED TEA-BRINED CAPON

DARJEELING OR CEYLON TEAS GIVE A CLEAN BRIGHTNESS AND ADDED COMPLEXITY TO THE CAPON, *without overwhelming the distinctive flavor of the bird. A capon is a kind of rooster specially raised for its tender, fatty meat, but you can easily substitute a chicken. The brined capon can either be roasted, as it is here, or smoked on the grill (instructions follow).*

Brining poultry aids in retaining moisture while cooking. This is useful while roasting and particularly important when grilling, since birds can dry out on a grill. Note: The capon or chicken needs to brine overnight, so plan accordingly.

Serves 6 to 8

TEA BRINE
½ cup/20 grams loose-leaf Darjeeling or Ceylon tea leaves

3 cups/720 milliliters boiling water (about 212°F/100°C)

½ cup/85 grams kosher salt

1 tablespoon (packed) light brown sugar

2 cinnamon sticks

1 tablespoon anise seeds

2 teaspoons allspice berries

2 bay leaves

1 teaspoon whole coriander seeds

1 teaspoon freshly ground black pepper

1 teaspoon whole black peppercorns

2 quarts/2 liters apple cider, chilled

1 capon or large chicken, about 7 pounds/3.2 kilograms

ROASTING INGREDIENTS
1 apple, quartered

1 tablespoon vegetable oil

2 large shallots, thinly sliced

4 garlic cloves

(continued)

TO MAKE THE TEA BRINE: Place the tea leaves in a glass measuring cup and pour boiling water over them. Steep, covered, for 5 to 6 minutes, then strain the tea into a large stockpot. If you will be grill-smoking the capon (see page 141), reserve the strained leaves; if not, discard them.

Add the salt, brown sugar, cinnamon, anise, allspice, bay leaves, coriander, and ground and whole black peppercorns to the tea and bring to a boil over high heat. Reduce the heat to medium and simmer for 3 to 4 minutes, then remove from heat.

Add the chilled cider. The liquid should now be room temperature—if not, let it cool completely.

Place the whole capon in the cooled brine. Oversize resealable plastic bags are great for this, but a non-reactive bowl will also work well. If needed, place a heavy plate over the bird to weigh it down so that it is fully submerged in the brine. Cover or seal and refrigerate for 24 hours. Remove, rinse well, and pat dry.

The bird may be smoked or roasted at this point. For smoking instructions, see page 137.

To roast the bird, preheat the oven to 375°F/190°C/gas 5. Have ready the roasting ingredients.

Place the apple into the cavity of the bird. Pour the oil in a Dutch oven or roasting pan and tilt to coat the bottom. Put the shallots and garlic in the pan and put the bird on top of them. Put the pan in the oven and roast until an instant-read thermometer inserted in the thigh reads 160°F/70°C, about 2¼ hours. *(continued)*

- ¾ cup/180 milliliters boiling water (about 212°F/100°C)

- 2 tablespoons loose-leaf Darjeeling or Ceylon tea leaves

- ½ cup/120 milliliters apple cider

- 1 teaspoon chopped fresh thyme, or ¼ teaspoon dried

- 2 tablespoons unsalted butter

- Dash fine sea salt, or more to taste

- Dash freshly ground black pepper, or more to taste

While the capon cooks, pour the boiling water over the tea in a small bowl and steep, covered, for 3 minutes. Strain and set aside, discarding the leaves.

When the capon is ready, tip the juices from the cavity of the bird into the roasting pan and remove the bird to a cutting board. Loosely tent with foil.

Pour the juices from the pan into a fat separator, then return the skimmed juices to the pan. Stir in the cider, steeped tea, and thyme. Bring the pan to a simmer over medium-high heat until reduced to about 1½ cups/360 millilters, 5 to 10 minutes. Turn off the heat and whisk in the butter. Season with the salt and pepper.

To serve, carve the capon and place carved pieces on a platter. Serve with the tea gravy on the side.

To conserve trees, more and more tea estates are packing tea in bags (*left*) rather than the classic wooden tea chests (*right*).

⌒ SMOKED TEA-BRINED CAPON ⌒

BRINING BEFORE SMOKING IS AN IDEAL WAY TO ADD ADDITIONAL MOISTURE AND FLAVOR TO YOUR FOOD.
This recipe is an example of grill-smoking, which involves cooking the food in a covered grill over a packet of smoking mix. This chicken is very nice with the Mango-Peach Salsa (page 163).

Serves 6 to 8

1 Roasted Tea-Brined Capon, uncooked (page 139)

½ cup/20 grams loose-leaf Darjeeling tea leaves

½ cup/100 grams rice

2 tablespoons (packed) light or dark brown sugar

1 apple, quartered

Prepare the Roasted Tea-Brined Capon through the overnight brining process. Remove the capon from the brine, rinse, pat dry, and cut into quarters. If time permits, let dry uncovered in the refrigerator for several more hours for a crisper skin, up to 24 hours.

Prepare the coals in a grill, light it, and allow them to turn grey and ash over. Mix together the tea leaves, rice, brown sugar, and apple. Place the mixture in the center of a large piece of heavy-duty aluminum foil. Fold over to make a loose packet, folding over the edges to seal. Cut several openings in the top of the packet for the smoke to release. Set aside.

Spread the coals and place the capon quarters on the grill. Cover and cook for 15 minutes. Using heavy gloves, remove the grill grid and place the prepared foil packet of tea leaves on the coals, cut-side up. Replace the grid, flip the capon pieces, and continue to cook, covered, until the internal temperature of the meat reaches 160°F/70°C on an instant-read thermometer (carryover cooking will bring the temperature to the necessary 165°F/75°C). Alternatively, you can sprinkle the used tea leaves from the brine directly over the coals, and replace the cover of the grill. The leaves will burn off without the rice to slow the process, but the fact that they are wet will slow it down enough to get some nice smoke imparted into the capon. If you'd like a more intense smoke flavor, prepare two packets. Add the first when you begin grilling the capon, and replace it with the second after 15 minutes.

Remove capon from the grill, cut into smaller pieces to serve, and place on a platter. Serve immediately.

❧ CLASSIC TEA-SMOKED DUCK ❧

THIS IS AN EXAMPLE OF HISTORIC CULINARY TEA, A CLASSICAL CHINESE METHOD USING A WOK, *updated for modern kitchens. This requires a large wok with a cover so that there is plenty of room for the duck without crowding. Traditionally, the duck would be rubbed and then hung, unwrapped, for a day to allow air to circulate freely around all sides and aid in its drying. As most home cooks do not have the ability to easily hang a duck or chicken, we offer an alternative technique of wrapping the duck and letting it rest, seasoned, in the refrigerator under a weight. The weight aids in pushing moisture from the duck, yielding similar results to the hanging technique. The duck is then steamed, smoked, and deep-fried. The final step of deep-frying gives the duck a spectacularly crisp skin. If preferred, it could instead be finished in an oven to slightly crisp the skin without the added traditional step of frying.*

Serves 4

1 (5-pound/2.3 kilogram) duck

2 teaspoons soy sauce

2 tablespoons kosher or fine sea salt

1 tablespoon crushed Szechuan or black peppercorns

4 (¼-inch/6-millimeter) slices fresh ginger

4 scallions, quartered

1 cup/40 grams loose-leaf black tea leaves, such as Keemun or lychee, divided

¾ cup/160 grams rice

½ cup/100 grams (packed) light brown sugar

4 whole star anise (optional)

1 cinnamon stick (optional)

Zest of 1 orange, preferably a Mandarin orange (optional)

2 tablespoons soy sauce

Wash and dry the duck thoroughly inside and out. Rub the inside and outside with the salt and sprinkle with the crushed peppercorns. Press down on the breastbone of the duck to break it slightly and allow the duck to be partially flattened. Wrap the duck loosely in foil and place in a shallow pan—the top of the duck should rise above the sides of the pan to allow you to press it. Place a sheet pan on top of the duck and weigh it down with a few canned goods. Refrigerate 24 to 48 hours.

When ready to cook the duck, bring 4 cups/960 milliliters water to a boil in a large wok over high heat. When it comes to a boil, add ¼ cup/10 grams of the tea leaves and 2 teaspoons soy sauce and reduce heat to a simmer.

While the water comes to a boil, remove the foil from the duck; rinse and pat dry. Place the ginger and scallions in the duck cavity. Prick the skin all over—this helps the fat drain during cooking—and place the duck on a wok rack over the steaming water in the wok. Cover and steam the duck over the simmering water for 1 hour or until juices run clear. Check every 15 minutes and add more boiling water if the water level appears too low. Remove the duck and set aside. Wipe and dry off the rack. Discard the water, wet tea leaves, and any fat from the wok. Run cold water over the wok to cool it so that you can comfortably handle it, then wipe dry and line it and the lid with heavy-duty aluminum foil. Place the remaining ¾ cup/30 grams of tea leaves, rice, and brown

2 tablespoons cornstarch

3 cups/720 milliliters peanut or corn oil for deep-frying

Toasted Peppercorn Salt (page 92)

sugar on the foil in the bottom of the wok, along with the star anise, cinnamon stick, and orange zest, if using. Mix well. Place the wok rack or a round splatter screen in the wok over the smoking mixture.

Place the duck on the rack, breast-side up. It is important that the wok be large enough that the domed lid does not touch the duck or the smoke will not circulate freely.

Turn the exhaust fan on. Place the wok over high heat. When the tea-rice mixture first begins to smoke after a few minutes, cover the wok and seal tightly with heavy-duty aluminum foil to prevent smoke from escaping. After 5 minutes, it should be heavily smoking. Reduce the heat to medium-low and smoke for an additional 15 minutes, keeping the lid on the whole time (don't peek!). Turn off the heat. Do *not* uncover wok. Leave the duck in the wok for an additional 20 minutes (this will allow the smoke to permeate the duck, rather than escape into your kitchen), then remove the cover and let the duck cool thoroughly until cool enough to handle. There will still be some smoke left at the end, however, so make sure the exhaust fan is still on when you uncover the wok.

Traditionally, the duck is finished with a very brief deep-frying that produces a wonderfully crisp skin. If preferred, especially if you do not intend to eat the skin, you can serve the duck now; the meat is still smoky-rich and delicious. If you plan to use the duck meat in a variation of the Wild Rice and Chicken Salad (page 72) or in the Fresh Springrolls (page 98), then you don't need to fry the duck to crisp the skin.

TO DEEP-FRY THE DUCK: Rub the cooled duck with the soy sauce and sprinkle with the cornstarch.

In the cleaned wok or a deep pot, heat peanut or corn oil to 375°F/190°C, very hot but not smoking. Lower the heat slightly and place the duck in, breast-side down, and fry for 5 minutes. Carefully turn over with large tongs and fry the second side for an additional 5 minutes. The skin will be a rich mahogany, and beautifully crisp at this point. Traditionally, the meat is cut into bite-size pieces with a cleaver, cutting through the bone, but you can also use a carving knife to cut the bird into 8 sections. Serve hot or at room temperature, with Toasted Peppercorn Salt on the side for dipping.

⨫ LYCHEE-SMOKED DUCK BREASTS ⨭

SMOKED DUCK IS WONDERFUL IN ALL ITS INCARNATIONS, BUT WHEN COMBINED WITH THE RICH
caramelization and crisp skin that grilling adds, this dish is a must! If you are using a charcoal grill, serve with the Whole Grilled Onions that accompany the Tea-Brined Pork Chops (page 167). Duck breasts vary in size depending on the type and age of the duck, but the most commonly available breasts are in the 12- to 14-ounce/340- to 400-gram range for a ready-to-split whole breast. Lychee tea has a sweet aroma that goes well with assertive meats such as duck, as well as with other poultry.

Serves 4

2 (12- to 14-ounce/340- to 400-gram) whole boneless duck breasts

¼ cup/10 grams Lychee Tea Spice Rub (page 84)

½ cup/100 grams uncooked rice

½ cup/20 grams loose-leaf lychee black tea leaves

2 whole star anise or 1 teaspoon anise seeds

1 teaspoon whole black peppercorns

2 cinnamon sticks

Zest of ¼ orange, removed in large strips

Split the duck breasts and trim off excess fat. Score the skin lightly several times on the diagonal with a sharp knife. Cut deeply enough to cut through the skin and well into the layer of fat, but not into the duck meat underneath. This will aid in draining the excess fat off during cooking.

Rub the breasts well with the Lychee Tea Spice Rub. Cover and refrigerate overnight.

When ready to cook the duck, light the grill and heat until coals are ashed over. While the grill heats, place the rice, tea, star anise, peppercorns, cinnamon sticks, and orange zest on a large piece of heavy-duty aluminum foil. Fold over to make a loose packet, folding over the edges to seal. Cut several small holes in the packet to allow the release of the aromatic smoke.

When the coals are ashed over, flatten the mound and place the tea-spice packet on top of the coals, with the holes facing upward.

When the packet has begun to smoke, place the duck breasts, skin-side down, on the grill. Cook over medium heat, covered. Turn after around 8 minutes and continue to cook, covered, until medium-rare, 135°F to 140°F/55°C to 60°C on an instant-read thermometer.

Remove the duck from the grill and let rest several minutes on a cutting board, tented with foil to keep warm. Slice the duck on the diagonal and serve immediately.

NOTES: The duck needs to sit in the rub overnight, so plan accordingly.

❧ OOLONG-BRINED TURKEY ❧

CHEFS JON RILEY AND EMMA ROBERTS OF CAPERS CATERING COMPANY IN STONEHAM, MASSACHUSETTS, *shared this oolong-based brined turkey with us. They created these recipes using Six Summits oolong tea, a cranberry-flavored oolong, but you can use any good quality oolong. The turkey can be served warm on its own, or used to make fabulous turkey sandwiches with Oolong Mayonnaise (page 77). Make sure to use turkey that has not already been brined.*

Serves 8 to 12

2 quarts/1.9 liters water

¼ cup/10 grams loose-leaf oolong tea leaves

½ cup/85 grams kosher salt

½ cup/100 grams (packed) light brown sugar

1 tablespoon whole Szechuan peppercorns or black peppercorns

1 (2-inch/5-centimeter) piece fresh ginger, sliced

8 whole cloves

3 bay leaves

1 tablespoon whole coriander seeds, lightly crushed

¼ cup/40 grams dried cranberries (optional)

1 (4- to 6- pound/1.8- to 2.7-kilogram) boneless turkey breast

2 tablespoons canola oil

In a large saucepan, heat water to steaming but not quite boiling. Add the tea, salt, and brown sugar and stir until the sugar and salt dissolve. Add the peppercorns, ginger, cloves, bay leaves, coriander seeds, and cranberries, if using. Let brine cool to room temperature.

Rinse the turkey breast. Place a gallon-size (3.8 liters) oven-roasting bag inside a second bag to form a double thickness. Place the bags inside a large stockpot. Place the turkey inside the bag and pour in the tea mixture. Secure the bags with twist ties. The bag keeps the brine around the turkey breast so that it is fully "submerged" during the brining period. Refrigerate for 12 to 24 hours.

When ready to roast the turkey, preheat the oven to 350°F/180°C/gas 4. Have ready a roasting pan with a rack.

Remove the turkey from the brine and lightly rinse off any excess brine and spices. Pat the turkey breast dry. Discard the brine.

Heat a large skillet over medium-high heat and add the oil. Place the breast, skin-side down, in the oil and sear until golden-brown on each side, about 2 to 3 minutes per side. Remove the turkey from the pan and place it on the rack in the roasting pan. Bake at 350°F/180°C/gas 4 until it reaches an internal temperature of 160°F/70°C on an instant-read thermometer. The time required for this will depend on the weight of the breast, roughly 15 minutes per pound/455 grams, or 60 to 90 minutes. Remove the turkey from the oven. Let it rest for 10 to 15 minutes before slicing. Serve warm.

NOTE: The turkey needs to brine 12 to 24 hours, so plan accordingly. The same amount of brine can be used for a 4-pound/1.8-kilogram or a 6-pound/2.7-kilogram turkey breast.

～ KEEMUN-SMOKED QUAIL ～

QUAIL ARE IDEAL FOR SMOKING AS THEY NEED SO LITTLE COOKING TIME THAT YOU CAN COOK THEM *completely with one smoking batch. Quail can be moist and flavorful, but be careful not to overcook them due to their small size. Keemun gives a sweet earthiness to the quail, but you will also get excellent results with other aromatic teas, such as lychee or rose congou or a nice Ceylon. This quail can be served whole as an entrée, or halved as an appetizer. Serve on a bed of mixed greens tossed with Darjeeling Vinaigrette (page 75), or with tea-braised bok choy.*

Serves 6

- ½ cup/20 grams loose-leaf Keemun tea leaves, divided
- ⅓ cup/75 milliliters boiling water (about 212°F/100°C)
- 2 tablespoons toasted sesame oil
- 2 tablespoons honey
- 2 tablespoons soy sauce
- 1 teaspoon freshly ground black or Szechuan pepper
- 1 tablespoon grated orange zest (preferably a Mandarin orange)
- 6 semi-boneless quail, rinsed and patted dry
- 8 long strips orange zest, divided (preferably a Mandarin orange)
- ½ cup/100 grams rice
- ½ cup/100 grams (packed) light or dark brown sugar
- 2 cinnamon sticks

Place 1 teaspoon of the tea leaves in a small bowl and add the boiling water. Steep, covered, for 4 minutes. Strain and discard the leaves.

In a small bowl, combine 2 tablespoons of the steeped tea with the sesame oil, honey, soy sauce, pepper, and grated orange zest. Whisk well and rub over each quail. Place a strip of orange zest in each quail. Place in a resealable plastic bag and refrigerate for 2 hours.

While quail marinates, line a wok with heavy-duty aluminum foil. Combine the remaining tea leaves, rice, brown sugar, cinnamon, and the remaining 2 strips of orange zest and place in the bottom of the wok. Oil or spray a rack and place it over the tea mixture.

Remove the quail from the marinade, let it come to room temperature, and place it on the rack. Heat the wok over high heat. Turn on the exhaust fan. When the tea-rice mixture begins to smoke, cover tightly and crimp foil to keep in smoke. After 2 minutes, reduce the heat to medium-low and continue to smoke for 12 more minutes. Remove the pan from the heat and let it rest, covered, for another 5 minutes, then carefully open while under the exhaust fan. The quail should be medium to medium-rare at this point. If you would like them cooked further, finish on the grill or in a 350°F/180°C/gas 4 oven for a few minutes, then serve.

NOTES: The quail needs to marinate 2 hours, so plan accordingly. Any kind of uncooked rice may be used, as it merely serves as a buffer for the tea leaves. The rice enables the tea leaves to smoke, rather than to just burn off (see "Smoking with Tea," page 56).

FILET MIGNON *with* CEYLON TEA BÉARNAISE

THIS RECIPE WAS CREATED BY ROHAN FERNANDOPULLE, EXECUTIVE CHEF AT THE HILTON COLOMBO *in Sri Lanka, as part of the Dilmah Tea Culinaire competition, using Dilmah Nuwara Eliya Pekoe Tea. You can substitute any good-quality high-grown Sri Lankan (Ceylon) tea. (The high-grown Ceylons are lighter and brighter than the richer low-grown teas.) You could also use a second flush Darjeeling. A béarnaise sauce is a traditional accompaniment to beef tenderloin, but this version has more complexity and layering of flavors than the original, giving the dish a little twist on tradition. Sautéed mixed mushrooms would be delicious on the side.*

Serves 4

BEEF

4 (6- to 8-ounce/170- to 225-gram)
   filet mignon (or beef tenderloin steaks)

Fine sea salt to taste

Freshly ground black pepper to taste

1 tablespoon Dijon mustard

2 tablespoons vegetable oil

BÉARNAISE SAUCE

¾ cup/180 milliliters steaming water
   (about 175°F/80°C)

1 teaspoon loose-leaf Ceylon tea leaves

2 tablespoons white wine vinegar

2 teaspoons finely chopped shallots

1 bay leaf

3 peppercorns, lightly crushed

3 egg yolks

½ pound/225 grams (2 sticks) plus 4
   tablespoons unsalted butter, melted

Fine sea salt to taste

Freshly ground black pepper to taste

TO MAKE THE STEAKS: Preheat the oven to 375°F/190°C/gas 5. Season the steaks with the salt and pepper and rub with the mustard. Heat the oil in a heavy ovenproof pan over high heat. When the oil begins to shimmer, add the meat and sear it briefly on all sides. Transfer the steaks to the oven and roast another 3 to 5 minutes until an instant-read thermometer reads 145°F/60°C for medium-rare, or to your preferred doneness. The meat will continue to cook slightly once removed from the oven. Remove and let rest, tented under foil, while preparing the sauce.

TO MAKE THE BÉARNAISE SAUCE: In a small bowl, pour the steaming water over the tea leaves and steep, covered, for 4 minutes. Strain and reserve both the steeped tea and the leaves. Finely chop the tea leaves and set aside.

Pour 6 tablespoons/90 milliliters of the tea into a small saucepan; discard any remaining tea. Add the vinegar, shallots, bay leaf, and peppercorns. Bring to a boil over medium-high heat; lower heat and simmer liquid until reduced by half. Strain and cool slightly, discarding the solids.

In a medium bowl, whisk the yolks until light in color. Whisk in the tea reduction and transfer to the top of a double boiler set over lightly steaming water. Slowly drizzle in the melted butter while whisking constantly. The sauce will slowly thicken and become creamy. Continue until the mixture clings to the whisk thickly, and you can glimpse the

SILVER TIP TEA OIL

½ cup/120 milliliters canola or other light vegetable oil

¼ cup/10 grams loose-leaf Silver Tip white tea leaves

bottom of the pan while whisking. Season with salt and pepper, then stir in the reserved chopped tea leaves. Set aside.

TO MAKE THE TEA OIL: Heat the oil over medium heat in a small saucepan until it reaches a light simmer. Add the tea and simmer on low for 5 minutes. Remove from heat and let cool. Do not strain.

To serve, place 1 steak on each of 4 plates and ladle béarnaise sauce around the meat. Drizzle each steak lightly with 1 to 2 teaspoons of tea oil. Serve warm.

NOTE: The beef is garnished with oil infused with Silver Tip white tea leaves. The recipe makes more than you'll need for the steaks; use any leftover infused oil in vinaigrettes and store, covered and refrigerated, for 5 to 7 days.

Left: Christ Church Warleigh, built in 1878 by the colonial English tea planters near Kenilworth Estate, Sri Lanka

Right: The view from behind the church

➣ TEXAS CHILI—NILGIRI-STYLE ➣

A FASCINATING TRIP TO SOUTHERN INDIA AND THE NILGIRI MOUNTAINS, WITH A RESULTING SUITCASE *full of incredibly fresh Nilgiri teas resulted in this multi-layered chili. Glendale Estate BOP Nilgiri is full-bodied, heady, and aromatic, the perfect tea to meld with all the herbs and spices. An Assam or a low-grown Ceylon will also work well. This chili is quite hot; feel free to cut back the cayenne if you prefer less heat. Serve it with fresh cornbread and coleslaw or a good vinegary salad.*

Serves 6 to 8

5 cups/1.2 liters boiling water (about 212°F/100°C)

6 tablespoons loose-leaf Nilgiri tea leaves, divided

3½ pounds/1.6 kilograms beef chuck, trimmed and chopped into ½-inch/ 12-millimeter cubes

Fine sea salt to taste

Freshly ground black pepper to taste

2 tablespoons vegetable oil

4 medium onions, chopped

5 garlic cloves, minced

2 (6-ounce/170-gram) cans tomato paste

3 tablespoons dried oregano

1 tablespoon dried basil

3 tablespoons chili powder, or more to taste

4 teaspoons ground cinnamon

1 tablespoon cayenne pepper

1 tablespoon sweet paprika

1 tablespoon Asian chili sauce, such as Sriracha

1 teaspoon ground cumin

Pour the boiling water over 3 tablespoons of the tea in a medium bowl. Steep, covered, for 5 minutes, strain, and set aside. Discard the leaves.

Grind the remaining 3 tablespoons tea in a spice grinder or with a mortar and pestle until very fine. There should be about 2 tablespoons ground tea. Reserve.

Sprinkle the beef cubes with salt and pepper. Heat the oil in a large pot over high heat. Sear the beef in small batches. Add additional oil if needed to caramelize the meat well in just a few minutes per batch. Transfer each batch to a plate as it is done.

When all the meat is seared, reduce heat to medium and add the onions and garlic. Cook until lightly browned, about 5 minutes, stirring up any remaining bits of meat from the bottom of the pan. Return the beef to the pot, stir in the tomato paste and continue to cook, stirring, another 10 minutes. Add the reserved ground tea, oregano, basil, chili powder, cinnamon, cayenne, paprika, chili sauce, and cumin. Stir for another 2 minutes, then add the steeped tea. Stir, bring to a boil over high heat, then reduce the heat to low and simmer, covered, over very low heat, stirring periodically, until meat is completely tender, about 2 hours. Serve in deep bowls with cornbread, coleslaw, and very large pitchers of Jasmine Tea and Brandied Fruit Sangria (page 261).

LAPSANG SOUCHONG-BRAISED
SHORT RIBS *of* BEEF

JON RILEY, EXECUTIVE CHEF OF THE CAPERS CATERING COMPANY IN STONEHAM, MASSACHUSETTS, *won first place in the 2009 New England Culinary Tea Competition, Savory Category, representing Johnson and Wales University, with this amazing short rib recipe. The meat cooks slowly in a flavorful marinade, with melt-in-your mouth results. Although we already had a short rib recipe which we love in the book, these ribs were too good to leave out!*

Serves 6

5 garlic cloves, sliced

3 tablespoons grated fresh ginger

3 cups/720 milliliters sake

1½ cups/360 milliliters port

1 cup/240 milliliters soy sauce

¼ cup/10 grams loose-leaf Lapsang Souchong tea leaves

6 whole star anise

4 cinnamon sticks

2 cups/480 milliliters water

1 tablespoon canola oil

6 (8-ounce/225-gram) portions boneless beef short ribs

Kosher or fine sea salt to taste

Freshly ground black pepper to taste

Preheat the oven to 350°F/180°C/gas 4. Have ready a deep casserole or glass baking dish just large enough to hold the ribs but not crowd them.

Combine the garlic, ginger, sake, port, soy sauce, tea, star anise, cinnamon sticks, and water in a large pot. Bring the mixture to a boil over high heat. Reduce the heat to low and simmer for 10 minutes.

While the tea mixture comes to a boil, heat a large skillet over medium-high heat. Add the oil. Sprinkle the short ribs on both sides with salt and pepper. As soon as the oil begins to shimmer, add the meat to the pan and brown thoroughly on each side, 1 to 2 minutes per side. Remove the ribs from the pan and arrange the browned meat in the deep casserole or glass baking dish.

Carefully pour the tea mixture over the browned beef to cover. If the liquid does not cover, steep some additional tea and add that to the mixture to make sure that the ribs are fully covered with the braising liquid. Cover the baking dish tightly with aluminum foil. Bake for 1½ to 2 hours, until ribs are fork-tender.

Using tongs or a slotted spoon, transfer the ribs to a serving platter. Tent with foil to keep warm.

Pour the remaining liquid through a sieve into a saucepan, discarding the solids. Use a fat separator or a spoon to remove all the oil and fat from the surface and discard. Reheat the sauce over medium heat. Pour some of the sauce over the ribs and serve the rest in a gravy boat on the side.

TEA-RUBBED SHORT RIBS
with SMOKY BARBECUE SAUCE

THIS RECIPE FEATURES SMOKY CHINESE LAPSANG SOUCHONG TEA AS WELL AS EARTHY AGED PU-ERH, *flavors that go particularly well with beef short ribs. Any full-bodied black tea, such as a Keemun or Nilgiri, will complement the ribs as well; pork ribs may be substituted for the beef. These ribs are slow-cooked in a low oven, which gives them a melting tenderness. For added flavor and texture, you can finish them on the grill or under a broiler. These ribs go well with polenta and sautéed bitter greens. The barbecue sauce can be used whenever you are looking for a rich, flavorful, slightly hot sauce.*

Serves 4

RIBS

2 to 3 pounds/910 grams to 1.4 kilograms beef short ribs

¼ cup/10 grams Eleven-Spice Tea Rub (page 83)

4 cups/960 milliliters boiling water (about 212°F/100°C)

⅓ cup/15 grams loose-leaf Pu-erh tea leaves

SMOKY BARBECUE SAUCE

1 cup/240 milliliters boiling water (about 212°F/100°C)

2 tablespoons loose-leaf Lapsang Souchong tea leaves

1 cup/300 milliliters ketchup

2 tablespoons molasses

2 tablespoons balsamic vinegar

2 tablespoons mustard, preferably grainy

2 teaspoons hot chili sauce, such as Sriracha

1 tablespoon (packed) light brown sugar

1 garlic clove, finely chopped

TO MAKE THE RIBS: Rinse the ribs well and pat dry. Rub well with the tea rub. Cover and refrigerate overnight or for up to 3 days.

TO MAKE THE BARBECUE SAUCE: Pour the boiling water over the Lapsang Souchong tea leaves in a medium bowl and steep, covered, for 6 minutes, then strain, discarding the leaves. Set aside.

In a small saucepan, combine ½ cup/120 milliliters of the steeped tea with the remaining sauce ingredients and bring to a simmer over medium-low heat. Simmer on medium-low for 10 minutes. Taste. Add more steeped tea if a smokier flavor is desired, or if the sauce seems too thick. Simmer an additional 5 minutes. Remove and use immediately or let the sauce cool completely, then store, covered and refrigerated, in a nonreactive sealed container for up to 1 week. Discard any unused steeped tea.

When ready to cook the ribs, preheat the oven to 300°F/150°C/gas 2. Pour the boiling water over the Pu-erh tea leaves in a medium bowl and steep, covered, for 6 minutes, then strain, discarding the leaves. Return tea to the bowl and add the barbecue sauce, mixing well.

Put the tea-rubbed ribs in a roasting or baking pan. Pour the barbecue sauce over the ribs. Cover with foil. Bake at 300°F/150°C/gas 2 for about 70 to 90 minutes, turning the ribs every 30 minutes, until the meat is tender and comes away easily from the bone; timing will depend on the size of the ribs used.

2 tablespoons olive oil

1 teaspoon paprika

1 teaspoon chili powder

½ teaspoon fine sea salt, or more to taste

¼ teaspoon freshly ground black pepper

The ribs may be eaten at this point, but you can also grill or broil them for a few minutes on each side to char them slightly. Serve immediately.

NOTE: The ribs need to sit with the spice rub at least overnight for the best flavor.

⁓ STEAK *au* POIVRE *et* THÉ ⁓

THIS IS FAST FOOD THAT TASTES LIKE IT TOOK MUCH LONGER. CLASSIC STEAK AU POIVRE USUALLY *contains one or more types of crushed peppercorns, but here we're also including allspice (another member of the pepper family) and Earl Grey tea, which both go well with bourbon. The butter and cream soften the pepper and tannin bite but still retain a very flavorful sauce. Sautéed wild mushrooms will accompany this steak nicely, or serve with simple roasted potatoes and steamed green beans.*

Serves 4

2 tablespoons loose-leaf Earl Grey tea leaves, divided

½ cup/120 milliliters boiling water (about 212°F/100°C)

1 teaspoon black or Szechuan peppercorns

1 teaspoon green or white peppercorns

½ teaspoon allspice berries

4 (6- to 8-ounce/170- to 225-gram) filet mignon steaks, each about 1½-inches/ 4 centimeters thick

Fine sea salt to taste

2 tablespoons unsalted butter, divided

1 tablespoon vegetable oil

2 tablespoons bourbon

½ cup/120 milliliters heavy whipping cream

Put 1 tablespoon of the tea leaves in a medium bowl and add the boiling water. Steep, covered, for 4 minutes, then strain, discarding the leaves. Set aside.

In a spice grinder or using a mortar and pestle, combine the remaining 1 tablespoon tea leaves, both peppercorns, and allspice. Coarsely crush; the mixture should be coarse. Pour onto a plate.

Preheat the oven to 250°F/120°C/gas 1/2. Lightly sprinkle each side of the fillets with salt and press into the pepper-tea mixture to lightly encrust.

Melt 1 tablespoon of the butter with the oil in a large skillet over high heat. Sear the fillets until well colored, about 4 minutes per side. Turn and finish until desired doneness. Check temperature with an instant-read thermometer. For medium-rare, steaks should be 145°F/60°C. Remove skillet from heat and transfer steaks to an oven-safe plate and place in oven to keep warm.

Pour the bourbon into the pan off the heat and ignite it using a long match. Let the alcohol burn off. Return pan to medium-high heat. Add 3 tablespoons of the reserved steeped tea and bring back to a simmer, scraping any bits from the pan to deglaze it. Reduce slightly, then add cream and let thicken over medium-low heat until the mixture coats the spoon. Stir in the remaining 1 tablespoon butter until smooth. Taste and adjust seasonings with salt or more of the steeped tea as desired.

To serve, pour sauce to coat each of four plates, remove cooked fillets from the oven, and slice and fan the steaks on each plate, or serve whole over the sauce. Serve immediately, with additional sauce on the side.

PRIME RACK *of* LAMB *with* EARL GREY TEA JUS

THIS LAMB RECIPE COMES FROM ROHAN FERNANDOPULLE, EXECUTIVE CHEF AT THE COLOMBO HILTON *in Sri Lanka. His team competed in the Dilmah Tea "Tea Culinaire" competition, going on to win in the European finals. Although rack of lamb makes an elegant and romantic dinner for two, multiplying this recipe for a dinner party would be easy; it's too good not to share. If you have a good butcher, you can ask them to french (trim) the lamb for you; just make sure to keep the trimmings. Serve with asparagus and a potato-and-onion gratin.*

Serves 2

1 (7- or 8-bone) single rack of lamb

2 tablespoons olive oil, divided

2 tablespoons minced shallots

½ teaspoon freshly ground black pepper, divided

1½ cups/360 milliliters lamb stock, veal stock, or chicken stock

¼ cup/10 grams loose-leaf Earl Grey tea leaves, divided

4 teaspoons unsalted butter, divided

½ cup/30 grams fresh breadcrumbs

Fine sea salt to taste

1 teaspoon Dijon mustard

1 cup/240 milliliters boiling water (about 212°F/100°C)

Clean and trim the rack of lamb, reserving the trimmings. A single rack of lamb has already been split so that you have 7 or 8 rib chops attached together. A trimmed rack, also known as a "frenched" rack, has had the meat and fat from between the ribs cut away, and scraped clean to expose the top couple of inches of the bone. Make sure to leave a layer of fat intact and not trim all the way down to the main portion of the meat.

Heat 2 teaspoons of the olive oil in a small saucepan over medium-high heat. Add the lamb trimmings and sauté until browned, about 1 minute. Add the shallots and ¼ teaspoon of the black pepper and cook, stirring, for 30 seconds. Add the stock and bring to a boil. Reduce the heat to medium-low and simmer until reduced by half (to ¾ cup/180 milliliters) 12 to 15 minutes. Remove from the heat and strain through a fine mesh sieve. Set aside.

Preheat the oven to 425°F/220°C/gas 7.

In a spice grinder or using a mortar and pestle, coarsely grind 2 tablespoons of the tea; you should have about 1 tablespoon ground tea. In a small saucepan over medium heat, melt 1 tablespoon of the butter. Stir in the ground tea and breadcrumbs and set aside.

Season the reserved rack of lamb with salt and the remaining ¼ teaspoon black pepper, or more to taste. Rub with mustard. Heat the remaining 4 teaspoons olive oil in a large skillet over high heat. Sear the lamb on both sides until it has good color, 1 to 2 minutes per side. Transfer to the roasting pan and roast the lamb bone-side down until very rare, 130°F/55°C on an instant-read thermometer, about 12 minutes.

While the lamb roasts, prepare the Earl Grey jus: Pour the boiling water over the remaining 2 tablespoons of the tea leaves and steep, covered, for 4 minutes. Strain and discard the leaves. In the small saucepan, combine the steeped tea and the strained stock. Bring to a boil over medium-high heat, then reduce the heat to maintain a low simmer. Reduce the sauce by half, around 15 minutes, and whisk in the remaining 1 teaspoon of butter to enrich and smooth out the sauce. Set aside.

When the lamb is done cooking, remove from the oven and turn on the broiler. Evenly pat the reserved tea-breadcrumb mixture all over the lamb, then broil the lamb for 1 minute or so until the crumbs are slightly brown. Set aside to rest for 2 to 3 minutes, then divide into 4 pieces, plating two per person, overlapping the bone-end on the plate and drizzling with the Earl Grey jus.

Tea pluckers, Kirkoswald Estate, Sri Lanka

LAPSANG SOUCHONG LEG *of* LAMB TWO WAYS

THE SMOKY EARTHINESS OF LAPSANG SOUCHONG TEA IS A NATURAL FOR LAMB. WE ENJOY THE TOUCH *of smoke, but an earthy Pu-erh or Keemun would also work very well here. Serve with polenta and sautéed Swiss chard.*

The procedure for grill-smoking is very similar to grilling—the only difference is that steeped tea leaves are added to the coals before or during the grilling. If the weather doesn't cooperate, you can roast the lamb in the oven.

Serves 6

1 cup/40 grams loose-leaf Lapsang Souchong tea leaves

2 quarts/1.9 liters boiling water (about 212°F/100°C)

¼ cup/40 grams coarse kosher salt

¼ cup/50 grams (packed) dark brown sugar

3 garlic cloves, thinly sliced

1 (4- to 5-pound/1.8- to 2.3-kilogram) boned butterflied leg of lamb

Matcha Mayo (page 78)

Place the tea leaves in a large bowl. Add the boiling water and steep, covered, for 5 to 6 minutes. Strain, reserving the leaves if you plan to grill-smoke the meat when grilling. Store the leaves, refrigerated, in a covered container. Immediately add the salt and sugar to the hot strained tea and stir until dissolved. Let cool to room temperature, about 20 to 30 minutes.

Insert the garlic slices at even intervals into the lamb using the tip of a sharp pairing knife, pushing the slices all the way into the meat so that no garlic is exposed. When tea brine is room temperature, put the lamb in the brine. Oversize resealable plastic bags are great for this, but a nonreactive bowl will also work well. If needed, place a heavy plate over the lamb to weigh it down so that it is fully submerged. Cover or seal and refrigerate for 12 to 24 hours.

When you're ready to cook the lamb, remove it from the brine, rinse, and pat dry. Discard the brine. The lamb may be grilled or grill-smoked at this point.

Prepare the coals and light the grill. When coals are ashed-over and grey, heap them on one side of the grill and place the oiled grid on the grill. If you are going to grill-smoke the lamb, have heavy duty oven mitts ready to use to lift the grill. For both grilling and grill-smoking, place the lamb over the hottest section of the grill (directly over the coals) to sear each side for 5 minutes uncovered. Move the lamb to indirect cooking where it is no longer directly over the main area of coals. If grilling, cover the grill and continue to cook another 15 minutes per side. If grill-smoking, remove the grill and lamb and sprinkle the coals with half of the reserved tea leaves. Return the grill and lamb, cover the grill, and continue to cook another 15 minutes per side or until an instant-read thermometer reads 140°F/60°C for medium-rare. (If you are grill-smoking, and the smoke being released through the vents slows, carefully remove the grill rack with the lamb still on it using heavy oven mitts. Sprinkle the remaining leaves over the coals, replace the grill rack, cover, and continue to cook.)

When it's cooked to desired doneness, transfer the lamb to a cutting board and let rest, tented with foil, for 5 minutes, then thinly slice to serve. Serve with Matcha Mayo on the side.

NOTE: The lamb needs to brine overnight, so plan accordingly.

Left: Preparing for a rustic Gong Fu ceremony in Wuyishan China, Fujian Province;
Right: The early morning mist in the Wuyi Mountains, Fujian Province, China

SLOW-COOKED CHINESE PORK SHOULDER

THIS DISH IS PERFECT FOR A CHILLY FALL OR WINTER NIGHT. CHINESE DRIED MUSHROOMS ARE ALSO *called Chinese black mushrooms (which is a little confusing since they are often brown or even gray or speckled). They are available at Asian markets, as is mushroom soy sauce (or you can use regular soy sauce instead). Chinese rice wine is also available at Asian markets or online, but if preferred, you can substitute gin, sake, dry vermouth, or dry sherry. Serve with sautéed bitter greens and rice or rice noodles to absorb the delectable sauce.*

Serves 6

11 cups/2.6 liters boiling water, divided

12 large Chinese dried mushrooms

1 cup/40 grams loose-leaf Pu-erh tea leaves

2 tablespoons mushroom soy sauce

1 cup soy sauce

12 whole star anise

¾ cup/180 milliliters molasses

3 tablespoons (packed) light brown sugar

10 tablespoons/150 milliliters Chinese rice wine

1 (5-pound/2.3-kilogram) pork shoulder

Pour 1 cup/240 milliliters of the boiling water over the dried mushrooms in a medium bowl. Soak for 30 minutes, then drain, reserving the liquid. Cut off and discard the stems. Set aside the mushroom caps.

Pour the remaining 10 cups/2.4 liters boiling water over the tea leaves in a large bowl. Steep, covered, for 6 or 7 minutes. Strain into a large pot, discarding the leaves. Add both soy sauces, the star anise, molasses, brown sugar, and rice wine. Bring to a simmer over medium-high heat.

Rinse the pork shoulder well and add to the pot. If the pork shoulder is not fully submerged, add the reserved mushroom water as needed. Bring to a boil, and then lower heat to a simmer and continue to cook for 3 hours, covered, over low heat. Add soaked mushroom caps and simmer an additional 30 minutes. The meat will be very tender, rich, and flavorful. Remove the pork from the sauce, slice or tear into chunks and place on a platter. Remove the mushrooms from the sauce and arrange around the pork on the platter. Pour the remaining sauce into a gravy boat and serve on the side.

PORK CHOPS *with* CABBAGE *and* DARJEELING

THIS IS A FLEXIBLE PREPARATION FOR PORK CHOPS THAT LENDS ITSELF TO SEVERAL VARIATIONS. THE *flavors reflect a German influence. Cooking the pork chops in tea here affects both flavor and texture of the meat, yielding meat that is tender and flavorful, but not too heavy. Serve over buttered egg noodles or spaetzle. A green salad on the side rounds out the meal.*

Serves 4

2 cups/480 milliliters boiling water (about 212°F/100°C)

3 tablespoons loose-leaf Darjeeling tea leaves

4 center-cut pork chops (about 2 pounds/910 grams)

½ teaspoon fine sea salt, or more to taste

⅛ teaspoon freshly ground black pepper, or more to taste

2 tablespoons vegetable oil

2 medium onions, thinly sliced

6 garlic cloves, finely chopped

1 medium head green cabbage, cored and sliced

2 bay leaves

2 teaspoons dried dill

1 teaspoon caraway seeds

¾ pound/340 grams new potatoes, halved

1 tablespoon finely chopped fresh dill or parsley for garnish

Pour the boiling water over the tea leaves in a medium bowl and steep, covered, for 3 to 4 minutes, then strain, discarding the leaves. Set aside.

Sprinkle the pork chops with the salt and pepper. In a large pot or Dutch oven heat the oil over medium-high heat. When the oil is shimmering, add the pork chops and brown them, about 2 minutes per side. Remove and set aside on a plate. Add the onions and garlic to the pan and lower the heat to medium-low. Cook until the onions are soft and translucent, 6 to 8 minutes.

Add the reserved tea, cabbage, bay leaves, dill, and caraway seeds, and stir. Return the pork chops to the pan, cover, and cook over medium-low heat. After 20 minutes, add the potatoes, stir and continue to cook another 25 to 30 minutes, until the pork is tender.

To serve, divide the cabbage among 4 plates or shallow bowls. Place a pork chop and a few potatoes on top, then sprinkle with fresh dill or parsley. Serve immediately.

Variation

PORK CHOPS WITH BOK CHOY AND PU-ERH: For an Asian twist, substitute Pu-erh tea for the Darjeeling. Use bok choy instead of cabbage. Replace the dill and caraway seeds with 1 teaspoon Chinese 5-spice powder (page 191) and 2 whole star anise.

❦ ORANGE SPICE TEA-ROASTED ❦
PORK TENDERLOIN *with* MANGO-PEACH SALSA

THE PORK MAY BE COOKED AHEAD AND SERVED COLD OR AT ROOM TEMPERATURE ON BABY GREENS AND *arugula lightly dressed with Darjeeling Vinaigrette (page 75). Or serve it hot from the oven with wilted greens or other vegetables. Firmer fruit works best for the salsa. Wear kitchen gloves when cutting the chile, to avoid getting the hot oils on your hands. If you like heat, use the whole habañero, otherwise half provides plenty of spice. This pork and salsa also make a nice tea sandwich.*

Serves 4

PORK

2 (1-pound/455-gram) pork tenderloins, cleaned of excess fat and silver skin

¼ cup/10 grams Eleven-Spice Tea Rub (page 83)

2 cups/480 milliliters orange juice, plus more as needed

MANGO-PEACH SALSA

1 fairly firm medium mango, peeled

1 fairly firm large peach, peeled

1 medium red bell pepper

1 small red onion

½ to 1 small habañero pepper, or 1 teaspoon red pepper flakes.

Juice from 2 limes

Zest and juice from ½ orange

1 tablespoon rice vinegar, or more to taste

½ teaspoon Eleven-Spice Tea Rub (page 83)

2 tablespoons (packed) light brown sugar, or more to taste

1 tablespoon chopped fresh cilantro, basil, or parsley

Fine sea salt to taste

Freshly ground black pepper to taste

PREPARE THE PORK: Rub the pork tenderloins with the tea rub; cover well and refrigerate overnight, or up to 3 days.

TO MAKE THE SALSA: Dice the mango, peach, bell pepper, and onion into ¼-inch/6-millimeter dice and add to a medium bowl. Seed and cut away the membranes of the habañero and finely mince. Add to the mango mixture. Add the lime juice, the orange zest and juice, and the rice vinegar. Sprinkle in the tea spice rub, brown sugar, and fresh herbs. Taste, then season with salt and pepper to taste. Stir well. Cover and chill until ready to serve.

When you are ready to cook the pork, preheat the oven to 375°F/190°C/gas 5. Remove the pork from the refrigerator and place it in a small roasting pan. Pour the orange juice in the pan ¼ to ⅓ of the way up the sides of the tenderloins; add more orange juice if needed.

Roast the pork uncovered, basting frequently with the orange juice (2 or 3 times) until desired doneness (if you prefer pink, around 150°F/65°C on an instant-read thermometer). Depending on the size of the tenderloins, this may take as little as 18 minutes or as long as about 30 minutes, so check frequently. If serving hot, allow pork to rest 8 to 10 minutes before slicing on the bias to serve. If serving cold, slice on the bias and arrange over dressed greens. Top with the salsa.

NOTE: The pork needs to develop overnight, so plan accordingly.

SPICED CEYLON-BRINED PORK LOIN

WITH TODAY'S LEANER PORK, AND PARTICULARLY WITH THE LOIN, IT IS VERY EASY TO UNINTENTIONALLY *dry it out. Brining helps to keep the meat moist and flavorful. Once brined, the pork can be finished with a tea-based rub, a mustard-based rub, or smoking; instructions follow for each method. After finishing with your chosen method, serve thick slices of the roast pork loin plated with Darjeeling-Roasted Sweet Potatoes (see page 87). A green salad will complete the meal nicely.*

Serves 6

2 quarts/1.9 liters water, divided

¼ cup/50 grams kosher salt

¼ cup/50 grams (packed) light brown sugar

¼ cup/50 grams granulated sugar

¼ cup/10 grams loose-leaf Ceylon tea leaves

4 cinnamon sticks

1 tablespoon allspice berries, lightly crushed

1 tablespoon whole black peppercorns, lightly crushed

2 bay leaves

7 garlic cloves, crushed

1 (3½-pound/1.6-kilogram) pork loin

TO MAKE THE TEA BRINE: In a large pot, combine 5 cups/1.2 liters of the water, salt, both sugars, tea, cinnamon, allspice, peppercorns, bay leaves, and garlic. Bring to a boil over high heat, then reduce the heat to medium-high and simmer for 2 minutes. Remove pot from the heat and add the remaining 3 cups/720 milliliters of water. Let cool to room temperature, about 30 minutes. When brine is completely cooled, add the pork loin. Make sure the loin is completely submerged, weight with a plate if necessary; cover and refrigerate 12 to 24 hours.

Remove pork from the fridge and rinse off spices and tea leaves. Pat dry. Cook using one of the three methods below: Tea-Rub Roasting, Mustard-Rub Roasting, or Smoking.

NOTE: The pork needs to brine 12 to 24 hours, so plan accordingly.

Tea-Rub Roasting

If you have time, let the tea-spice rub develop on the pork for a day, you will find that the aromatic, rich, clean flavor lingers on the palate.

1 teaspoon coriander seeds

1 teaspoon allspice berries

½ teaspoon whole black peppercorns

1 tablespoon ground loose-leaf Ceylon tea leaves

Olive oil as needed

Combine the coriander, allspice, and peppercorns in a small skillet. Heat over medium heat until you can smell the spices, around 2 minutes. Remove from the heat and let cool. Using a spice grinder or mortar and pestle, grind spices well, then combine with the tea in a small bowl. Add enough olive oil to make a thick paste. Score the side of the pork that has a covering of fat with a sharp knife. Rub the tea-spice paste over the brined, rinsed, and dried pork loin. Cover and return to the refrigerator for at least 2 hours and up to 24 hours.

When ready to roast, preheat the oven to 375°F/190°C/gas 5. Remove the pork from the refrigerator and bring to room temperature. Roast until meat reaches 150°F/65°C on an instant-read thermometer, about 1 hour and 10 minutes (about 20 minutes per pound). Remove to a cutting board and let rest, tented with foil, about 10 minutes before serving.

Mustard-Rub Roasting

This traditional method of preparing a pork roast for cooking is a classic for a reason. Its piquant flavors highlight and contrast with the pork, and it has the benefit of not requiring additional time for flavor development.

½ cup/120 milliliters whole-grain mustard 3 garlic cloves, finely chopped ¼ teaspoon freshly ground black pepper	Preheat the oven to 450°F/230°C/gas 8. In a small bowl, combine the mustard, garlic, and pepper. Score the side of the pork loin that has a covering of fat with the tip of a sharp knife. Rub completely with the mustard mixture. Place the loin in a shallow roasting pan. Cook for 12 minutes at 450°F/230°/gas 8, then reduce the heat to 350°F/180°C/gas 4 and continue cooking until meat reaches 150°F/65°C on an instant-read thermometer, about 1 hour and 10 minutes (around 20 minutes per pound). Remove to a cutting board and let rest, tented with foil, for about 10 minutes before serving.

Smoking

This is an example of smoking a larger item, so you'll need more than one round of smoking mix for both the smoke penetration and to cook the pork through. Alternatively, if you want a subtler smoky flavor, after the first 15 minutes of smoking, you can finish cooking the pork loin in the oven. This combination of smoking and oven-roasting is particularly nice with the tea-spice rub method above.

2 tablespoons olive oil (if pork has not been tea-rubbed) 1 teaspoon fine sea salt (if pork has not been tea-rubbed)	Remove the pork from the refrigerator and allow it to come to room temperature. If you have not previously seasoned the pork with the tea-spice rub, then score the fat cap of the loin now and rub it lightly (*continued*)

½ teaspoon freshly ground black pepper
(if pork has not been tea-rubbed)

1 cup/215 grams rice

½ cup/100 grams (packed) light
brown sugar

1 cup/40 grams loose-leaf Ceylon
tea leaves

Zest from ¼ orange, in large strips

2 cinnamon sticks

½ teaspoon cracked black peppercorns

with olive oil and sprinkle with salt and pepper. Set aside. Line a large wok or deep skillet with heavy-duty foil so that bottom and sides are fully covered and some foil sticks out over the edge.

In a medium bowl, combine the rice, brown sugar, tea leaves, orange zest, cinnamon sticks, and peppercorns. Place half of this mixture on a piece of heavy-duty aluminum foil with the sides turned up to allow for easy handling. Make a second tray to hold the remaining half. Place the first tray in the bottom of the foil-lined wok. Place a wok rack or a splatter shield over the smoking mixture, making sure that you have 2 inches between the smoking mixture and the rack that will hold the pork.

Preheat the oven to 375°F/190°C/gas 5. Also, you'll have it ready if you want a subtler smoky flavor and only want to use one batch of smoking mix for the pork. Plan on between 1 hour and 10 minutes and 1½ hours total cooking between smoking and oven time.

Turn on the exhaust fan. Place the wok without the pork over high heat until the tea mixture begins to smoke. Place the pork on the rack. Cover with foil, then with the wok lid or a sheet pan and lower the heat to medium. After 15 minutes, turn off the heat and let the pork continue to smoke for 5 more minutes. Carefully remove the foil and lid. Using oven mitts, lift out the pork and rack and set aside. Remove the foil tray containing the smoking mixture and replace with the second tray. (At this point for a lighter smoke, you could also finish cooking the pork in the preheated oven for about 1 hour.) Turn the heat to high and watch for the second tray to begin to smoke. When it does, replace the rack and pork in the wok, cover, and lower the heat to medium. Continue cooking an additional 15 minutes and turn off the heat. Let the pork sit in the smoke an additional 10 minutes and then uncover. Test for doneness: the internal temperature of the pork loin at the thickest part should be 150°F/65°C on an instant-read thermometer. If the temperature reads less than 150°F/65°C, which is very likely, finish cooking the pork in the preheated oven. Probably an additional 20 to 30 minutes in the oven will be needed to completely cook the pork. Transfer to a cutting board and let rest, tented with foil, about 10 minutes before serving.

TEA-BRINED PORK CHOPS
with WHOLE GRILLED ONIONS

AS WITH OTHER PORK DISHES, BRINING ADDS NOT ONLY MOISTURE TO THE MEAT, BUT IT ALSO ALLOWS *you to infuse it with added depth of flavor and aromatics. These pork chops can be grilled on a gas or charcoal grill, but the onions can only be made using a charcoal grill, as they need to be buried in the ashes to cook. They come out moist and smoky and wonderful. You may find yourself tempted to add onions to your coals every time you light the grill! A green vegetable or salad will round out the meal.*

Serves 4

¼ cup/10 grams loose-leaf Chinese congou or low-grown Ceylon tea leaves, divided

3 cups/720 milliliters boiling water, divided

¼ cup/50 grams granulated sugar

¼ cup/40 grams kosher salt

1 tablespoon molasses

6 whole star anise

1 tablespoon whole black peppercorns

2 cups/480 milliliters cold water

4 (6-ounce/170-gram) center-cut pork chops, each 1¼-inches/3.5 centimeters thick

4 large onions, washed and unpeeled, left whole

Place 2 tablespoons of the tea leaves in a medium bowl and pour 1 cup/240 milliliters of the boiling water over them. Steep, covered, for 5 minutes, then strain into a large bowl. If planning to smoke the chops, reserve the strained leaves; otherwise, discard. Add the sugar, salt, and molasses while the tea is still hot. Stir until dissolved. Add the star anise and peppercorns. Add the cold water. When brine is fully cool, add the pork chops. Cover and refrigerate 8 hours.

An hour or more before you are ready to grill, place the remaining 2 tablespoons of loose-leaf tea in a small bowl and pour the remaining 2 cups/480 milliliters of boiling water over them. Steep, covered, for 5 minutes, then strain into a large bowl. If planning to smoke the chops, reserve the strained leaves; otherwise, discard. Place the whole onions in the bowl and add enough room temperature water to cover the onions completely. Let sit for at least 1 hour; the onions can sit in the tea for up to a day, but you will not find much difference between 1 hour and many, so drain them at whatever time is convenient for you as you are preparing the coals.

When ready to cook the chops, remove the pork chops from the brine and rinse well. Pat dry with paper towels and let come to room temperature while you preheat the grill. When coals are ashed over, remove the onions from the tea and, using long tongs, bury them fully in the coals, evenly dispersed in the mound.

NOTE: The pork needs to brine several hours before cooking, so plan accordingly.

COOK THE CHOPS USING ONE OF THE METHODS BELOW: grilling or grill-smoking. Grill-smoking allows the added flavors of the smoke to complement the caramelized flavors produced by grilling.

When the meat is cooked through using either method, using heavy oven mitts, lift the grill grate off and carefully remove the onions from the coals using tongs (the exterior of the onions will be completely charred). Transfer the onions one at a time to a cutting board and, using a paring knife, carefully cut the charred exterior away while holding the onions stable with a fork. Serve the smoky, moist, tender interior of the onions alongside the pork chops.

Grilling

Oil the grill grate and set it in place.

Briefly sear the chops on both sides over a very hot grill directly over the coals, then move the chops to a cooler area of the grill (not directly over the coals). Cover the grill and cook until an instant-read thermometer reads 150°F/65°C, about 15 to 18 minutes total cooking time for a 1-inch/2.5 centimeter chop. When the chops are ready, transfer them to a warmed plate and tent with foil while you prepare the onions for serving (see above).

Grill-Smoking

Used tea leaves from tea-brined pork chops and onions

¼ cup/10 grams loose-leaf Chinese congou or low-grown Ceylon tea leaves

½ cup/120 milliliters room temperature water

Place the dry tea leaves in a small bowl and add the room temperature water; let soak until soft, at least 3 minutes or until they are needed. The leaves will absorb most of the water so there should be no need to drain.

Sprinkle the wet leaves from the brine over the coals in which you have buried the onions. Place the grill rack in place and put the pork chops over medium heat (not directly over the coals) and cover. After 10 minutes, uncover and turn the pork chops. When the smoke slows down, carefully remove the grill rack with the chops still on it using heavy oven mitts. Sprinkle the soaking leaves over the coals and replace the grill rack and cover. Continue to cook until pork chops read 150°F/65°C on an instant-read thermometer, 18 to 20 minutes total cooking time for 1-inch/2.5 centimeter chops.

When the chops are ready, remove them to a warmed plate and tent with foil while you prepare the onions for serving (see main recipe).

ᗌ PAN-SEARED OOLONG PORK ᗌ
with ROOT VEGETABLES AND GREENS

THIS DISH COMES TO US FROM CHEF CORY COTTER, WHO CREATED IT WHILE A CULINARY STUDENT AT *Bunker Hill Community College in Boston. Note the use of maple syrup rather than sugar in his brine, which melds well with the oolong tea and vanilla. Grade B maple syrup has a more assertive maple flavor than grade A, which makes it preferable for cooking.*

Serves 4

PORK

5 cups/1.2 liters water

¾ cup/30 grams loose-leaf oolong tea leaves

1 vanilla bean, split in half lengthwise, or 1 tablespoon pure vanilla extract

1 stalk lemon grass, ends trimmed, coarsely chopped

⅓ cup/75 milliliters maple syrup, preferably grade B

¼ cup/40 grams kosher salt

4 (5- to 6-ounce/140- to 170-gram) boneless pork chops, each ¾ to 1 inch/2 to 2.5 centimeters thick

1 tablespoon olive oil

ROOT VEGETABLE PURÉE

3 carrots, diced

2 parsnips, diced

1 purple-top turnip, diced

2 tablespoons unsalted butter, melted

Fine sea salt to taste

Freshly ground black pepper to taste

(continued)

TO MAKE THE BRINE: In a medium saucepan bring the water to a bare simmer (do not let boil). Add the tea, vanilla bean, and lemon grass. Remove from heat and let stand for 5 minutes. Strain the tea mixture into a medium bowl. Discard the solids. Remove 2 cups/480 milliliters of the liquid to use in the vegetable purée and for cooking the pork. To the remaining 3 cups/720 milliliters tea, add the maple syrup and salt and stir well so the salt dissolves. Let cool to room temperature, about 20 to 30 minutes.

Pour the brining marinade into a resealable plastic bag or a large container with an airtight lid. Add the pork, turning to coat each chop thoroughly. Refrigerate for at least 4 hours and up to 12 hours.

About 30 minutes before you plan to cook the pork, prepare the root vegetable purée: In a large pot, add 1 cup/240 milliliters of the reserved steeped tea to the diced carrots, parsnips, and turnip. Bring to a simmer over medium-high heat and cook until tender, about 25 minutes. Transfer the vegetables to the bowl of a food processor and pulse to purée. As you pulse, add butter and 2 tablespoons of the reserved tea to make a smooth consistency. Add additional tea if needed. Add salt and pepper to taste and set aside.

TO MAKE THE PORK: Preheat the oven to 375°F/190°C/gas 5. Spray a 13 x 9-inch/33 x 23-centimeter baking pan with vegetable cooking spray.

Remove the pork from the brining liquid, rinse well, and pat dry. Discard the brine. Heat a large skillet or sauté pan over medium-high heat. Add the oil, then brown the pork, about 5 to 7 minutes on each side.

WILTED SWISS CHARD

1 tablespoon olive oil

1 bunch Swiss chard, well cleaned, thick stems discarded, leaves coarsely chopped

1 small onion, halved and thinly sliced

1 teaspoon chopped garlic

1 tablespoon herbes de Provence

Fine sea salt to taste

Freshly ground black pepper to taste

Once there's a nice, crisp crust, transfer the chops to the prepared pan. Sprinkle 1 tablespoon of the remaining reserved tea over the pork. Bake for 10 to 15 minutes, until the internal temperature of the pork reaches 150°F/65°C on an instant-read thermometer. Remove the pork from the oven, tent with foil, and let it rest 5 minutes.

TO MAKE THE CHARD: Wipe the skillet clean. Heat the oil over medium-high heat. Add the onion and cook until translucent, about 5 minutes, then add the garlic and let it brown slightly, about 1 minute. Add the Swiss chard and herbes de Provence and cook, stirring occasionally, until Swiss chard is soft, about 5 minutes.

To serve, divide the vegetable purée among 4 plates, placing it in the center of the plate. Slice the chops on the bias into $^1/_2$-inch-/12-millimeter-thick slices, if desired. Divide among the 4 plates, placing in a circle around the purée, overlapping the purée slightly. Place an equal amount of chard on each plate, in the center, and serve immediately.

NOTE: The pork needs to brine several hours (or overnight) before cooking, so plan accordingly.

DESSERTS

Confections

Cookies

Cakes and Pastries

Custards, Pies, and Fruit

Frozen

EARL GREY TRUFFLES

CHOCOLATE AND TEA WORK BEAUTIFULLY TOGETHER. FOR THE BEST FLAVOR, USE AN EARL GREY TEA *with an assertive level of good-quality bergamot oil. Alice Medrich, author of several award winning cookbooks and a noted pastry chef, developed the groundbreaking technique of using water instead of cream in her truffles; naturally, we turned that water into tea.*

Makes about 4 dozen

5 teaspoons loose-leaf Earl Grey
   tea leaves

1 cup/240 milliliters boiling water
   (about 212°F/100°C)

2 egg yolks

1 pound/455 grams bittersweet
   chocolate, chopped

12 tablespoons (1½ sticks)/170 grams
   unsalted butter

1 orange

2 teaspoons Grand Marnier (optional)

Dash fine sea salt

½ cup/50 grams unsweetened cocoa
   powder, or more as needed

Put the tea leaves in a glass measuring cup or bowl and add the boiling water. Steep, covered, for 4 minutes. Meanwhile, whisk the egg yolks in a medium bowl. Strain a small amount of the tea into the egg yolks, whisking to temper the yolks with the hot tea. Gradually strain remaining tea into yolks and mix gently but thoroughly. Set aside. Discard the leaves.

Melt the chocolate and butter in a double boiler over medium heat. The water in the bottom pot should be just barely steaming. Stir frequently. When the chocolate has completely melted, remove from the heat and stir in the egg yolk mixture and the salt. Stir until smooth.

Zest the orange over the chocolate mixture to catch any of the fragrant oils released while zesting. Gently stir the zest into the chocolate, along with the Grand Marnier, if using. Reserve the rest of the orange for another use. Refrigerate the chocolate to chill in a covered container at least 3 hours, and up to 5 days.

When you're ready to make the truffles, remove the chocolate from the fridge and allow to soften slightly at room temperature for a few minutes. Scoop scant teaspoons and roll into a balls between your palms. Roll the balls in cocoa. Serve immediately or store in a resealable container refrigerated for up to 1 week, or in the freezer for up to 1 month. If storing for later use, roll the truffles in the cocoa just before serving.

Variations

• Add a few drops of food-grade bergamot oil or 1 teaspoon vanilla
   extract when adding the zest.
• Replace the Earl Grey with a black tea like Nilgiri or Assam instead of
   the Earl Grey and ½ teaspoon cinnamon and ¼ teaspoon (or more)
   cayenne pepper.

ROSY GREEN TEA TRUFFLES

GREEN TEA TAKES VERY WELL TO FLORAL OR FRUIT ADDITIONS. ROSE PETALS ARE AVAILABLE FROM *many produce markets, natural food stores, and from online tea purveyors (see Sources, page 277). If you grow your own roses without pesticides, you could use those rose petals. This recipe, inspired by Alice Medrich also works well with other floral variations.*

Makes about 4 dozen

¼ cup/10 grams fresh or dried rose petals

1 cup/240 milliliters boiling water (about 212°F/100°C)

2 egg yolks

2 teaspoons matcha green tea powder, plus additional for rolling, if desired

1 pound/455 grams bittersweet chocolate, chopped

12 tablespoons/170 grams (1½ sticks) unsalted butter

½ cup/50 grams unsweetened cocoa powder, or more as needed

Dash fine sea salt

Place the rose petals in a glass measuring cup and pour the boiling water over them. Steep, covered, for 6 minutes for dried rose petals, 15 minutes for fresh. Meanwhile, whisk the egg yolks in a medium bowl. When the rose petals are done steeping, strain a small amount of the liquid into the egg yolks, and whisk to temper the yolks with the hot liquid. Gradually strain the remaining liquid into the yolks and mix gently but thoroughly. Discard the petals. Whisk in the matcha and set aside.

Melt the chocolate and butter in a double boiler over medium heat. The water in the bottom pot should be just barely steaming. Stir frequently. When the chocolate has completely melted, remove from the heat and stir in the egg yolk mixture and the salt. Stir until smooth. Refrigerate the chocolate in a covered container at least 3 hours, and up to 5 days.

When you're ready to make the truffles, remove the chocolate from the fridge and allow to soften slightly at room temperature for a few minutes. Scoop scant teaspoons and roll into balls between your palms. Roll balls in cocoa, a blend of cocoa and matcha, or straight matcha. Serve immediately or store in a resealable container, refrigerated, for up to 1 week, or in the freezer for up to 1 month. If storing for later use, roll the truffles in the cocoa or matcha just before serving.

Variation
LAVENDER GREEN TEA TRUFFLES: Substitute lavender for the rose petals.

MILK CHOCOLATE KEEMUN TRUFFLES

IRISH CREAM LIQUEUR MELDS WONDERFULLY WITH FULL-BODIED TEAS LIKE KEEMUN, WHICH ADD *depth to the chocolate and the liqueur. These delectable truffles could be served with the Keemun Cream (page 256), a tea cocktail that also features a combination of Keemun and Irish cream.*

Makes about 4 dozen

1¼ cups/300 milliliters heavy whipping cream

6 tablespoons loose-leaf Keemun or other full-bodied black tea leaves, divided

⅓ cup/75 milliliters Irish cream liqueur, such as Bailey's

⅓ cup/75 milliliters boiling water (about 212°F/100°C)

10 ounces/280 grams milk chocolate, chopped

6 ounces/170 grams bittersweet chocolate, chopped

6 tablespoons/85 grams unsalted butter

Dash fine sea salt

½ cup/50 grams unsweetened cocoa powder, or more, as needed

In a small saucepan, bring the cream just to a boil and add ¼ cup/10 grams of the tea. Remove from the heat and set aside to steep, covered, for 45 minutes.

While the tea steeps in the cream, place 1 tablespoon of the remaining tea leaves in a small bowl and cover with the boiling water. Steep, covered, for 4 minutes, then strain and set aside.

Strain the cream, pressing the tea leaves to extract as much cream as possible; this should yield about ⅔ cup/165 milliliters. Add enough Irish cream to equal 1 cup/240 milliliters of liquid. Return to small saucepan and warm over low heat to slightly above body temperature.

Melt the milk and bittersweet chocolates and butter in a double boiler over medium heat. The water in the bottom pan should be just barely steaming. Stir frequently. When the chocolate has completely melted, remove from the heat and slowly stir in the warmed cream mixture and the salt. Measure 1 tablespoon of the reserved tea and stir into the chocolate mixture. Taste and add more of the reserved tea to taste. Refrigerate the chocolate in a covered container at least 3 hours, and up to 5 days. Discard any remaining tea.

When ready to make the truffles, remove the chocolate from the fridge and allow to soften slightly at room temperature for a few minutes.

Grind the remaining 1 tablespoon tea leaves to a fine powder in a spice grinder or using a mortar and pestle. Mix with the cocoa in a small bowl. Scoop out teaspoons of the chocolate mixture, roll into balls between your palms, and roll in the cocoa-tea mixture.

Serve immediately or chill in a resealable container for up to 1 week, or store in the freezer for up to 1 month. If storing for later use, roll the truffles in the cocoa mixture just before serving.

⤜ TEA TOFFEE *with* TEA-SMOKED SALT ⤏

SALTED CARAMELS HAVE BECOME QUITE POPULAR LATELY, AND WE'RE PARTICULARLY FOND OF THAT
salty-sweet blend when combined with chocolate. A full-bodied black tea, such as low-grown Ceylon, Nilgiri, or Assam, stirred into the toffee, helps balance the sweetness. The garnishes are flexible—if you like a higher chocolate-to-toffee ratio, increase the chocolate. If you like a sweeter chocolate flavor, use milk chocolate, or a blend of milk and dark chocolates, instead of bittersweet.

Makes 2 pounds / 910 grams

1 pound/455 grams (4 sticks) unsalted butter

2 cups/400 grams granulated sugar

1 tablespoon light corn syrup

1 tablespoon bourbon

½ teaspoon cream of tartar

1 tablespoon ground loose-leaf Ceylon tea leaves

8 ounces/225 grams sliced almonds

4 ounces/115 grams bittersweet chocolate, chopped

2 teaspoons Tea-Smoked Salt (page 81) or coarse sea salt, or more to taste

Line a baking sheet with parchment paper and set aside.

Combine the butter, sugar, corn syrup, bourbon, and cream of tartar in a large, heavy saucepan and heat over medium-low heat. Melt, stirring occasionally. When the mixture is blended and bubbling lightly, add the almonds and ground tea and increase the heat to medium. Stir slowly, gently, and constantly from this point, about 10 to 15 minutes. The mixture will thicken, and then thin out slightly just before it is ready. It will also go from opaque to translucent, and you may see a wisp or two of smoke.

When translucent and rich golden in color, remove from the heat and pour onto the prepared baking sheet. Spread out evenly and thinly with a spatula. Be careful not to touch the candy as it will be very hot. Sprinkle the chopped chocolate over the toffee. Wait a few minutes for it to melt and then use a rubber spatula to spread the chocolate over the surface. Allow 10 to 15 minutes for the chocolate to begin to set; it will start to lose some of its shine. Sprinkle lightly with the salt and refrigerate to cool completely.

When cool, break the toffee into small pieces. Serve at room temperature. Store in an airtight container at room temperature, or refrigerate in warmer weather.

DARJEELING TEA BARK

TEA AND CHOCOLATE GO BEAUTIFULLY TOGETHER, AND CHOCOLATE BARK IS AN EASY AND UNEXPECTED *way to enjoy the delicate flavors of various teas. Use coarsely ground or crushed tea, and keep this in mind: the better the chocolate, the better the bark. Darjeeling adds a floral perfume to dark chocolate, but experiment with different combinations of teas and styles of chocolate, as indicated in our suggested variations.*

Makes 1 pound/455 grams

1 pound/455 grams finely chopped bittersweet or semisweet chocolate

2 tablespoon coarsely ground or crushed loose-leaf Darjeeling tea leaves

Line a baking sheet with parchment paper or a silicone baking mat.

In the top of a double boiler set over just steaming water, melt the chocolate slowly, stirring frequently. When about $^3/_4$ of the chocolate is melted, remove the pan from the heat and stir until all the chocolate is melted. The chocolate should feel just slightly warm to the touch. Stir in the tea and mix well to distribute.

Pour the chocolate onto the prepared pan and spread it about $^1/_8$-inch/3 millimeters thick. Let the bark set at room temperature until completely solid, about 4 to 6 hours. When it is set, break into pieces that are about 2 square inches. Store at room temperature in an airtight container.

Variations

Use an equal amount of chocolate and replace the Darjeeling with the suggested amount of tea below in the following variations.

WHITE ON WHITE: White chocolate, with 4 teaspoons coarsely ground white tea

JASMINE WHITE: White chocolate with 2 tablespoons coarsely ground jasmine tea

MILK CHOCOLATE CHAI: Milk chocolate with 4 teaspoons ground chai tea blend

LEMON BLACK: Dark chocolate with 2 tablespoons of any ground black tea and $^1/_2$ teaspoon grated lemon zest

EARL GREY BLACK: Dark chocolate with 2 tablespoons ground Earl Grey tea
HOLIDAY BARK: White chocolate with 2 teaspoons matcha green tea powder and crushed peppermint candies
SMOKY PECAN: Dark chocolate with Smoky Tea-Spiced Pecans (page 86); omit the tea

---

Melting Chocolate

The key to good bark is to melt the chocolate slowly, bringing it to a temperature just above body temperature. If chocolate melts at too high a temperature, it will loose temper, and when it solidifies again, it will be crumbly, with patches of white called "bloom," which is a separation of the cocoa butter. Milk and white chocolates can be trickier to melt, as the milk content in each makes them burn more easily. If you use a double boiler with steaming, not simmering water, you can control the way you melt chocolate, and then enjoy the delectable results.

⤪ EARL GREY ZEBRA COOKIES ⤨

THESE COOKIES HAVE A LOVELY CHEWY TEXTURE, AND GAIN A DOUBLE SHOT OF FLAVOR FROM BOTH *steeped tea and ground tea leaves. As with the Earl Grey Truffles (page 174), this is a classic flavor combination of chocolate and citrus, enhanced by the earthiness of tea. Orange zest highlights the citrus notes of Earl Grey tea. The cookies will keep at room temperature for several days, or in the freezer for at least 1 month.*

Makes about 4 dozen

½ cup/120 milliliters boiling water (about 212°F/100°C)

2 tablespoons loose-leaf Earl Grey tea leaves, divided

1¾ cup/215 grams all-purpose flour

¼ teaspoon baking soda

⅓ cup/35 grams unsweetened cocoa powder

½ pound/225 grams (2 sticks) unsalted butter

1 cup/200 grams granulated sugar

½ cup/100 grams (packed) dark brown sugar

1 teaspoon bourbon

1 egg

1 teaspoon finely grated orange or tangerine zest

1 cup/135 grams chopped white chocolate

Preheat the oven to 350°F/180°C/gas 4. Line 2 baking sheets with parchment paper or spray with vegetable cooking spray.

In a small bowl, pour the boiling water over 1 tablespoon of the Earl Grey tea leaves. Steep, covered, for 5 minutes. Strain and discard tea leaves. Set aside the steeped tea to cool.

In a spice grinder or using a mortar and pestle, grind the remaining 1 tablespoon tea; there should be about 2 teaspoons. Combine the ground tea with the flour, baking soda, and cocoa in a medium bowl.

In a large bowl, use an electric mixer on medium-high to beat the butter until light and fluffy. Add both sugars and beat until smooth. Beat in bourbon, egg, orange zest, and 2 tablespoons of the cooled tea. (Reserve remaining tea for another use, or discard.) On low speed, slowly add reserved flour mixture and beat until fully incorporated.

Scoop the dough by the teaspoonful and form into balls, placing them on the prepared baking sheets about 1½ inches/4 centimeters apart. If the dough does not easily roll into balls, chill for 15 minutes and then roll. Flatten dough balls slightly. Bake until just barely firm, about 10 minutes. Let cool on the baking sheet several minutes, then transfer to a cooling rack to cool.

Melt the white chocolate gently in the top of a double boiler set over steaming water. Transfer to a resealable plastic bag and snip one corner, or use parchment paper to make a small piping bag. Pipe white chocolate in a zig-zag pattern over the cookies and let sit at room temperature for at least 30 minutes, or until the white chocolate is firm. Store cookies in an airtight container.

❧ WHITE PEONY FINANCIERS ❧

Judy Mattera of Sweet Solutions is an extraordinarily talented Boston pastry chef who *specializes in pairing desserts and wines. Her study of wine and these pairings translates beautifully to understanding the flavors and aromatics of fine teas. It can often be difficult to pair against or cook with the subtlety of white teas, but Mattera combines a heartier style of open leaf white tea with a delicate almond cake, with intriguing and delicious results. A slightly sweet confection, the edges of the financiers are a little crunchy, while the inside is moist and chewy.*

Makes 1 dozen

1½ tablespoons warm water (100°F to 110°F/38°C to 45°C)

2 teaspoons loose-leaf white peony tea leaves

4 tablespoons unsalted butter

¼ cup/35 grams almond meal or finely ground almonds

2 tablespoons cake flour, sifted

¼ teaspoon baking powder

Pinch fine sea salt

½ cup/50 grams confectioners' sugar, sifted

2 egg whites, at room temperature

Pour the warm water over the tea in a small bowl and steep, covered, for 15 minutes.

In a small saucepan, melt the butter, then continue heating until butter begins to brown slightly—watch carefully. Remove from heat and let cool to room temperature.

Preheat the oven to 350°F/180°C/gas 4. Spray 12 mini-muffin cups with vegetable cooking spray, then line with small paper baking cups.

In a large mixing bowl, combine the almond meal, cake flour, baking powder, salt, and confectioners' sugar. Stir to mix well.

In a separate bowl, whisk the egg whites just until foamy, about 30 to 60 seconds. Fold into the dry ingredients. Add the steeped tea and the tea leaves. Add the reserved butter. Mix well, then refrigerate the batter for 30 minutes.

Divide the batter evenly among the prepared muffin cups. Bake for 12 to 15 minutes, until surface springs back when pressed. Cool in pan for 5 minutes, then remove the cakes and cool on a cooling rack. Store in an airtight container. Serve at room temperature.

Note: Almond meal (also called almond flour) is very finely ground almonds. It can be found in natural food markets and online baking supply stores. If you can't find it, grind ¼ cup/35 grams blanched almonds with 1 tablespoon of the confectioners' sugar in a food processor.

ANISE LYCHEE BISCOT-TEA

THIS RECIPE USES LYCHEE CONGOU BLACK TEA, GROUND AS CLOSE TO A POWDER AS POSSIBLE. LYCHEE *black tea is a classic Chinese scented tea that can be found almost anywhere that has a good selection of loose teas. The flavor goes particularly well with the anise in these biscotti. If you can't find lychee tea, substitute with a Chinese black or strongly oxidized oolong. You will probably need at least 3 tablespoons of loose-leaf tea to yield the 4 1/2 teaspoons of ground tea needed for the recipe. And, yes, the 4 1/2 teaspoons of anise extract is correct! We love the intense bite, which seems to go well with the tea and the crunchy texture of the cookies.*

Makes about 3 dozen

2 tablespoons unsalted butter, chilled

1 1/3 cups/265 grams granulated sugar

4 eggs, divided

4 1/2 teaspoons anise extract

3 cups/385 grams sifted all-purpose flour

2 teaspoons baking powder

Pinch fine sea salt

4 1/2 teaspoons finely ground loose-leaf lychee congou tea leaves

1 tablespoon water

Preheat the oven to 350°F/180°C/gas 4. Line 2 baking sheets with parchment paper or spray with vegetable cooking spray.

In a large mixing bowl, use an electric mixer on medium-high speed to cream the butter until smooth. Add the sugar and continue to beat. Add 3 of the eggs, one at a time, beating after each addition, then add the anise extract and beat until smooth.

In a medium bowl, sift together the flour, baking powder, salt, and ground tea. Slowly stir the flour mixture into the egg mixture on low speed. Mix until thoroughly incorporated. The dough will be stiff.

Divide the dough in two and shape each half into a log on each of the prepared pans. (The dough will spread while baking, so don't put two on the same sheet pan.) In a small bowl, lightly whisk the remaining egg with the water until smooth and combined. Brush the loaves with the egg wash. Bake until the loaves are puffed slightly and firm, and a tester inserted in the center comes out clean, about 35 minutes.

Remove from the oven and let cool 5 minutes, then transfer the loaves to a cutting board. Cut into 1/2-inch/12-millimeter slices on an angle, and place the slices back on the baking sheets standing up so that both cut sides are exposed and none of the biscotti touch each other. Bake an additional 10 to 15 minutes, until the slices are dry and beginning to gain a golden color. They will still be slightly soft, but will crisp up as they cool. Cool completely on a cooling rack. Store in an airtight container at room temperature for up to 3 weeks.

CHAI CHOCOLATE WAFERS

A VERSION OF THIS RECIPE ORIGINALLY APPEARED IN HANNAFORD SUPERMARKETS' *FRESH* **MAGAZINE,** *for an article on afternoon tea. Chocolate goes nicely with warm spices like cinnamon, and malty Assam enhances the chocolate.*

Makes about 8 dozen

4 ounces (1 stick)/115 grams unsalted butter

¼ cup/50 grams (packed) light brown sugar

¼ cup/50 grams granulated sugar

½ teaspoon vanilla extract

¼ teaspoon ground cinnamon

½ teaspoon ground cardamom

⅛ teaspoon ground cloves

1½ teaspoons ground loose-leaf black tea leaves, preferably Assam or Ceylon

1 egg white

1 cup/130 grams all-purpose flour

½ teaspoon baking powder

¼ teaspoon fine sea salt

½ cup/85 grams semisweet chocolate chips

In a large mixing bowl, use an electric mixer on medium-high speed to cream the butter until light and fluffy, about 1 minute. Add both sugars and mix on medium-high until well blended, about 2 minutes. Add the vanilla, cinnamon, cardamom, cloves, and tea and blend, about 1 minute. Add the egg white and mix well, about 1 to 2 minutes.

Scrape the sides of the bowl. Sprinkle the flour, baking powder, and salt over the surface. Fold in lightly with a rubber spatula, then mix on low speed until all the flour is incorporated, about 45 seconds.

Add the chocolate chips to the bowl of a food processor. Pulse until the chips are finely ground into very small pieces. Add the crushed chips to the batter and mix on medium speed until combined, about 30 seconds.

Place an 18-inch/46-centimeter length of plastic wrap or parchment paper on a work surface. Scoop ⅓ of the dough onto the wrap, making a log shape that is about 1 inch/2.5 centimeters in diameter and 10 to 11 inches/25 to 28 centimeters long. Wrap the plastic completely around the dough and roll the log to even out the dough. Place the wrapped log in the freezer for at least 30 minutes; repeat with the remaining dough, for 3 logs. The dough may be stored up to 3 weeks in the freezer, double-wrapped.

When ready to bake, preheat the oven to 350°F/180°C/gas 4. Line 2 baking sheets with parchment paper or spray with vegetable cooking spray.

Remove the logs from the freezer one at a time. Slice into rounds about ¼ inch/6 millimeters thick. Place in rows on the prepared baking sheets, about 1 inch/2.5 centimeters apart. Bake for 8 to 9 minutes, until the cookies are just set and pale gold at the edges. Remove and let the cookies cool on the pan for 2 minutes, then transfer to a cooling rack to continue cooling. Store in an airtight container at room temperature for 2 days, or in the freezer.

HONEY JASMINE WAFERS

CRÈME FRAÎCHE GIVES THESE DELECTABLE BITE-SIZE COOKIES A LIGHT TEXTURE, AND HONEY *accentuates the floral flavors of jasmine tea. These are the perfect cookies to enjoy at the end of an Asian-themed meal. White chocolate also goes well with jasmine, but these cookies are just as delicious without the white chocolate garnish.*

Makes about 8 dozen

- 4 ounces (1 stick)/115 grams unsalted butter, softened
- ¼ cup/60 millileters crème fraîche or sour cream
- ¼ cup/50 grams granulated sugar
- ¼ cup/60 milliliters honey
- 1 egg yolk
- 1½ teaspoons vanilla extract
- 1½ teaspoons coarsely ground jasmine tea leaves
- ¼ teaspoon fine sea salt
- 1¼ cups/160 grams all-purpose flour
- Coarse sugar, such as turbinado sugar for sprinkling (optional)
- ½ cup/70 grams finely chopped white chocolate for garnish (optional)

In a large bowl, use an electric mixer on medium-high speed to cream the butter until light, about 1 minute. Add the crème fraîche and beat on medium-high speed until thoroughly combined. Add the sugar and beat on medium-high until well mixed. Beat in the honey and egg yolk and mix until mixture is light and fluffy, about 2 minutes. Add the vanilla, jasmine tea, and salt and mix to combine. Add the flour and mix until just combined. The dough should be stiff and not too sticky.

Place an 18-inch/46-centimeter length of plastic wrap, parchment paper, or waxed paper on a work surface. Scoop ⅓ of the dough onto the wrap, making a log shape that is about 1¼ inches/3.5 centimeters in diameter and 10 to 11 inches/25 to 28 centimeters long. Wrap the plastic completely around the dough and roll the log to even out the dough. Repeat with the remaining dough, for a total of 3 logs. Refrigerate for at least 2 hours, or freeze for 30 minutes. Dough may be stored up to 3 weeks in the freezer, double-wrapped.

When ready to bake, preheat the oven to 350°F/180°C/gas 4. Line 2 baking sheets with parchment paper.

Remove the logs from the freezer or fridge one at a time. Unwrap and roll a log against a work surface to even it out and make the edges smooth and round. If desired, sprinkle edges with coarse sugar and roll slightly so that the sugar crystals adhere to the sides of the roll. Slice the roll into ¼-inch-/6-millimeter-thick slices and place on the prepared baking sheets about 1 inch apart.

Bake one or two sheets at a time for 8 to 10 minutes, until edges are pale gold and cookies are firm; the undersides of the cookies should be golden.

Remove the pans from the oven and allow cookies to rest on the baking sheet for 2 minutes. If using white chocolate, immediately sprinkle a pinch of the finely chopped chocolate over each cookie. The heat will melt the white chocolate. Transfer cookies to a cooling rack and let cool completely until the chocolate is firm, about 2 hours. Store in an airtight container.

Left: Tea pluckers awaiting transport of their leaves in from the fields, Glendale Estate, southern India;
Right: Tea pluckers in the fields at Havakul Estate, southern India

⊘ ASSAM SHORTBREAD DIAMONDS ⊘

SHORTBREAD COOKIES ARE ONE OF THE MOST BASIC—AND DELICIOUS—STYLES OF COOKIES, CONSISTING *of butter, sugar, flour, and a few optional flavorings. They're not too sweet, and the flavor of the tea comes through very nicely. Assam imparts a wonderful, subtle nuttiness with just a hint of malt to shortbread. A Nilgiri or an African black tea also works well. Grind the tea in a spice grinder, or with a mortar and pestle. Make sure it's coarsely ground, not powdered, which gives the cookies an appealing crunch. These cookies are baked at a very low heat, which keeps them a lovely ivory color and brings out a creamier texture that contrasts with the texture of the tea. For a crisper cookie, you can increase the temperature to 325°F/165°C/gas 3 and bake them until lightly golden around the edges and underneath.*

Makes about 5 dozen

1 pound (4 sticks)/455 grams
   unsalted butter, chilled

1 cup/200 grams granulated sugar

2 teaspoons bourbon

4 cups/500 grams all-purpose flour

½ teaspoon fine sea salt

4 teaspoons coarsely ground
   loose-leaf Assam tea leaves

In a large bowl, use an electric mixer on medium speed to cream together the butter and sugar until smooth. Add the bourbon and mix until incorporated. Add the flour, salt, and tea. Mix on low speed until dough just pulls together.

Divide dough in two and flatten into two rectangles. Place one between two sheets of parchment or waxed paper and roll out to ¼-inch/6-millimeter thickness; repeat with the second rectangle of dough and transfer each to separate baking sheets to help the dough stay flat as it chills. Chill dough in the refrigerator for at least 20 minutes, or until firm enough that you can cut the dough and lift it cleanly without stretching it. You can chill the dough for up to 3 days or freeze it for up to a month at this point.

When ready to bake, preheat the oven to 250°F/120°C/gas 1/2. Line two baking sheets with parchment paper or spray with vegetable cooking spray.

Remove the dough rectangles from the fridge one at a time. Cut into diamonds or another shape. Place on the prepared baking sheets about ½ inch/12 millimeters apart (the cookies will not spread very much).

Bake for 40 to 45 minutes, until the shortbread is firm and takes on a sandy, dry appearance; the color will not change much due to the low oven temperature. Cool on a cooling rack and store in an airtight container at room temperature for up to 1 week or freeze well wrapped for up to a month.

Variations

CHOCOLATE-ORANGE: Add $^1/_2$ cup/70 grams finely chopped bittersweet or semisweet chocolate and the grated zest of $^1/_2$ orange with the tea.

CHAI SPICE: Add $^1/_4$ teaspoon ground cloves, 1 teaspoon ground cardamom, $^1/_8$ teaspoon freshly ground black pepper, and $^1/_4$ teaspoon ground cinnamon with the flour.

SAVORY PEPPER: Reduce the sugar to $^1/_2$ cup/100 grams and add $^1/_2$ to 1 teaspoon freshly ground black pepper, depending on how spicy you want the shortbread to be. This version goes very nicely with a wedge of blue cheese, some lightly dressed greens, and roasted figs.

DARJEELING-LAVENDER: Change the ground tea to Darjeeling and add 1 teaspoon dried lavender; substitute vanilla for the bourbon.

CRANBERRY-KEEMUN SHORTBREAD

A full-bodied Chinese Keemun adds chocolaty overtones to this shortbread, which goes *particularly well with cranberries. If Keemun is not available, substitute any strong Chinese black tea. These cookies may also be prepared by rolling out and cutting into shapes, using the technique described in the recipe for Assam Shortbread Diamonds (page 186).*

Makes about 5 dozen

3 tablespoons loose-leaf Keemun tea leaves, divided

²/₃ cup/165 milliliters boiling water (about 212°F/100°C)

½ cup/85 grams dried cranberries, coarsely chopped

1 pound (4 sticks)/455 grams unsalted butter, chilled

1 cup/200 grams granulated sugar

2 teaspoons vanilla extract

4 cups/500 grams all-purpose flour

¼ teaspoon fine sea salt

Place 1 tablespoon of the tea leaves in a small bowl and pour over the boiling water. Steep, covered, for 4 minutes. Put the chopped cranberries in another small bowl and strain the tea over the berries, discarding the leaves. Let sit until cooled to room temperature, about 15 minutes. Remove the plumped cranberries from the tea and lightly pat dry. Discard the tea.

In a large bowl, use an electric mixer on medium speed to cream together the butter and sugar until smooth. Beat in the vanilla.

Grind the remaining 2 tablespoons tea in a spice grinder until relatively fine but not powdered—there should be some texture. Add to the butter with the flour and salt and mix until the dough just comes together. Gently stir in the chopped cranberries.

Place a 12-inch/30.5-centimeter length of plastic wrap, parchment paper, or waxed paper on a work surface. Scoop ¹/₃ of the dough onto the wrap, making a log shape that is about 2 inches/5 centimeters in diameter and 6 to 8 inches/15 to 20 centimeters long. Wrap the plastic completely around dough and roll the log to even out the dough. Repeat with the remaining dough, for a total of 3 logs. Refrigerate for at least 1 hour, or freeze for 20 minutes. Dough may be stored up to 3 weeks in the freezer, double-wrapped.

When ready to bake, preheat the oven to 250°F/120°C/gas1/2. Line 2 baking sheets with parchment paper.

Working with 1 log at a time, remove dough from the freezer or fridge. Unwrap and roll log against a work surface to even it out and make the edges smooth and round. Slice the roll into ¹/₄ -inch-/6-millimeter-thick slices and place on the prepared baking sheets about $^1\!/_2$-inch/12 millimeters apart (the cookies will not spread very much).

Bake for 40 to 45 minutes, until the shortbread is firm and takes on a sandy, dry appearance; the color will not change much due to the low oven temperature. Cool on a cooling rack and store in an airtight container at room temperature for up to 1 week or freeze well-wrapped for up to a month.

Variations

Use the same plumping technique for other dried fruit: currants, raisins (regular and golden sultanas), blueberries, cherries.

CHOCOLATE-CHERRY: Substitute cherries for the cranberries. Add $^1\!/_2$ cup/70 grams finely chopped bittersweet chocolate with the cherries and substitute bourbon for the vanilla.

CRANBERRY-ORANGE: Substitute Grand Marnier liqueur for the vanilla. Add 1 teaspoon grated orange zest with the Grand Marnier. If desired, add $^1\!/_2$ cup/70 grams diced candied orange peel with the plumped cranberries.

LEMON-CURRANT: Substitute currants for the cranberries. Add 1 teaspoon grated lemon zest with the vanilla.

PEAR-GINGER: Substitute dried pears for the cranberries. Add $^1\!/_2$ teaspoon ground ginger and/or 2 tablespoons chopped crystallized ginger.

MATCHA "TEA LEAVES"

MATCHA IS THE FINELY GROUND JAPANESE GREEN TEA USED IN CHANOYU, THE JAPANESE TEA CEREMONY.
The better quality the matcha, the brighter green the color and the fresher the taste. These same characteristics will carry over to the cookies as well, which are formed into a leaf shape to match their green color.

Makes about 3 dozen

8 ounces (2 sticks)/225 grams unsalted butter, chilled

½ cup/100 grams granulated sugar

1 teaspoon Grand Marnier liqueur

2 cups/255 grams all-purpose flour

2 teaspoons matcha green tea powder

½ teaspoon Chinese 5-spice powder

¼ teaspoon fine sea salt

In a large bowl, use an electric mixer on medium speed to cream together butter and sugar until smooth. Blend in the Grand Marnier, then add the flour, matcha, 5-spice powder, and salt. Mix until the dough just pulls together.

Flatten dough into a disk and place between two sheets of parchment or waxed paper. Roll out to $1/8$-inch/3-millimeter thickness and chill on a baking sheet to help the dough stay flat as it chills for at least 20 minutes, or until it is firm enough that you can cut the dough and lift it cleanly without stretching it.

When ready to bake, preheat the oven to 300°F/150°C/gas 2. Line two baking sheets with parchment paper or spray with vegetable cooking spray.

Remove the sheet of dough from the fridge. Using a sharp paring knife, cut into leaf shapes roughly 2 inches/5 centimeters long and 1 inch/2.5 centimeters wide, or use a leaf-shaped cookie cutter.

Transfer the leaves to the prepared pans with roughly $1/2$-inch/12 millimeters between them, and very lightly score a center vein into the tea leaf, if desired. Work quickly; if the dough becomes too soft to transfer easily to the baking sheet, return to the fridge and chill for a few minutes.

Bake until the cookies take on a dry powdery look and are firm, around 15 minutes. Let cool on the baking sheets 2 minutes, then transfer to a cooling rack to cool completely. Store in an airtight container at room temperature for up to 1 week or freeze.

NOTE: Five-spice powder is a Chinese spice blend that includes star anise, anise, ginger, cinnamon, and cloves.

GLAZED HOLIDAY SHORTBREADS

THE PALE GREEN OF THE MATCHA TEA LOOKS PARTICULARLY FESTIVE WITH THE CRUSHED RED-AND- *white peppermint candy. This recipe is a tea-oriented variation on the first place-winning Peppermint Candy Shortbread submitted by Tasha Schlake Festel to the Boston Park Plaza Hotel during a holiday cookie competition.*

Makes about 3 dozen

SHORTBREAD

2 cups/255 grams all-purpose flour

½ cup/30 grams cornstarch

2 teaspoons matcha green tea powder

⅛ teaspoon fine sea salt

½ pound (2 sticks)/225 grams
  unsalted butter, chilled

¼ cup granulated sugar

¼ cup crushed peppermint candies

1 teaspoon vanilla extract

GLAZE

1 cup/100 grams confectioners' sugar

¼ teaspoon matcha green tea powder

½ teaspoon vanilla extract

1 to 2 tablespoons milk

2 tablespoons crushed
  peppermint candies

Preheat the oven to 300°F/150°C/gas 2. Line 2 baking sheets with parchment paper or spray with vegetable cooking spray.

To make the shortbread: In a medium bowl, stir together the flour, cornstarch, matcha, and salt.

In a large bowl, use an electric mixer on medium speed to cream together the butter and sugar until smooth. Add the crushed peppermint and vanilla and blend until evenly distributed. Add the flour mixture slowly and blend until the dough just pulls together.

Form the dough into 1-inch/2.5-centimeter balls and place on the prepared baking sheets. Flatten each ball slightly. Leave 1 inch/2.5 centimeters between each cookie.

Bake until the bottom of the cookies begins to color, about 22 to 25 minutes. Remove from the oven and let cool on the baking sheet.

When cookies are cool, prepare the glaze: Sift together the confectioners' sugar and matcha in a medium bowl. Stir in the vanilla and 1 tablespoon of the milk until smooth. Add additional milk if needed to create a smooth, pourable consistency. Drizzle the icing over the cooled cookies, then sprinkle a pinch of crushed peppermint candy over each cookie. Let set about 30 minutes before serving.

To store, place cookies carefully in a flat airtight container in single layers, with sheets of waxed paper between the layers. Store for up to 2 days at room temperature, or in the freezer well-wrapped up to 2 weeks.

GREEN TEA LIME TUILES
with VINEGARED STRAWBERRIES

TUILES ARE VERY THIN COOKIES THAT ARE SOFT AND MOLDABLE THE MOMENT THEY COME OUT OF THE *oven; they then firm up into whatever shape you've formed—cigars, bowls, spirals, etc. They are easy to prepare and make an elegant presentation. Nonstick baking mats such as those made by Silpat are ideal for these cookies; if you don't have one, parchment paper or nonstick foil can work, or make sure to grease the baking surface generously. Vegetable cooking spray is very good for this. The measurements for the sugar and flour may seem odd, but tuiles can be very tricky, and the ratios for the different ingredients need to be very precise.*

The strawberries are especially delicious with Mango-Peach Oolong Granita (page 226) or Jasmine Rhubarb Sorbet (page 228), but any good peach, apricot or mango sorbet, or vanilla or mango ice cream would be lovely.

Serves 6

VINEGARED STRAWBERRIES

1 pint/350 grams strawberries, hulled and quartered

2 tablespoons red wine vinegar

2 tablespoons granulated or superfine sugar

Pinch freshly ground black pepper, or to taste

2 tablespoons coarsely chopped fresh basil

2 tablespoons coarsely chopped fresh mint

TUILES

¼ cup/50 grams plus 1 teaspoon granulated sugar

1 egg white

1 tablespoon unsalted butter, melted

¼ teaspoon grated lime zest

(continued)

TO MAKE THE STRAWBERRIES: Put the strawberries in a medium bowl. Toss with the vinegar, sugar, pepper, basil, and mint. Cover and refrigerate while you prepare the tuiles.

TO MAKE THE TUILES: Preheat the oven to 325°F/165°C/gas 3. Line a baking sheet with a nonstick mat, nonstick foil, or spray generously with vegetable cooking spray.

In a medium bowl, whisk together the sugar, egg white, and melted butter until smooth. Blend in the lime zest and juice, then sprinkle in flour, tea, salt, and pepper and stir until smooth. Batter will be thin.

Take 1 tablespoon of the batter and pour it onto the prepared pan. Use the back of a spoon to spread it out to a very thin, even disk, about 5 to 6 inches/12 to 15 centimeters in diameter. Make 1 more disk on the pan. (Because tuiles firm up so quickly once they are baked, it is best to make only two at a time when you are going to form the baked cookies into shapes, until you get some practice working with tuiles.) Bake until the edges are golden and the center appears fully dry, about 6 minutes.

While the tuiles bake, take a sheet of foil and loosely crush it into a ball 2 to 3 inches/5 to 7.5 centimeters in diameter. Flatten it slightly so it doesn't roll. Repeat to make 1 more foil ball. As soon as the cookies are

½ teaspoon fresh lime juice

¼ cup/30 grams plus 1 teaspoon all-purpose flour

1 tablespoon finely ground (but not to a powder) loose-leaf green tea leaves, such as sencha or Dragonwell

Pinch fine sea salt

⅛ teaspoon freshly ground black pepper

Sorbet or ice cream of your choice, for serving

Mint or basil sprigs, for garnish

done baking, working very quickly, carefully remove one disk at a time from the pan with a large spatula. Drape the tuile over a foil ball and press down slightly to form the bowl shape. You need to work very quickly, as the tuiles will harden as soon as they cool. Alternatively, you could use 2 (6 ounce/175 milliliter) ramekins to form bowls. As an alternative serving suggestion, you can make smaller tuille cookies and not form them into bowls.

Let the pan cool slightly, then form 2 more disks of batter. Repeat the baking instructions. Just before the second batch of tuiles are ready, remove the formed tuiles from the foil balls—they should be set before the next set are ready. Form the next 2 tuiles into bowls using the foil balls and repeat for the third set. If made in advance, store in an airtight container at room temperature.

To serve, place each tuile bowl on a dessert plate. If the bottom of your tuile is not sitting well on the plate, a dollop of whipped cream for it to settle into will keep it steady. Place a scoop of sorbet or granita in the tuile bowl, and top with the strawberries. Garnish with a sprig of fresh mint or basil.

Variations

TUILE CIGAR: Instead of draping the tuile disk over the foil ball to form a bowl, wrap around the well-oiled handle of a wooden spoon or a wooden dowel to form an elegant thin cigar-shaped tuile. Use to garnish bowls of sorbet or ice cream.

BLACK TEA AND COCOA TUILES: Substitute ground Ceylon, Keemun, or Nilgiri tea for the green tea. Increase the butter by 1 more teaspoon and add 2 teaspoons unsweetened cocoa power with the flour. Replace the lime zest and juice with orange zest and orange juice.

❧ CEYLON-PEPPER BISCUITS ❧

THESE BISCUITS ARE A GREAT BREAKFAST OR BRUNCH TREAT. TRY THEM WITH SCRAMBLED EGGS AND *bacon. They also go nicely with poached eggs and sliced ham.*

Makes 18

2 cups/255 grams all-purpose flour

1 tablespoon baking powder

½ teaspoon fine sea salt

2 teaspoons coarsely ground loose-leaf Ceylon tea leaves

½ teaspoon freshly ground black pepper

⅓ cup/75 milliliters olive oil

⅔ cup/165 milliliters milk, plus more as needed

Preheat the oven to 425°F/220°C/gas 7. Line a baking sheet with parchment paper or spray with vegetable cooking spray.

Sift together the flour, baking powder, and salt into a large bowl. Using a fork, stir in the tea and pepper. Add the olive oil and milk, stirring gently with a wooden spoon, being careful not to overmix. If dough is too crumbly, add more milk 1 tablespoon at a time. The dough should come together into a loose ball.

Roll or pat the dough to a thickness of $^1/_2$ inch/12 millimeters. Cut into biscuits using a glass or a 1$^1/_2$ inch/4 centimeter round cookie cutter and place the biscuits about 1 inch/2.5 centimeters apart on the prepared pan. Bake for 10 minutes, until the biscuits are lightly golden on top. Serve immediately.

Variation

Add crumbled crisp bacon or diced ham right after adding in the liquid ingredients.

❧ BREAKFAST TEA SCONES ❧

SCONES ARE THE QUINTESSENTIAL ACCOMPANIMENT TO A POT OF TEA FOR A CLASSIC ENGLISH TEATIME *experience. In America, they've become breakfast fare as well. What better way to enjoy tea than in the scone itself? The scones get their tea flavor both from steeping the leaves in buttermilk and from the steeped leaves themselves, which you add to the batter. These not-too-sweet-scones are great with jam and crème fraîche or clotted cream and lemon curd. Try substituting coarse or sanding sugar for the granulated sugar on top of the scones. Maple sugar is also great. This recipe is easily adapted to other flavors; see the variations for more ideas.*

Makes 1 dozen

1¼ cups/300 milliliters buttermilk

1 tablespoon loose-leaf black breakfast tea leaves (like English or Irish)

1½ cups/190 grams all-purpose flour

½ cup/65 grams white whole wheat flour

3 tablespoons (packed) light brown sugar

2 teaspoons baking powder

¼ teaspoon fine sea salt

5 tablespoons/70 grams chilled unsalted butter, cut into ½-inch cubes

1 tablespoon granulated sugar

Put the tea leaves and buttermilk in a small saucepan. Heat over medium-high heat until just beginning to boil. Remove from the heat and let steep about 5 to 10 minutes while you start to prepare the scones. Do not strain. The mixture may separate and look curdled; this is okay.

Preheat the oven to 400°F/200°C/gas 6. Line a baking sheet with parchment paper or spray with vegetable cooking spray.

In a large mixing bowl, combine both flours, the brown sugar, baking powder, and salt. Mix well. Add the butter and mix with an electric mixer on medium-high speed or use a pastry blender to mix until the texture looks like cornmeal, with small pea-size bits of butter here and there.

Pour the buttermilk-tea mixture into a blender, or use an immersion blender to blend. If it previously looked curdled, it will become a uniform texture when blended; it's okay if the tea leaves are not chopped up. Strain the buttermilk into a glass measuring cup; add the tea leaves to the butter-flour mixture. Measure out ²⁄₃ cup of the remaining buttermilk and add it to the bowl. Reserve any remaining liquid.

Mix on low speed just until the dough starts to come together. It will be wet but manageable. Divide the dough into 2 disks and place on a lightly floured surface. Pat each disk into a circle about 6 inches/15 centimeters in diameter. Cut each circle into 6 wedges and transfer to the prepared baking sheet, placing them about 1 to 2 inches/2.5 to 5 centimeters apart.

Lightly brush the surface of each scone with the reserved buttermilk. Sprinkle each scone with about $^1/_4$ teaspoon of the granulated sugar. Bake at 400°F/200°C/gas 6 for 14 to 16 minutes, until firm. The scones should be pale gold on top and darker gold on the bottom. Transfer to a cooling rack and cool a few minutes. Serve warm or at room temperature. These scones are best when eaten the day that they are baked, but unbaked scone dough can be wrapped well and frozen for up to 2 weeks.

Variations

JASMINE-VANILLA: Use 1 tablespoon loose-leaf jasmine tea, and add 1 teaspoon vanilla to the buttermilk mixture.
CHAI SPICE: Use 1 tablespoon loose-leaf chai tea, and add $^1/_2$ teaspoon ground cardamom and $^1/_8$ teaspoon freshly ground black pepper to the dry ingredients.
KEEMUN-PECAN: Use 1 tablespoon loose-leaf Keemun tea and add $^1/_2$ cup chopped toasted pecans immediately after mixing in the buttermilk.

SMOKY ALMOND PEACHES-AND-CREAM SHORTCAKES

THIS RECIPE WAS CREATED BY BOSTON CHEF AND WRITER LINDSAY MCSWEENEY. THE BISCUITS—THE *shortcakes—at the base of this dish are very versatile. This dessert is one variation that she recommends, but they are also great served sliced and layered with ham and pepper jelly for breakfast. This recipe gains its depth of flavor from the pine tar smokiness of a good Lapsang Souchong tea. If amaretti cookies are not available, coarsely chopped lightly toasted almonds or toasted, crushed granola can be used instead.*

Serves 6

2½ cups/600 millimeters heavy whipping cream, divided

5 teaspoons loose-leaf jasmine tea leaves

2 tablespoons loose-leaf Lapsang Souchong tea leaves

¼ cup/50 grams plus 2 teaspoons granulated sugar, divided

¼ cup/60 milliliters water

2 ounces/60 milliliters amaretto liqueur

3 ripe peaches, peeled, pitted, and sliced

2 cups/255 grams all-purpose flour

2 teaspoons baking powder

½ teaspoon fine sea salt

1 egg white, lightly beaten

12 amaretti cookies (6 pairs) crushed

In a medium saucepan, heat the cream to scalding over medium heat. Remove from heat and pour 1 cup/240 milliliters into a bowl. Add the jasmine tea leaves. Steep, covered, for 4 minutes. Add the Lapsang Souchong tea to the remaining 1½ cups/360 milliliters cream in the saucepan. Steep, covered, for 4 to 5 minutes. At the end of the steep, strain each tea-cream mixture into separate bowls, discarding the leaves. Let cool to room temperature, about 20 minutes. Cover the jasmine cream and refrigerate.

Rinse out the saucepan and add ¼ cup/50 grams of the sugar and the water. Bring to a boil over high heat and boil for 2 minutes to make a syrup. Remove from heat and pour into a medium bowl. Add the amaretto liqueur and the sliced peaches. Set aside to macerate.

Preheat the oven to 425°F/220°C/gas 7. Line a baking sheet with parchment paper or spray with vegetable cooking spray.

When the Lapsang cream has cooled to room temperature, make the biscuits: In a large bowl, whisk together the flour, baking powder, salt, and remaining 2 teaspoons sugar. Reserve ¼ cup/60 milliliters of the Lapsang cream, and pour the rest over the flour. Using a large wooden spoon, stir the cream into the flour mixture until a rough dough is formed. If the dough is dry and crumbly, add additional cream 1 tablespoon at a time. Transfer the dough onto a lightly floured work surface. Knead briefly until shiny. Pat into circle about ¾ inch/2 centimeters thick. Save any remaining cream for another use.

With a 2 3/4-inch/7-centimeter round cookie cutter, cut out 4 biscuits and place on the prepared baking sheet. Take the scraps of the dough and pat them into an oval, then cut out 2 more biscuits; there should be a total of 6 biscuits. Brush the egg white on the top of the biscuits and bake until light golden brown, 18 to 20 minutes. Remove and cool on a cooling rack.

When the jasmine cream is cold, use an electric mixer on medium-high to whip to form soft peaks.

To assemble the shortcakes; slice open each biscuit. Brush on some of the amaretto peach juice from the macerated peaches on the cut sides. Divide the peaches among the bottom halves of each biscuit, then top each with some of the whipped jasmine cream. Tilt the top half of the biscuit on the peaches to form a slant. Sprinkle the crushed amaretti cookies on top of the cream. Serve immediately.

Left: The sculpted plantings on the Havakul Estate, Southern India;
Right: A shy smile from the daughter of a tea plucker, Adderly Estate, India

⊙ WALNUTMEG TEACAKE ⊙

A VERSION OF THIS RECIPE ORIGINALLY APPEARED IN HANNAFORD SUPERMARKETS' *FRESH* **MAGAZINE,** *for an article on afternoon tea. The flecks of tea in the baked bread give an appearance that resembles banana bread. It's low in fat and not too sweet, and makes a nice afternoon snack with jam.*

Serves 12

1⅓ cups/170 grams all-purpose flour

⅔ cups/85 grams white whole wheat flour

¼ teaspoon fine sea salt

1 teaspoon baking soda

1 teaspoon baking powder

½ teaspoon grated nutmeg

1½ teaspoons ground black tea leaves, such as Nilgiri, Ceylon, or English Breakfast

1 egg

2 tablespoons walnut oil or canola oil

½ cup/100 grams plus 2 teaspoons granulated sugar, divided

1 teaspoon vanilla extract

1 cup/240 milliliters low-fat or nonfat buttermilk

½ cup/55 grams coarsely chopped walnuts

Preheat the oven to 350°F/180°C/gas 4. Spray a 9 x 5-inch/23 x 13-centimeter loaf pan with vegetable cooking spray.

In a medium bowl, combine both flours, salt, baking soda, baking powder, nutmeg, and tea. Stir until well mixed. Set aside.

In a large bowl, beat the egg using an electric mixer on medium speed until well beaten. With the mixer running, pour in the oil and beat on medium speed for 1 minute. With mixer running, slowly add ½ cup/100 grams of the sugar, then the vanilla. Beat until light and lemon-colored, about 2 minutes.

Use a rubber spatula to stir in half the flour mixture just until blended. Add the buttermilk and mix on medium-low speed just until combined. Add the remaining flour and mix on low just until combined. Gently stir in the walnuts. The batter will be thick.

Scrape the batter into the prepared pan. Smooth the surface, then sprinkle with the remaining 2 teaspoons sugar. Bake for 45 to 55 minutes until light gold, and a tester inserted in the center comes out clean. Cool in the pan on a cooling rack for 1 hour, then remove from the pan and transfer to a plate. Serve at room temperature.

BLACK TEA CUPCAKES *with* LEMON BUTTERCREAM

THE REFRESHING LEMON FLAVOR NICELY COMPLEMENTS THE BLACK TEA IN THE CUPCAKES. CREATED BY *Tracy Sisco while she was a student at the Cambridge School of Culinary Arts in Boston, the cupcakes originally included a very rich Italian meringue lemon buttercream. This simplified version is inspired by a technique used by baker Judy Rosenberg in her book,* The All-Butter, Fresh Cream, Sugar-Packed, No-Holds-Barred Baking Book. *Make the frosting just before serving.*

Makes 1 dozen

CUPCAKES

¾ cup/180 milliliters whole milk

4 teaspoons loose-leaf black tea leaves

1¼ cups/155 grams all-purpose flour

1½ teaspoons baking powder

¼ teaspoon fine sea salt

¾ cup/150 grams granulated sugar

12 tablespoons (1½ sticks)/170 grams unsalted butter, at room temperature

1 egg

2 egg whites

1½ teaspoons vanilla extract

LEMON BUTTERCREAM

4 ounces (1 stick)/115 grams unsalted butter, at room temperature

Grated zest of 2 lemons

1⅓ cups/135 grams confectioners' sugar

1 cup/240 milliliters chilled heavy whipping cream

TO MAKE THE CUPCAKES: In a small saucepan over low heat, combine milk and tea leaves and heat just until small bubbles begin to appear around the edges—do not boil. Remove from the heat and let steep until the milk cools to room temperature and is the color of milk chocolate, about 30 minutes. Strain the tea, pressing down on the leaves to extract liquid. Discard the leaves.

Preheat the oven to 350°F/180°C/gas 4. Line a 12-cup muffin pan with paper liners. In a medium bowl, whisk together the flour, baking powder, and salt. Set aside.

In a large bowl, use an electric mixer on medium-high speed to beat the butter and sugar until fluffy, about 3 minutes. Add the egg and egg whites, one at a time, beating after each addition. Beat in the vanilla. Add the flour mixture and tea-infused milk, beginning and ending with the flour, beating on low until just combined after each addition. Scrape down sides of bowl as needed. After the last addition of flour, mix on medium for just under a minute, until thoroughly combined.

Divide the batter evenly among the 12 muffin cups. Bake until a tester inserted in the center of a cupcake comes out clean, about 17 to 20 minutes. Remove cupcakes from tins and cool on a cooling rack for about 1 hour.

TO MAKE THE BUTTERCREAM: In a large bowl, combine the butter and lemon zest. Cream together with an electric mixer on medium-high for 1 minute, then add the confectioners' sugar and the cream. Beat on high for 15 to 20 minutes, until mixture is light and fluffy. Initially it will appear curdled, but will become a light, creamy, not-too-sweet pale yellow buttercream. Frost the cooled cupcakes with the buttercream. Serve immediately.

APPLE CEYLON TEA CAKE

THIS CAKE WORKS WELL WITH DIFFERENT KINDS OF TEA, TAKING ON THE SUBTLE FLAVORS. NILGIRI AND *Ceylon complement the apples, but any good black or oolong tea will work well. The cake is spectacularly moist and will keep for several days. Try it with a dollop of Tea-Spiced Chantilly Cream (page 220) or a scoop of vanilla ice cream on the side.*

Makes 1 (10-inch) cake

CAKE

1¼ cups/300 milliliters water

3 tablespoons loose-leaf Ceylon or oolong tea leaves

1 cup/240 milliliters unsweetened applesauce

2 tablespoons plus 1 teaspoon bourbon or brandy

2¼ cups/450 grams plus 2 tablespoons granulated sugar, divided

½ pound/225 grams (2 sticks) cold, unsalted butter

2 eggs

2¾ cups/340 grams all-purpose flour

2 teaspoons baking powder

1½ teaspoons cinnamon

½ teaspoon ground ginger

½ teaspoon fine sea salt

1¼ cups thinly sliced peeled tart apple, such as Granny Smith

PECAN TOPPING

5 tablespoons unsalted butter, chilled, cut into 5 pieces

⅓ cup (packed) light brown sugar

1 teaspoon ground ginger

¾ cup/85 grams coarsely chopped lightly toasted pecans

Preheat the oven to 325°F/163°C/gas 4.

TO MAKE THE CAKE: If using Ceylon tea, bring the water to a boil (about 212°F/100°C) and pour over the tea leaves in a medium bowl. Steep, covered, for 4 to 5 minutes. If using oolong tea, bring the water just to heavy steaming (about 185°F/85°). Pour the water over the oolong leaves and steep, covered, for 4 minutes. Strain and discard the leaves; there should be 1 cup/240 milliliters of liquid. Stir in the applesauce and bourbon or brandy. Set aside.

Meanwhile, spray a 10 x 2-inch/25 x 5-centimeter springform or standard cake pan with nonstick cooking spray. Sprinkle the inside of the pan with 2 tablespoons of the sugar, shaking the pan to coat the surface evenly.

In a large mixing bowl, use an electric mixer on medium-high to cream the butter. Add the remaining 2¼ cups/450 grams sugar and beat until light and fluffy. Beat in the eggs one at a time until smooth.

In a medium bowl, sift together the flour, baking powder, cinnamon, ginger, and salt. Add ⅓ of the flour mixture to the butter mixture. Beat just until incorporated. Add ½ of the applesauce mixture, again beating just until incorporated. Alternate adding dry and liquid ingredients, ending with dry. Mix until the batter is smooth, scraping down the sides of the bowl as needed. Gently stir in the apples. Spoon the batter into the prepared pan and lightly smooth the surface.

TO MAKE THE PECAN TOPPING: In a large bowl, use an electric mixer on medium-high to beat the butter until soft. Add brown sugar and ginger and beat until smooth. Add pecans and beat until just incorporated. Crumble pecan mixture over top of the batter, distributing evenly. Bake until the surface is firm and a tester comes out moist but clean, about 80 to 90 minutes. Serve warm or at room temperature.

❧ FLOURLESS KEEMUN-CHERRY ❧
CHOCOLATE TORTE

THIS DENSE, RICH CAKE KEEPS WELL FOR SEVERAL DAYS, OR CAN BE FROZEN FOR SEVERAL WEEKS, SO
it's a good one to make ahead. You can even make several, and freeze them before topping with the ganache. Keemun has choco-
laty nuances that go particularly well with dark chocolate. A small amount of port accentuates the fruity undertones of the tea
and the cherry flavor as well. This cake is dense and rich, so serve small slices.

Makes 1 (9-inch) cake

TORTE

²/₃ cup/165 milliliters boiling water
(about 212°F/100°C)

1½ tablespoons loose-leaf Keemun
tea leaves

²/₃ cup/115 grams dried cherries

2 tablespoons port

8 ounces/225 grams bittersweet chocolate,
finely chopped

½ pound (2 sticks)/225 grams
unsalted butter, at room temperature

1⅓ cups/260 grams plus 2 tablespoons
granulated sugar, divided

6 eggs, separated

1 teaspoon almond extract

²/₃ cups/90 grams almond meal

⅛ teaspoon fine sea salt

KEEMUN GANACHE

8 ounces/225 grams bittersweet
chocolate, finely chopped

½ cup/120 milliliters heavy
whipping cream

TO MAKE THE TORTE: Pour the boiling water over the tea leaves in a small bowl. Steep, covered, for 5 minutes and strain. Discard the leaves. Return the steeped tea to the bowl, and add the cherries and the port. Soak for at least 1 hour. Reserve ¼ cup/60 milliliters of the tea-port liquid to use for the ganache. The cherries and any remaining soaking liquid will be used in the cake.

Preheat the oven to 325°F/165°C/gas 3. Spray a 9-inch/23 x 3.5-centimeter round baking pan with vegetable cooking spray, line the bottom with a circle of parchment or waxed paper, then spray the paper with cooking spray.

Melt the chocolate in the top of a double boiler over just steaming water. Stir until smooth and let cool slightly.

In a large bowl, use an electric mixer on medium speed to cream the butter and 1⅓ cups/260 grams of the sugar until light and fluffy, about 2 minutes. With the mixer running, beat in yolks one at a time. Scrape the sides, add the almond extract, and mix until smooth, about 30 seconds. Add the melted chocolate while mixing on low speed, and mix until well combined. Fold in almond meal, then the cherries and their soaking liquid.

In a separate bowl, add egg whites and sprinkle in salt. Use clean beaters to whip egg whites. Start on a low speed, then gradually increase speed. While mixing, gradually add remaining 2 tablespoons sugar. Beat until soft peaks appear. Use a rubber spatula to fold in about ⅓ of the

¼ cup/60 milliliters reserved tea-port liquid (from the torte)

Pinch fine sea salt

Toasted sliced almonds for garnish (optional)

whites into the chocolate batter to lighten it, then gently fold in remaining whites, just until incorporated.

Pour the batter into the prepared pan, smoothing the top. Cover the pan with foil. Bake until a tester comes out with very moist crumbs, about 22 to 25 minutes. Remove the foil and cool completely in pan on a cooling rack, at least 45 minutes. (If you try to remove the cake from the pan before it is fully cooled, it is likely to crack. If this happens, the cake is so moist that you can push it back together and re-form.) When completely cooled, invert the cake onto a flat plate or cardboard cake round, removing the parchment paper from the bottom side of the cake. (The cake may be frozen at this point. Wrap completely in plastic wrap, then wrap in foil.)

WHEN READY TO SERVE, MAKE THE GANACHE: Place chopped chocolate in a large bowl. In a small saucepan, scald the cream over low heat with the reserved ¼ cup/60 millilters tea-port liquid. Add the salt, then pour the hot mixture over the chocolate and cover the bowl with a plate or with aluminum foil. Let sit for several minutes, then uncover and stir slowly until smooth. Pour onto the center top of the cooled torte; immediately turn and tilt the cake until the ganache covers the entire torte smoothly. If needed, use a spatula to smooth the sides.

If desired, garnish the torte with toasted sliced almonds. Let the ganache set for 10 to 15 minutes, and then serve. (The finished torte may be refrigerated for up to 2 days, but allow it to come to room temperature before serving.)

NOTE: Almond meal (also called almond flour) is very finely ground almonds. It can be found in natural food markets and online baking supply stores. If you can't find any, grind ¾ cup/95 grams blanched almonds with ¼ cup/50 grams of the sugar in a food processor.

⊶ EARL GREY CHOCOLATE CAKE ⊷

THIS CAKE IS A VARIATION ON A CLASSIC BUTTERMILK CHOCOLATE CAKE. THE CITRUSY UNDERTONES OF *the tea give the cake a subtle "mmm...just what is that?" flavor. The cake is easy to make, is great for a party, and keeps well.*

Makes 1 Bundt cake

CAKE

1⅓ cups/315 milliliters boiling water (about 212°F/100°C)

2½ teaspoons loose-leaf Earl Grey tea leaves

1¾ cups/215 grams all-purpose flour

2 cups/400 grams granulated sugar

¾ cup/65 grams unsweetened cocoa powder

2 teaspoons baking soda

1 teaspoon baking powder

¼ teaspoon fine sea salt

2 eggs

1 cup/240 milliliters buttermilk

4 ounces (1 stick)/115 grams unsalted butter, melted and cooled slightly

1 teaspoon vanilla extract

CHOCOLATE GLAZE

¼ cup/60 milliliters steeped Earl Grey tea (from the cake)

4 ounces/115 grams bittersweet chocolate, finely chopped

4 tablespoons salted butter

TO MAKE THE CAKE: Preheat the oven to 350°F/180°C/gas 4. Spray a Bundt or tube pan with vegetable cooking spray. Rub cooking spray into all crevices of the pan with a paper towel, then lightly flour the pan, tipping out any excess.

Pour the boiling water over the tea leaves in a small bowl. Steep, covered, for 5 minutes, then strain, discarding the leaves. Set aside.

In a large bowl, combine the flour, sugar, cocoa, baking soda, baking powder, and salt. Whisk or mix thoroughly. Add 1 cup of the steeped tea, reserving the remaining ¼ cup/60 milliliters or so for the glaze. Add the buttermilk, melted butter, and eggs. Using an electric mixer on medium-high, beat the mixture for 2 minutes. Scrape down the sides of the bowl and mix for another 2 minutes, until smooth. The batter will be thin. Pour into the prepared pan.

Bake for 30 to 45 minutes, until a tester inserted in the middle of the cake comes out clean and the surface springs back when lightly touched. Cool in the pan for 15 minutes, then invert the cake onto a cooling rack. When the cake is cool, transfer to a serving plate.

TO MAKE THE GLAZE: In the top of a double boiler over steaming water, heat the chocolate and the butter just until melted. Heat the reserved ¼ cup/60 milliliters tea in the microwave for 30 seconds until hot, then stir it into the chocolate. The mixture will thicken; stir until smooth and pourable. Spoon the glaze over the cake, using the back of the spoon to spread it slightly. It should drip down the sides, but will not cover the cake completely. Let set for 1 hour, then serve at room temperature. Store in an airtight container at room temperature or refrigerated; the cake may also be frozen.

⟡ EARL GREY CREAM TEA CAKE ⟡

CHRISTIE MORRISON CREATED THIS RECIPE WHILE SHE WAS A STUDENT AT THE CAMBRIDGE SCHOOL *of Culinary Arts. The cake was inspired by her experiences in London enjoying afternoon tea, so she created this superb cake combining the components that she most loved: Earl Grey tea, cakes, clotted cream, and marmalade. The génoise (which is similar to a sponge cake), buttercream, and syrup can each be prepared several days in advance, and ideally, as with all soaked génoise, the finished cake should be assembled a day before you plan to serve it, so the tea and other flavors have a chance to merge and develop.*

Makes 1 double-layer 9-inch/23 x 3.5 centimeter cake

EARL GREY SOAKING SYRUP

1½ cups/360 milliliters boiling water (about 212°F/100°C)

5 teaspoons loose-leaf Earl Grey tea leaves

¾ cup/150 grams granulated sugar

EARL GREY GÉNOISE

⅓ cup/70 grams unsalted butter

1 teaspoon vanilla extract

2 tablespoons brewed Earl Grey tea (from the soaking syrup)

6 eggs

1 cup/200 grams granulated sugar

¼ teaspoon fine sea salt

1 cup/130 grams cake flour, sifted

½ cup/170 grams orange marmalade

(continued)

TO MAKE THE SOAKING SYRUP: Pour the boiling water over the tea leaves in a small bowl. Steep 4 minutes, strain into a small saucepan, and discard the leaves. Remove 2 tablespoons of the steeped tea to use for the génoise and set aside.

Add the sugar to the remaining tea in the saucepan and bring to a low simmer over medium-low heat, stirring periodically. When fully dissolved, increase heat to medium-high and let simmer 3 minutes or until the syrup has thickened. Remove from heat. Set aside to cool to room temperature. The syrup may be prepared in advance and stored, covered, 1 day at room temperature, or refrigerated for up to 5 days.

TO MAKE THE GÉNOISE: Preheat the oven to 350°F/180°C/gas 4. Butter or spray with vegetable cooking spray 2 round cake pans (9-inch/23 x 3.5-centimeter. Line each with a circle of parchment paper, then butter or spray the paper and flour the pans.

Melt the butter in a small saucepan. Stir in the vanilla and the reserved 2 tablespoons tea and set aside.

In a large mixing bowl, whisk the eggs using an electric mixer on medium-high speed. Gradually add the sugar and salt with the mixer running. Continue beating until light and lemon-colored, sugar is completely dissolved, and the mixture has tripled in volume, about 5 to 8 minutes. Fold in the flour.

Take a spoonful of the génoise batter and mix it into the reserved butter mixture. Pour the butter-batter mixture into the génoise batter and

CLOTTED CREAM MOUSSELINE

½ cup/120 milliliters heavy
   whipping cream

1 tablespoon loose-leaf Earl Grey
   tea leaves

1 (6-ounce/170-gram) jar clotted
   cream or double Devon cream

ORANGE-EARL GREY
BUTTERCREAM

3 tablespoons Grand Marnier

1½ teaspoons loose-leaf Earl Grey
   tea leaves

8 egg yolks

Pinch fine sea salt

½ cup/120 milliliters water

1¼ cups/250 grams granulated sugar

⅛ teaspoon fresh lemon juice

12 ounces (3 sticks)/340 grams plus 4
   tablespoons unsalted butter, softened
   and cut into 1 tablespoon pieces

Candied citrus peel or fresh flowers,
   such as violets, lavender, or pansies
   for garnish (optional)

fold gently until the mixture is uniform. Pour immediately into the pre-pared cake pans, smoothing the top, and bake for 20 to 25 minutes, or until a toothpick inserted into the center comes out clean.

Let cool in pans a few minutes, then tap the bottom of each pan against the counter or other hard surface to loosen. Turn the cakes out onto cooling racks and cool completely. If you will not be assembling the cake that day, wrap well and store at room temperature for up to 2 days, or freeze for up to 2 weeks.

To make the mousseline: Combine the cream and tea leaves in a small saucepan. Scald the cream over medium-high heat, immediately remove from the heat, and steep, covered, for at least 1 hour at room temperature or overnight in the fridge. Strain into a large metal bowl and chill. When cold, whip the cream to stiff peaks. Add the clotted cream to a large bowl. Mix with a spatula to loosen, then gently fold the whipped cream into the clotted cream. The mixture should have a spreadable consistency. The cream may be infused with tea the day before, and once strained, kept chilled for up to 3 days, but you should whip the mousseline the day you plan to assemble the cake.

To make the buttercream: Combine the Grand Marnier and tea leaves in a small bowl and steep, covered, for several hours at room tem-perature, preferably overnight. Strain and set aside, discarding the leaves.

In a large mixing bowl, beat the egg yolks and salt until pale yellow in color, thick, and creamy, about 2 to 3 minutes.

Combine the water, sugar, and lemon juice in a small saucepan. Heat over medium-high, stirring to dissolve the sugar, then bring to a boil. Once the syrup comes to a boil, do not stir. Cook the syrup until it reaches the soft ball stage: when you drip some syrup into ice water it will form a soft, malleable ball (238° F/115°C on a candy thermometer).

With an electric mixer running on medium-high speed (fit with a whisk attachment if your mixer has one) carefully pour the hot sugar syrup into the egg yolks along the side of the bowl so it doesn't splash. Continue beating on medium speed until the yolk mixture (which is cooked by the hot syrup) thickens, increases in volume, lightens in color, and cools to body temperature, about 5 minutes. Reduce speed to low and continue to beat until room temperature, about 5 to 6 more minutes.

Return the mixer to medium speed, and, while beating, slowly add the softened butter 1 tablespoon at a time. Allow the butter to incorporate completely before adding the next piece. The mixture may look lumpy, or slightly curdled during this process; if this occurs, turn the speed up to high until it smoothes out, then reduce to medium and continue adding more butter. Continue to beat until the buttercream begins to pull away from the sides of the bowl and holds stiff peaks. If, after all of the butter has been added, the mixture is not completely smooth, add 1 tablespoon at a time of cold butter and mix until fully homogeneous and smooth. Add the tea-infused Grand Marnier and mix until incorporated. If making in advance, refrigerate for up to 1 week, or freeze for up to 1 month. (After freezing, transfer from the freezer to the fridge the night before you plan to use it. Remove from the fridge an hour before using, then beat with an electric mixer on medium-high until it reaches a good, spreadable consistency. It may appear curdled during the beating, but continue beating, and it will smooth out completely. This will take several minutes.)

TO ASSEMBLE THE CAKE: Using a serrated knife, carefully trim the edges and tops from each fully cooled génoise layer. This trimming of the edges flattens the top, allows the syrup to soak in more evenly, and prevents the exterior of the cake from getting gummy when the syrup is brushed on it. Place one layer on a serving plate and liberally brush the entire surface, including the sides, with the soaking syrup (the syrup carries lots of flavor, so you want to make sure it penetrates throughout each layer). To ensure an even distribution, brush on several layers, dipping the brush back into the syrup frequently.

Spread the marmalade over the surface of the cake, then spread the mousseline on top. Place the second cake layer atop the mousseline. Brush the top layer with the soaking syrup. Cover the entire cake with the buttercream and decorate as desired by piping on any remaining buttercream. Garnish with candied citrus peel or fresh flowers, if desired. Ideally, refrigerate overnight. Remove from fridge 1 hour before serving.

GREEN TEA TIRAMISÙ

YUN-JEONG HWANG, REPRESENTING THE NEWBURY COLLEGE CULINARY ARTS PROGRAM, CAME IN FIRST *place at the 2009 New England Culinary Tea Competition for this visually stunning dessert. She makes use of four different teas in this gluten-free interpretation of a tiramisù.*

Serves 8

LEMON-GINGER TEA GELÉE

2 cups/480 milliliters boiling water (about 212°F/100°C)

2 teaspoons lemon-ginger tea (2 tea bags)

⅓ cup/65 grams granulated sugar

12 gelatin sheets

GREEN TEA CAKE

1 tablespoon matcha green tea powder

1 cup/160 grams white rice flour

4 eggs, separated

½ cup/100 grams plus 2 tablespoons granulated sugar

2 tablespoons vegetable oil

2 tablespoons honey

2 tablespoons whole milk

½ teaspoon rum

¼ cup/60 milliliters Black Tea Simple Syrup (page 239)

GREEN TEA PASTRY CREAM

10 gelatin sheets

2½ cups/600 milliliters whole milk

1 teaspoon vanilla extract

½ cup/100 grams plus 1 tablespoon granulated sugar, divided

6 egg yolks

TO MAKE THE TEA GELÉE: In a medium bowl, pour the boiling water over the tea. Steep, covered, for 7 minutes. Strain the tea, discarding the leaves and stir in sugar until dissolved.

Soak gelatin sheets in cold water to cover until soft, about 5 minutes. When soft, squeeze out excess liquid. Place hot, strained tea in the top of a double boiler and add the softened gelatin sheets. Stir over steaming water until fully melted, about 2 minutes. Pour the liquid to an 8 x 8-inch/20 x 20-centimeter pan. It will form a shallow layer. Place in the freezer to fully chill, about 20 minutes. If you are making it in advance (up to 3 days) transfer after 20 minutes to the refrigerator until you are ready to assemble the final dessert. It will have the consistency of firm gelatin, but when removed from the fridge for a few minutes will be spreadable.

TO MAKE THE CAKE: Preheat the oven to 375°F/190°C/gas 5. Spray a 13 x 9 inch/33 x 23 centimeter pan with vegetable cooking spray.

Sift together the rice powder and green tea powder and set aside.

In a large bowl, use an electric mixer on medium-high speed to whip the egg whites. When soft peaks form, gradually beat in the sugar with the mixer running until stiff peaks form. With mixer running, add egg yolks one at a time, then stir in oil, honey, milk, and rum. Fold in the dry ingredients until just mixed.

Pour the batter into the prepared pan and bake until just set and a tester comes out clean, about 10 to 15 minutes. Remove from the oven and cool in the pan on a rack. Brush with simple syrup.

TO MAKE THE PASTRY CREAM: Soak the gelatin sheets in a pan of cold water to cover until softened, at least 5 minutes or until ready to use.

In a medium saucepan, combine milk, vanilla, and half the sugar; bring just to a boil, then remove from heat.

1/4 cup/55 grams unsalted butter

2 teaspoons matcha green tea powder

5 ounces/140 grams white chocolate, chopped

2 cups/480 milliliters heavy whipping cream

EARL GREY TEA SAUCE

3/4 cup/180 milliliters heavy whipping cream

6 tablespoons granulated sugar

3 teaspoons loose-leaf Earl Grey tea leaves

1 teaspoon cornstarch

Additional matcha or cocoa powder for garnish

NOTE: If the lemon-ginger tea in the gelée is not available, substitute 2 teaspoons of black tea leaves, 2 thin slices fresh ginger, and 1/2 teaspoon grated lemon zest.

In a medium bowl, whisk together the remaining sugar and the egg yolks.

Slowly temper the egg mixture with half the hot milk, whisking constantly. Pour the warmed-egg mixture into the saucepan with the milk and continue to whisk.

Cook over low heat, stirring constantly, until the mixture thickens and coats the back of the spoon, several minutes. Remove from the heat.

Gently squeeze out any excess water from the soaking gelatin sheets and add the sheets to the warm thickened pastry cream, stirring slowly and constantly until they are fully incorporated. Combine pastry cream and the butter in the bowl of an electric mixer and beat on low speed for 2 minutes. Stir in the matcha powder and mix until thoroughly combined, 1 to 2 minutes.

Melt the white chocolate and stir into the warm pastry cream.

In a clean bowl, whip the cream on medium-high speed to form firm peaks, about 2 minutes, then fold into the pastry cream. It will have a soft consistency, making it easy to spread, but it will firm up after it is assembled and chilled.

TO MAKE THE TEA SAUCE: Heat the cream in a saucepan over medium-high heat until bubbles just begin to form. Add the tea and sugar, stirring until the sugar dissolves. Remove from the heat and steep, covered, for 10 minutes. Strain, discarding the leaves. Stir in the cornstarch and heat over high heat, stirring constantly for 2 to 3 minutes, until the mixture thickens. Remove from the heat and set aside until you are ready to serve the dessert. (If it will be more than 1 hour, store covered in the refrigerator.)

TO ASSEMBLE THE CAKE: Cut the green tea cake into four equal rectangles. Place the first layer on a serving plate, spread a third of the tea gelée onto the moistened cake, then top with a quarter of the pastry cream. Top with a second layer of cake, and repeat the layers twice, ending with the final rectangle of cake and a thin layer of the pastry cream spread over it. If desired, sprinkle the top with matcha or cocoa powder. Chill for at least 1 hour for the gelatin to fully set, then serve chilled or at room temperature with the Earl Grey Tea Sauce on the plate. Leftover cake can be wrapped and refrigerated for up to 3 days.

⤳ EARL GREY CRÈME BRÛLÉE ⤳

CRÈME BRÛLÉE IS AN IDEAL SHOWCASE FOR TEA, AS DAIRY HOLDS THE TEA FLAVOR VERY WELL AND *buffers the tannins. In addition to this, with the added "burnt sugar" top, some crème brûlées can be overly sweet. The use of tea in the custard balances that sweetness, while adding complexity. Vanilla extract may be used instead of a vanilla bean, but a vanilla bean gives custard a wonderful flavor that goes well with the Earl Grey.*

Crème brûlée is very rich, so a small amount goes a long way. Use 4- to 6-ounce/125- to 175-milliliter ramekins or oven-safe espresso or tea cups. This crème brulee has been enjoyed at the Boston Park Plaza for years as the third course of their Afternoon Tea.

Makes 8

1½ cups/360 milliliters heavy whipping cream

1½ cups/360 milliliters half-and-half

½ cup/100 grams plus 1 tablespoon granulated sugar, divided

¼ cup/10 grams loose-leaf Earl Grey tea leaves

¼ teaspoon grated orange zest

¼ teaspoon dried lavender (optional)

½ vanilla bean or 1 teaspoon vanilla extract

8 egg yolks

Granulated sugar for brûléeing

In a medium saucepan over medium heat, bring the cream, half-and-half, and ¼ cup/50 grams of the sugar just to a boil (scald) then immediately reduce the heat to low. Add the tea leaves, orange zest, and lavender, if using. Halve the vanilla bean lengthwise and scrape the seeds into the mixture, then add the pod. Stir and remove from the heat and let steep, covered, for 10 to 40 minutes, tasting periodically, until it reaches the flavor you like. Strain and discard the leaves. If you did not use the vanilla bean, add the vanilla extract.

Preheat the oven to 275°F/135°C/gas 1. Have ready 8 ramekins or other containers for baking the custard.

In a medium bowl, combine the egg yolks and remaining 5 tablespoons sugar and whisk lightly until thickened and pale yellow ribbons form when the whisk is lifted, about 2 minutes. To avoid cooking the yolks, temper them by adding the warm infused cream a few tablespoons at a time, whisking continuously, until the temperature of the cream roughly equals that of the eggs. Then add the remaining cream and whisk gently.

Divide the custard among 8 ramekins or espresso cups. Place the ramekins in a baking pan with sides at least 2 inches/5 centimeters high. Pour hot tap water into the pan, being careful not to splash into the custard, so that it comes halfway up the sides of the ramekins. Cover the pan with foil and bake until the custard is just set. Depending on the depth of the ramekins, the timing will vary. If they are small and shallow, begin checking at 20 minutes; deeper or larger ramekins can take as long as 45 minutes or more. Be careful not to overcook. The edges should be firm but the center should still jiggle; the custard will continue baking after being removed from the oven.

Remove the custards from the water bath, let cool for 15 minutes at room temperature, then chill completely, at least 2 hours or overnight.

Just before serving, sprinkle surface of each custard with a thin layer of sugar. Tilt and turn the ramekin until the entire surface is covered, and then gently tap the tilted ramekin to release any extra sugar. If you have a brûlée torch or a blow torch, melt the sugar until golden and bubbling. Alternatively, place the ramekins on a baking sheet and broil (close to the broiler) for about 1 minute, just until sugar melts and turns dark gold. Serve immediately.

Variations

Substitute different teas and flavorings for the Earl Grey, lavender, vanilla, and orange zest. Try the following:

• Green tea, slices of fresh ginger, and rose petals

• Jasmine tea and vanilla

• Black tea, 1 tablespoon bourbon, and $^1/_4$ teaspoon each cinnamon and mace

• Any masala chai tea blend

❧ JASMINE FRESH FRUIT TART ❧

THIS TART WAS A STAPLE AT THE BAKERY COUNTER OF CINDY'S RESTAURANT, TEA-TRAY IN THE SKY. *A classic pastry cream is infused with jasmine tea, which complements fresh fruit. A thin layer of white chocolate seals the pre-baked crust and goes very nicely with the jasmine. The fruits used can vary according to what's in season and the quantities can vary depending on whether you prefer arranged thin slices of fruit or a heaped look. The various components of the tart need to be prepared in advance—the tart shell and the pastry cream need time to chill. Prepare the components a day in advance, and then assemble a few hours before you want to serve the tart. It's a show-stopping finish to a meal. If preferred, this tart can be made with a standard tart shell.*

Makes 1 (10-inch/ 25-centimeter) tart

CRUST

1 baked 10-inch/25-centimeter Ceylon Tea Tart Shell (page 217)

2 ounces/55 grams white chocolate, chopped (about ⅓ cup)

JASMINE PASTRY CREAM

1 cup/240 milliliters plus 2 tablespoons whole milk

¼ cup/50 grams granulated sugar, divided

½ vanilla bean, scraped, or 1 teaspoon vanilla extract

1 tablespoon loose-leaf jasmine tea leaves

3 egg yolks

2 tablespoons all-purpose flour

2 tablespoons unsalted butter

TO PREPARE THE TART SHELL: Gently melt the white chocolate in a double boiler over steaming water. Pour the melted white chocolate onto the pre-baked, cooled tart shell and let set until completely hardened, about 30 minutes.

TO MAKE THE JASMINE PASTRY CREAM: Place the milk, 2 tablespoons of the sugar, and the vanilla bean in a medium saucepan. Heat over medium-high heat to just boiling, then remove from the heat and stir in the tea leaves. Steep, covered, for 30 minutes, or more to taste. Strain the milk and return it to the saucepan. Discard the leaves and vanilla bean.

While the tea steeps, whisk the egg yolks in a large mixing bowl with remaining 2 tablespoons sugar. Whisk in flour until smooth.

Reheat the jasmine-infused milk over medium heat. Slowly pour half the heated milk into the egg mixture, whisking constantly. Return the egg-milk mixture to the saucepan with remaining milk and continue to stir constantly with a wooden spoon over medium-low heat until it comes to a boil, 1 to 2 minutes. Continue to stir constantly over medium-low heat until it is smooth and thick, about 2 more minutes. Remove from heat, stir in the butter until it is fully incorporated, and pour through a fine-mesh sieve to remove any lumps. Cover with plastic wrap to prevent a skin from developing; poke the plastic with a knife in several places to allow steam to escape. Let the pastry cream cool

FRUIT

¾ cup/240 grams apricot, currant, or quince jelly

1 tablespoon Grand Marnier, brandy, or steeped Ceylon tea

1 pint/350 grams strawberries, stemmed and halved

1 cup/150 grams fresh blueberries

2 kiwis, peeled and thinly sliced

1 cup/120 grams fresh raspberries or blackberries

½ mango, peeled, pitted, and sliced

completely at room temperature or in the fridge. It may be stored in an airtight container, refrigerated, for several days.

When ready to assemble the tart, heat the jelly in a small saucepan over low heat, just until slightly melted. Stir in the Grand Marnier until smooth. Remove from the heat.

Spread the fully chilled pastry cream on the white chocolate-lined tart shell. Arrange the fruit in a decorative pattern on top of the cream so that no pastry cream is exposed. Gently brush the fruit with the glaze. Let the tart rest at room temperature until the glaze is set, about 10 to 15 minutes, then chill until ready to serve. Serve chilled or at cool room temperature.

Variations

Infuse the milk with other teas and flavorings, such as the following:

• Keemun or Ceylon with a cinnamon stick (use dark chocolate instead of white chocolate in the tart shell)

• Green tea with ½ teaspoon orange zest and a slice of fresh ginger

CEYLON BROWN SUGAR TART

THIS RICH TART IS WONDERFUL ON ITS OWN, WITH A DOLLOP OF WHIPPED CREAM OR TEA-SPICED *Chantilly Cream (page 220), or with fresh figs, lightly spiced poached plums, or a winter dried-fruit compote alongside. It can also be made with a standard tart shell, but the ground tea in the tart shell really adds something special to this dessert.*

Makes 1 (9- or-10 inch/ 23- or 25-centimeter) tart

1 tablespoon loose-leaf Ceylon
   tea leaves

½ cup/120 milliliters boiling water
   (about 212°F/100°C)

2 cups/480 milliliters heavy
   whipping cream

1 teaspoon vanilla

1 egg

½ cup/100 grams granulated sugar

½ cup/100 grams (packed)
   dark brown sugar

1 tablespoon all-purpose flour

1 pre-baked Ceylon Tea Tart shell
   (page 217)

Confectioners' sugar for garnish

Whipped cream for garnish (optional)

Preheat the oven to 400°F/200°C/gas 6.

Place the tea leaves in a small bowl and add the boiling water. Steep, covered, for 5 minutes, then strain, discarding the leaves, and let cool to room temperature, about 10 minutes.

In a medium bowl, whisk together the cream, vanilla, egg, and cooled tea.

In a large bowl, stir together both sugars and the flour, making sure any lumps in the brown sugar are fully broken up. Whisk in the liquid ingredients until completely smooth. Pour into the parbaked shell and bake until the filling is set and the top is golden, about 20 minutes. Serve warm or chilled, dusted with confectioners' sugar and topped with a dollop of whipped cream, if desired. Leftovers (if there are any) will keep for 2 or 3 days, covered and refrigerated. Dust with more confectioners' sugar before serving.

⁓ CEYLON TEA TART CRUST ⁓

AROMATIC BLACK TEAS WORK WONDERFULLY IN BUTTERY CRUSTS. THIS IS A CLASSIC FRENCH PÂTÉ *sucré crust, with the addition of coarsely ground Ceylon tea. The nuttiness of ground tea complements a wide variety of fillings, such as chocolate, pecan, walnut, apples, or cranberries. It's used as the base for the Jasmine Fruit Tart (page 214) and for the Ceylon Brown Sugar Tart (page 216). Depending on the original leaf size, it will take from 2 1/2 to 4 teaspoons loose-leaf tea leaves to produce 2 teaspoons ground tea. The grind should be coarse—not too powdery, as you want the texture as well as the flavor. This recipe uses a low-grown Ceylon tea, good with a fruit tart. For a chocolate or caramelized tart, use Assam or Nilgiri.*

Makes 2 (9- or 10-inch/ 23- or 25-centimeter) tart shells

2 1/2 cups/320 grams all-purpose flour

1/8 teaspoon fine sea salt

2 teaspoons coarsely ground loose-leaf Ceylon tea leaves

1/2 cup/100 grams granulated sugar

1/2 pound (2 sticks)/225 grams unsalted butter, chilled, cut into 1/2-inch/ 12-millimeter cubes

1 egg

1 teaspoon vanilla extract

In the bowl of a food processor, combine the flour, salt, tea, and sugar. Pulse a few times to mix thoroughly. Scatter the butter cubes over the flour mixture and process until it resembles coarse meal, about 15 seconds.

Whisk together the egg and vanilla in a small bowl. With the processor running, pour the egg mixture in a steady stream through the feed tube and process just until the dough comes together.

Remove the dough from the processor and knead very gently into a smooth, homogeneous ball. Form the dough into 2 disks. Wrap each disk in plastic and chill for at least 1 hour. The dough may be refrigerated for up to 2 days, or frozen, double-wrapped, for up to 1 month.

When ready to use, if pre-baking the crust, preheat the oven to 350°F/180°C/gas 4. Spray two 9- or 10-inch/23 x 3.5- or 25 x 5-centimeter tart or pie pans with vegetable cooking spray. If not pre-baking, follow the instructions of your chosen filling recipe.

On a lightly floured surface, roll out one of the dough disks into a circle 1/8 inch/3 millimeters thick. Transfer the circle of dough to a prepared pan and press into the pan. Repeat with the second disk of dough. Chill for at least 10 minutes before baking.

Pierce the bottom of the crust here and there with the tines of a fork. Bake until lightly golden in color and the pastry looks completely dry, about 15 to 18 minutes. Five minutes into the baking, check the shell for any bubbling. If the pastry is lifting away from the pan, carefully prick at any raised point to allow the steam to escape and the shell to bake flat. Let cool and use in the recipe of your choice.

JASMINE TEA PHIRNI *with* DICED MANGOES

THIS RICH AND FRAGRANT RICE CUSTARD WAS CREATED BY PASTRY CHEF VASANT KHOT AT LE ROYAL *Meridian Hotel in Mumbai, India. Try to find the ripest mangos possible; alternatively, consider serving this dessert with whatever is at peak ripeness: cherries, berries, or fresh figs. Cashew nut meal (also called powder) can be found at Asian markets and online. To make your own, pulse $^2/_3$ cup/95 grams dry-roasted unsalted cashews with 1 tablespoon cornstarch in a food processor until finely powdered.*

Serves 8

8½ cups/2.1 liters whole milk, divided

¼ cup/55 grams white basmati rice

½ cup/100 grams granulated sugar

2 tablespoons loose-leaf jasmine tea leaves

2½ ounces/70 grams cashew nut meal

Pinch saffron

1 tablespoon sweetened condensed milk (optional)

2 mangoes, peeled, sliced to fan on plate or diced

Soak the rice in 2 cups/480 millilters of the milk for 4 hours, then place in a blender or food processor and process until finely ground. Transfer to large saucepan, add the remaining 6 ½ cups/1.5 liters milk and sugar and heat over medium heat until it reaches a simmer.

Place the tea leaves in a tea sack or oversized tea ball, or wrap loosely and tie in a piece of cheesecloth, making sure that the leaves have plenty of expansion room, and place in the simmering rice-milk mixture. Reduce the heat to medium-low and steep the tea in the simmering mixture for 15 minutes, stirring occasionally with a wooden spoon, then remove the tea sachet and discard. Continue to cook on low, stirring occasionally, until the mixture reduces by at least a third and starts to thicken. This can take quite a while, well over an hour. Add the cashew meal and saffron. Continue to stir until the mixture coats the spoon and holds a line drawn with your finger. Remove from heat and stir in the condensed milk, if using. Let cool to room temperature, then transfer to a sealed container and refrigerate until chilled. The end result will have a thick, pudding-like texture.

To serve, ladle chilled phirni into individual small bowls and top with diced mango or other fresh fruits, or fan the mango decoratively on the plate next to the phirni. Serve chilled.

When we first received the recipe for the Jasmine Tea Phirni served with fresh fruit from a pastry chef in Mumbai, India, Cindy read through it eagerly. She had not previously been familiar with Indian phirni, but after reading the recipe, she realized that this was an Indian parallel to crème pâtissière, or French pastry cream. In the case of the phirni, the thickening agent for the dairy is ground rice and nut flour, as opposed to the French use of egg yolk and sometimes flour or cornstarch.

Chef Khot's dessert is a lovely dish, but what was particularly fascinating is the fact that in India, he was inspired to create this as his very first foray into tea cuisine. A decade or so ago, Cindy's very first culinary tea recipe was a fresh fruit tart with jasmine-scented pastry cream (page 214). Some culinary concepts and flavor palettes are seemingly universal, no matter how different the style of cuisine.

FRUITS *in* TEA SYRUP

FRESH FRUIT IS COMPLEMENTED BEAUTIFULLY BY TEA-INFUSED SIMPLE SYRUP. ADJUST THE FLAVORS *and fruits seasonally—berries and stone fruits in the summer, melon in the winter. In the Beverages chapter, there are recipes for a variety of different simple syrups, all of which can be used to drizzle over cut fresh fruit. Serve with Matcha "Tea Leaves" (page 191) or Green Tea Lime Tuiles (page 193) on the side.*

Serves 8

½ cup/120 millilters Earl Grey Simple Syrup (page 240), or other tea-infused simple syrup

6 cups/750 grams mixed fresh fruit (melon, papaya, mango, pineapple, apples, pears, peaches, plums, oranges, clementines, blueberries, strawberries) cut into cubes or rounds

Mint sprigs for garnish

If you want a slightly softer fruit, heat the syrup, then pour it over the fruit in a large bowl and chill. For fresh, crisp fruit, use cool syrup. Toss it with the fruit, garnish with fresh mint sprigs, and serve.

Variation: **FRESH FRUIT IN TEA-INFUSED PORT**
Substitute ½ cup/120 millilters White Port with Black Tea, Rose, and Lavender (page 260) for the simple syrup. For fruit, use peaches, plums, apricots, nectarines, and blueberries and add ¼ teaspoon grated lime zest. Chill well.

✑ TEA-SPICED CHANTILLY CREAM ✑

THIS SIMPLE WHIPPED CREAM GOES WELL WITH MANY DESSERTS. TRY IT WITH THE APPLE CEYLON
Cake (page 202), or any apple, pear, plum, or peach pie or tart, gingerbread, chocolate spice cake, or the Flourless Keemun-Cherry Chocolate Torte (page 204). It's also flexible—try creating your own variations with different spices and teas.

Makes about 2 cups/ 480 milliliters

1 cup/240 milliliters heavy whipping
  cream

1 tablespoon granulated sugar

1 tablespoon loose-leaf full-bodied
  black tea leaves, such as low-grown
  Ceylon, Nilgiri, or Assam

1 cinnamon stick

2 whole star anise

½ teaspoon allspice berries

½ teaspoon cracked black peppercorns

1 teaspoon brandy (if using Ceylon)
  or bourbon (if using Nilgiri or Assam)

Place cream, sugar, tea leaves, cinnamon, star anise, allspice, and peppercorns in a small saucepan and scald by bringing just to a boil over medium-high heat. Immediately remove from the heat. Let steep, covered, for at least 30 minutes or up to several hours for the flavors to infuse and develop. Taste periodically. When you are happy with the flavor development, strain completely and chill. May be made up to 5 days in advance up to this point. When you are ready to use, whip the infused cream with the brandy or bourbon until soft peaks form. Serve immediately.

∽ DULCE DE LECHE TEA ICE CREAM ∽

CHRIS CASON, THE TEA SOMMELIER AND CO-FOUNDER OF TAVALON TEA IN NEW YORK, SHARED THIS *recipe with us. The recipe list for the book was already considered final at that point, but this ice cream was so good, we just had to include it. The slight sharpness of the tea nicely balances the sweetness of the caramel. It's great with a drizzle of a bittersweet chocolate sauce or served with a brandied winter-fruit compote.*

The base needs to chill several hours before freezing, and the ice cream needs to ripen overnight, so plan accordingly.

Makes 1 quart/950 milliliters

2 (14-ounce/414-milliliters) cans sweetened condensed milk

2 cups/480 milliliters whole milk

1 cup/240 milliliters heavy whipping cream

¼ cup/10 grams loose-leaf English or Irish Breakfast tea leaves

⅛ teaspoon vanilla extract

Preheat the oven to 425°F/220°C/gas 7.

To make the dulce de leche: Pour both cans sweetened condensed milk into a 1-quart/1-liter soufflé dish or casserole. Cover the dish with foil and place inside an 8- or 9-inch/20- or 23-centimeter round cake pan. Fill the cake pan with hot water to about ½ inch/12 millimeters from the top. Place in the oven and bake for 50 to 60 minutes, until the milk darkens to a caramel color.

While the condensed milk bakes, combine the whole milk, cream, and tea leaves in a medium saucepan. Bring to a full boil over medium-high heat, then remove from heat. Steep for 15 minutes, then strain, discarding the tea leaves.

When the dulce de leche is ready, whisk until smooth. Whisk in the vanilla and the steeped milk-cream mixture and stir until smooth. Let cool to room temperature, then transfer to an airtight container and refrigerate until completely chilled, at least 6 hours or overnight.

When mixture is completely chilled, freeze in an ice-cream maker according to the manufacturer's instructions. Mixture will be soft, like very soft frozen custard. Transfer to an airtight container and freeze overnight. The ice cream will firm up as it sets.

CHAI ICE CREAM *with* HIBISCUS ALMOND BRITTLE

CHEF MAGGIE LAMONT OF BOSTON CREATED THIS RECIPE. SHE RECOMMENDS A GOLDEN TIP ASSAM *tea, which imparts a nice maltiness and is a classic tea for a masala chai. Any good Assam or Nilgiri tea would be ideal. A low-grown Ceylon or African black tea would also work well.*

Hibiscus is a flower with a tangy, fruity flavor that nicely balances the sweet spices of the ice cream. If you can't find dried hibiscus flowers, use a Celestial Seasonings Red Zinger tea bag—hibiscus is a key component of Red Zinger.

The custard base needs to chill several hours before freezing, and the ice cream needs to ripen overnight, so plan accordingly.

Makes about 3 cups/720 milliliters ice cream and about 1 dozen large pieces brittle

CHAI ICE CREAM

4 cardamom pods, husks removed

1 cinnamon stick

2 whole star anise

¼ whole nutmeg, grated

3 cloves

5 black peppercorns

2 allspice berries

2 tablespoons minced fresh ginger

½ cup/120 milliliters whole milk

2 cups/480 milliliters heavy whipping cream

4½ teaspoons loose-leaf Assam tea leaves

¾ cup/150 grams granulated sugar, divided

5 egg yolks

1 egg

(continued)

TO MAKE THE ICE CREAM: In a spice grinder, combine cardamom seeds, cinnamon, star anise, nutmeg, cloves, peppercorns, and allspice. Grind into a coarse powder. Heat a medium saucepan over low heat. Add the spices and toast until fragrant, about 1 minute, being careful not to burn. Add the milk and cream to the spices and heat over medium heat, stirring occasionally, until mixture just comes to a boil. Remove from heat and add tea, stirring. Steep by taste until you enjoy the level of flavor and until the cream-milk mixture is a golden color with a flowery, not bitter, tea flavor, anywhere from 5 to 20 minutes.

Strain the cream mixture into a bowl; discard the spices and leaves. Rinse out the saucepan, and return the mixture to the saucepan. Heat over low heat. Stir in 6 tablespoons of the sugar.

In a medium bowl, whisk together yolks and whole egg until combined, then whisk in the remaining 6 tablespoons sugar until pale yellow ribbons form when you lift the whisk out of the bowl. Whisk a few tablespoons of the hot cream into the yolks to temper them, and continue to whisk in more cream, about 2 tablespoons at a time, until egg mixture is warmed. Stir warmed eggs into the remaining milk in the saucepan. Stir continuously with a wooden spoon over medium-low heat until the custard thickens and coats the back of a spoon. The temperature should be around 165°F to 170°F/75°C (it should not come to a full boil or you risk the egg yolks curdling). This can take 8 to 12 minutes.

HIBISCUS ALMOND BRITTLE

1 teaspoon dried hibiscus flowers
   ground coarsely or 1 Red Zinger
   tea bag, cut open

⅓ cup/75 milliliters water

1 cup/200 grams granulated sugar

2 pinches fine sea salt

⅛ teaspoon fresh lemon juice

½ cup/70 grams blanched almonds,
   toasted and coarsely chopped

Remove the custard from the heat and strain through a fine sieve. Let cool to room temperature, then transfer to an airtight container and refrigerate until chilled, at least 6 hours or overnight.

WHILE THE ICE CREAM BASE CHILLS, MAKE THE BRITTLE: Line a baking sheet with a Silpat, parchment paper, or foil. If using foil, spray with vegetable cooking spray.

Put sugar and salt in a saucepan and sprinkle with water. Stir until sugar resembles moist sand. Add lemon juice and stir briefly. Heat moistened sugar over medium heat. The sugar will melt gradually; no need to stir. When syrup has formed with small bubbles, it will change in color from white to golden to amber. When it becomes amber, remove from heat. Add ground hibiscus flowers, or contents of opened teabag, stirring the caramel, then add the toasted almonds, stir again briefly and immediately pour the mixture onto the prepared sheet pan. Spread to a thickness of $^1/_8$ inch/3 millimeters or less. Let cool. When completely cool and set (about 2 hours), break into shards. Extra brittle may be stored at room temperature in an airtight container for over a week.

When ice cream mixture is fully chilled, freeze in an ice-cream maker according to the manufacturer's instructions. Transfer ice cream to a sealed container and let freeze overnight.

To serve, scoop ice cream into dessert bowls and decorate with shards of brittle.

ASIAN-SPICED TEA, HONEY, and PINK PEPPERCORN ICE CREAM

THIS RECIPE WAS CREATED BY ANNE SIROIS, A BOSTON CHEF WHO STUDIED AT THE CAMBRIDGE SCHOOL *of Culinary Arts. After being inspired by a tea and tea cuisine seminar at the school, she did her final class practicum creating this culinary tea dish. The pink peppercorns add an unexpected bite, which along with the tea give wonderful complexity, and contrast nicely with the richness of the ice cream. The custard needs to chill several hours before freezing, and the ice cream needs to ripen overnight, so plan accordingly.*

Makes about 3 cups

2 tablespoons whole pink peppercorns, divided

1½ cups/360 milliliters whole milk

1 cup/240 milliliters heavy whipping cream

2 tablespoons loose-leaf chai tea

6 egg yolks

½ cup/120 milliliters honey

Pinch fine sea salt

1 teaspoon vanilla extract

Lightly crush 1 tablespoon of the pink peppercorns with a mortar and pestle or using the edge of a heavy pan.

Combine the milk and cream in a heavy saucepan and heat over medium heat, stirring occasionally, until mixture just comes to a boil. Remove from heat and add the crushed peppercorns and the tea. Steep, covered, for 15 minutes or to taste. Strain and discard the tea and pepper. In a large bowl, whisk together the egg yolks, honey, and salt until foamy and light yellow in color. Whisk a few tablespoons of the warm cream infusion into the eggs to temper them, then continue to whisk in more cream, about 2 tablespoons at a time, until the egg mixture is warmed.

Stir warmed eggs into the remaining milk in the saucepan. Stir constantly with a wooden spoon over medium-low heat until the custard thickens and coats the back of a spoon; the temperature should be around 165°F/75°C to 170°F/80°C (it should not come to a full boil or you risk the egg yolks curdling). This can take 8 to 12 minutes. Remove from the heat and strain the cooked custard through a fine-mesh sieve into a bowl. Coarsely grind the remaining 1 tablespoon peppercorns in a pepper grinder and add to the custard along with the vanilla. Let cool to room temperature, then refrigerate, covered, for at least 6 hours or overnight.

When custard mixture is completely chilled, freeze in an ice-cream maker according to the manufacturer's instructions. Transfer the ice cream to a sealed container and freeze overnight.

‿ MANGO-PEACH OOLONG GRANITA ‿

GRANITA IS THE ORIGINAL ITALIAN ICE. BECAUSE IT IS FROZEN WITHOUT AN ICE-CREAM MAKER, THE *result is granular rather than smooth, making it incredibly refreshing—the flavors just burst on your tongue. Alternatively, if you have an ice-cream maker, you can use this recipe to make a sorbet. A version of this recipe originally appeared in Hannaford Supermarkets' fresh magazine.*

Serves 8

2 cups/400 grams granulated sugar

2½ cups/600 milliliters water, divided

1½ teaspoon fresh lemon juice, divided

½ cup/10 grams loose-leaf Chinese or Formosa oolong tea leaves

5¼ pounds/2.4 kilograms ripe peaches

2 ripe mangos

1½ teaspoons grated fresh ginger

Dash fine sea salt

Mint leaves for garnish

Combine the sugar with 1 cup/240 milliliters of the water and ½ teaspoon of the lemon juice in a medium saucepan. Bring to a simmer over medium-high heat. Reduce the heat to medium and simmer for 3 to 5 minutes, until the sugar has completely dissolved and the liquid is clear and slightly thickened. Remove the simple syrup from the heat and let cool.

Place the tea leaves in a large bowl. Bring the remaining 1½ cups/360 milliliters water to a boil and pour over the tea. Let steep, covered, for 3½ minutes; strain and let cool. Discard the leaves.

Reserve 1 peach to use for garnishing. Peel, pit, and slice the remaining peaches and the mangoes. Purée them in a food processor or blender until smooth. Add the purée to the bowl of cooled tea with the cooled simple syrup, remaining 1 teaspoon lemon juice, ginger, and salt. Stir until smooth.

Pour the mixture into a shallow glass or metal baking or roasting pan. Place in the freezer. Stir briefly every 30 minutes or so with a fork or whisk, pulling the frozen bits away from the edges into the center. Repeat until frozen into a granular mass, about 2½ to 3 hours. If wrapped well, at this point the granita will hold for several days.

Serve by scraping the granita out of the pan with a large spoon or scoop. Serve in martini glasses or small bowls. Peel, pit, and slice the remaining peach and garnish the granita with the peach slices and mint leaves.

RHUBARB JASMINE TEA SORBET

MATTHEW J. MAUE, CHEF DE CUISINE AT TASTINGS WINE BAR & BISTRO IN FOXBORO, MASSACHU-SETTS, *created this pale pink sorbet as an intermezzo—it is served between courses as a palate cleanser. The jasmine adds a nice floral element to the tartness of the rhubarb—it is a perfect union of flavors, and especially refreshing as part of a summer meal. Note that the sorbet base needs to chill overnight.*

Makes 1 quart/960 milliliters

- 4 cups/960 milliliters steaming water (about 175°F/80°C)
- 2 tablespoons loose-leaf jasmine tea leaves
- 2 cups/400 grams granulated sugar
- 2½ cups/300 grams coarsely chopped rhubarb

Pour steaming water over tea leaves in a medium bowl. Steep, covered, for 10 minutes. Strain into a large saucepan and discard the leaves.

Add the sugar and rhubarb to the tea. Bring to a simmer over medium-high heat and cook until the rhubarb is soft, about 10 to 12 minutes.

Remove from the heat and purée until smooth using a blender, food processor, or immersion blender. Cool to room temperature, then chill overnight in the fridge.

Freeze in an ice-cream maker according to manufacturer's instructions.

The Egg Test

Getting the right sugar to water ratio for a granita or a sorbet can be tricky when the sugar levels (ripeness) of the fruits vary. An easy trick is to take a whole egg (after rinsing the shell) and place it into the bowl of mixture. It should break the surface with a round the size of a dime showing. If more than a dime is showing, then the mixture has too much sugar and you need to add more water (or steeped tea). If it sinks lower and shows less than a dime size, than you need to add additional sugar or simple syrup.

TEA BEVERAGES

Non-alcoholic Infusions

Tea Cocktails

VODKA INFUSIONS

WHITE PORT INFUSIONS

SANGRIAS

OTHER ALCOHOLIC INFUSIONS

TEA IS A BEVERAGE, BUT IT ALSO MAKES A TERRIFIC BASE FOR OTHER BEVERAGES. THIS CAN TAKE two forms: tea steeped in water with other ingredients added, and tea steeped directly in other liquids. In this chapter, we explore nonalcoholic tea-infused beverages and tea cocktails.

For non-alcoholic tea beverages, iced tea is a natural place to start. Refreshing, delicious, with infinite varieties—just check out the local supermarket or convenience store shelves.

Tea cocktails provide a whole new world of culinary tea options. Some cocktails are based on water-steeped tea, while others incorporate tea-infused spirits. We have found that for subtle complexity in your cocktails, combined with shelf stability, direct, slow infusions of tea leaves into the base alcohol are often the best.

Vodka is one of the easiest and most flexible alcohols to work with. A good-quality neutral vodka can be infused with virtually any tea; the next step is to choose the secondary ingredients (fruits, spices, etc.) to complement the chosen tea in the finished cocktail. These can be infused into the alcohol as well, used in simple syrups that are added later, or muddled in fresh. Other alcohols such as gin, white port, sake, or rum are less neutral, so you need to be more particular in choosing the teas that you pair with them. You may also find that different brands may give different results, but taste-testing and experimenting is part of the fun of creating tea cocktails.

When infusing loose-leaf tea and other ingredients into alcohol, the infusion time can vary for different ingredients. A convenient way to work while developing new recipes and combinations is to divide each ingredient to be infused into separate disposable tea bags such as T-Sacs (see page 50) or tied cheesecloth sachets. For instance, a recipe might include a combination of tea leaves, spices, herbs, fresh or dried flower petals, and dried fruits. If you want one flavor to dominate or be more subtle, you can remove the sachets of ingredients at different times.

Whatever the balance of ingredients in the infusion, the key to shelf stability of the infused alcohol is thorough straining. Strain through a coffee filter, several layers of cheesecloth, or T-Sacs. The resulting infusion should be crystal clear. If any bits of tea leaves or other ingredients remain, the product will change over time, and, depending on the ingredient not properly removed, that change could begin very quickly. If strained completely and thoroughly, then the shelf life of the infused alcohol could be several months.

MASALA CHAI CONCENTRATE

CHAI LITERALLY MEANS "TEA" IN INDIA, BUT IN AMERICA IT HAS COME TO MEAN AN INDIAN MASALA-
style tea—strong black tea that is slowly simmered with spices. Chai can traditionally be made by simmering the tea and spices in water, but simmering the tea and spices initially in milk allows the fat-soluble components of the spices to be more fully released and developed. This recipe makes a generous amount of spiced concentrate, good for a party. It is the base recipe to use with tea in the Masala-Style Chai (page 235).

This flavor base can be used for several other recipes, including the Chai Martini (page 266) and Park Plaza Tea-Nog (page 266). Try it drizzled over oatmeal, blended into French toast batter, or as part of the base when making ice cream, crème brûlée, spiced whipped cream or other dairy-based recipes.

Makes 1 quart / 950 milliliters

1 vanilla bean

Zest of 1 small orange, in 2- to 3-inch strips

5 quarter-size slices fresh ginger

2 tablespoons cracked black peppercorns

2 tablespoons whole black peppercorns

2 tablespoons allspice berries

3 cinnamon sticks

4 teaspoons anise seeds or 8 whole star anise

2 bay leaves

4 teaspoons whole coriander seeds

4 teaspoons whole cloves

4 teaspoons whole cardamom pods

2 pinches saffron (optional)

¼ cup/50 grams granulated sugar

5 cups/1.2 liters whole milk

3 cups/720 milliliters half-and-half

¼ cup/10 grams loose-leaf Assam or Nilgiri tea leaves

Combine all ingredients except the tea leaves in a large, heavy stockpot. Heat to a simmer over low heat and keep at a bare simmer for 5 hours. Add the tea leaves and continue to simmer for an additional hour, until the mixture is reduced by about a third. It is important to keep the heat very low. If the milk comes to a boil, turn it down immediately. Alternatively, place in a slow-cooker with the lid off and cook on low for 5 hours. Add the tea leaves and cook on low for an additional hour.

Strain the reduced spiced milk concentrate into a large bowl, preferably nonreactive stainless steel, and place the bowl in a larger bowl of ice, stirring to quick-chill the milk. Once chilled, pour into an airtight container and refrigerate. This quick chill helps increase the shelf life of the concentrate, which should last about 10 days, refrigerated in an airtight container.

NOTE: When using it as part of a hot beverage, it is best to start with warm chai concentrate. If the concentrate was made ahead and chilled, it can be easily heated with a steamer wand on an espresso machine, gently in the microwave, or, when making large batches, in a small saucepan.

❧ MASALA-STYLE CHAI ❧

THIS CHAI IS PARTICULARLY NICE TO SIP IN THE MIDDLE OF WINTER. THE REDUCED MILK CONCENTRATE *has a natural sweetness and some prefer this chai without further sweetener. Special thanks to Mark Yedvabny, who played a strong role in early renditions of this recipe at the first Tea-Tray in the Sky location.*

Serves 4

2 tablespoons loose-leaf Assam or Nilgiri tea leaves

6 cups/1.4 liters boiling water (about 212°F/100°C)

¼ cup/60 milliliters Masala Chai Concentrate (page 234), or more to taste, warmed

Sugar or Basic Simple Syrup (page 237) to taste

Put the tea leaves in a large, pre-warmed teapot or saucepan and pour the boiling water over them. Steep, covered, for 4 to 5 minutes. Strain into a large teapot, discarding the leaves. Stir in the chai concentrate. Sweeten to taste, or serve with sugar or simple syrup on the side. Serve immediately.

Variations

CREAMY CHAI: Replace the boiling water with whole milk. Heat till bubbles just begin to form, then add the tea leaves and steep for 5 minutes. Strain and proceed with the recipe. Alternatively you can add steamed milk as well as additional Masala Chai Concentrate to your normally steeped tea for a similarly rich and creamy result.

CHAI-CHINO: Chai flavors for coffee fans. Blend equal parts warmed Masala Chai Concentrate and espresso, then finish with steamed milk.

SPICY CHAI: When steeping the tea, add ¼ teaspoon crushed black peppercorns for added heat.

Simple Syrups

SIMPLE SYRUP IS A BLEND OF SUGAR AND WATER, HEATED TO DISSOLVE THE SUGAR. IT'S THE PERFECT way to sweeten beverages—no grainy undissolved sugar crystals sinking to the bottom of the glass. Simple syrups are quick and easy to make, and keep for weeks in the refrigerator. A small amount of acid is added to prevent the sugar from re-crystallizing. Typically lemon juice is used when making simple syrup for drinks, but lime juice or even vinegar work as well. More heat-stable items such as dried herbs, dried fruits, and spices can be added while the syrup simmers. Less heat-stable teas, fresh herbs, or flower petals can be added once the syrup is removed from the heat.

For simple syrups made with tea, vary the amount of tea that you add depending on how delicate or assertive you want the tea flavor to be. When increasing the tea, unless you want a more concentrated syrup, add a little more water to allow for the water that the leaves will absorb and hold.

✑ BASIC SIMPLE SYRUP ✑

Makes about 1 cup/240 milliliters

1 cup/200 grams granulated sugar
1 cup/240 milliliters water
A few drops fresh lemon or lime juice

Combine the sugar, water, and juice in a medium saucepan. Stir and bring to a boil over high heat. Reduce the heat and simmer until all the sugar is dissolved and the mixture is slightly syrupy, about 2 to 3 minutes. Remove from the heat and cool completely. Store covered. If keeping for more than a day or two, refrigeration is recommended but not required.

GINGER-OOLONG SIMPLE SYRUP

Makes about 1 cup/240 milliliters

1 cup/200 grams granulated sugar

1¼ cups/300 milliliters water

A few drops fresh lemon juice

3 quarter-size slices fresh ginger

1 tablespoon loose-leaf oolong tea leaves

Combine the sugar, water, juice, and ginger in a medium saucepan. Stir and bring to a boil over high heat. Reduce the heat, stir, and simmer until all the sugar is dissolved and the mixture is slightly syrupy. Add the tea leaves and simmer for another minute. Remove and cool completely. Strain and discard the ginger and tea leaves. Store in an airtight container in the refrigerator for up to 2 weeks.

Variation

GINGER SIMPLE SYRUP: Make the above recipe, but omit the tea. This is good to use when you are adding the syrup to a different style of tea cocktail and don't want the oolong to compete. For instance, it would be an excellent addition to a green-tea-based cocktail.

GREEN TEA SIMPLE SYRUP

Makes about 1 cup/240 milliliters

1 cup/200 grams granulated sugar

1 cup/240 milliliters water

A few drops fresh lemon or lime juice

1 tablespoon loose-leaf green tea leaves

Combine the sugar, water, and juice in a medium saucepan. Stir and bring to a boil over high heat. Reduce the heat and simmer until all the sugar is dissolved and the mixture is slightly syrupy, about 2 to 3 minutes. Add the tea leaves and let simmer 1 more minute. Remove and let cool fully. Strain and discard the tea leaves. Store in an airtight container in the refrigerator for up to 2 weeks.

Variations

GREEN TEA AND LEMONGRASS SIMPLE SYRUP: Add 2 tablespoons chopped fresh lemongrass with the water and sugar. Discard after straining.

GREEN TEA-ZER SIMPLE SYRUP: Add 2 tablespoons chopped fresh lemongrass with the sugar and water. Discard after straining. When completely cool, add 2 tablespoons chopped fresh basil leaves and purée in a blender. Because this syrup contains fresh basil, it won't keep as long, about 3 days in the refrigerator.

BLACK TEA
SIMPLE SYRUP

Makes about 1 cup/240 milliliters

1 cup/200 grams granulated sugar
1 cup/240 milliliters water
A few drops fresh lemon juice
1 cinnamon stick
1 tablespoon loose-leaf Ceylon or Nilgiri tea leaves

Combine the sugar, water, lemon juice, and cinnamon in a medium saucepan. Stir and bring to a boil over high heat. Reduce the heat and simmer until all the sugar is dissolved and the mixture is slightly syrupy, about 2 to 3 minutes. Add the tea leaves and simmer 1 more minute. Remove from the heat, let cool completely, then strain. Discard the cinnamon stick and tea leaves. Store in an airtight container in the refrigerator for up to 2 weeks.

RASPBERRY TEA
SIMPLE SYRUP

ISRAELI CHEF SHARONE ARTSI DEVELOPED THIS *syrup for his award-winning Vanilla Green-tea-ni (page 270).*

Makes about 1 cup/240 milliliters

1 cup/240 milliliters water
¾ cup/150 grams granulated sugar
4 teaspoons loose-leaf black tea leaves with raspberries

Combine water, sugar, and tea in a saucepan and bring to a boil over high heat until the sugar is dissolved and the mixture is slightly syrupy, about 2 to 3 minutes. Remove from heat and let steep, covered, for 10 minutes, then strain, discarding the leaves, and let cool completely. Store syrup in an airtight container in the refrigerator for up to 2 weeks.

KEEMUN-SPICED PLUM SIMPLE SYRUP

Makes about 2 cups/480 milliliters

2 cups/400 grams granulated sugar

2½ cups/600 milliliters water

A few drops fresh lemon or lime juice

1 plum, pitted and sliced

½ teaspoon whole black peppercorns

Zest of 1 orange in large strips

2 whole star anise (optional)

2 teaspoons loose-leaf Keemun tea leaves

Combine all ingredients except the tea in a medium saucepan. Stir and bring to a boil over high heat. Place the tea leaves in a cheesecloth or tea sack and add to the mixture. Reduce the heat and simmer until the sugar is dissolved and the mixture is slightly syrupy, about 2 to 3 minutes. Remove from the heat and let cool completely. Remove the tea package, but keep the remaining ingredients in the syrup until ready to use to intensify the flavors. Strain off a small amount as needed. Store in an airtight container in the refrigerator for up to 2 weeks.

EARL GREY SIMPLE SYRUP

THIS WAS INSPIRED BY ONE OF THE HOUSE SIG-nature tea blends at the Boston Park Plaza. Swan's Grey combines Italian oil of bergamot with lavender and vanilla in a blended black tea base.

Makes about 2½ cups/600 milliliters

2½ cups/600 milliliters boiling water (about 212°F/100°C)

¼ cup/10 grams loose-leaf Earl Grey tea leaves

2 cups/400 grams granulated sugar

1 vanilla bean, split in half lengthwise

1 teaspoon dried lavender

Grated zest of 1 orange

Grated zest of 1 lime

Pour the boiling water over the tea leaves in a glass measuring cup or medium bowl and steep, covered, for 5 minutes. Strain into a medium saucepan, discarding the leaves. Add the sugar, vanilla bean, lavender, and orange and lime zest. Stir and bring to a boil over high heat, then reduce the heat to medium-low and simmer until the sugar is dissolved and the mixture is slightly syrupy, about 2 to 3 minutes. Remove from the heat and let cool completely. Since the tea leaves have already been strained out, you can strain each portion of syrup as needed. Store in an airtight container in the refrigerator for up to 2 weeks.

ROSE CONGOU TEA SYRUP: Substitute 3 tablespoons rose congou tea and 2 teaspoons dried lavender for the Earl Grey tea and vanilla bean. Omit orange zest and use only zest of $^1/_2$ lime.

OOLONG AND PEACH SYRUP: Substitute 2 tablespoons oolong tea for the Earl Grey tea. Omit lime zest and use just 1 teaspoon orange zest. Replace vanilla bean with 1 cinnamon stick and 1 sliced peach.

MATCHA GREEN TEA SIMPLE SYRUP

THIS SIMPLE SYRUP IS USED IN THE VANILLA *Green-tea-ni cocktail (page 270). Although it is ideal in that drink, the matcha powder makes the syrup opaque, which may limit its uses elsewhere. It tends to separate after a day, so make just what you will use at the time.*

Makes $^1/_4$ cup/60 milliliters

$^1/_4$ cup/60 milliliters Simple Syrup (page 237)
$1^1/_2$ teaspoons matcha green tea powder

In a small saucepan, heat the simple syrup just until small bubbles form. Remove from the heat and add the matcha. Whisk until fully combined. Let cool to room temperature.

VANILLA-CLOVE SIMPLE SYRUP

THIS SYRUP INCLUDES FOUR VANILLA BEANS FOR *an intensely rich vanilla flavor and aroma. If you decide to use fewer beans, it will still give a very nice syrup. Use any extra syrup for other drinks or to drizzle over fresh fruit. This recipe was created by Max Solano, the mixologist for Emeril's Table 10, for his award-winning Genevrier Verte cocktail (page 267).*

Makes about $1^1/_2$ cups/360 milliliters

$1^1/_2$ cups/300 grams granulated sugar
$1^1/_2$ cups/360 milliliters water
1 tablespoon whole cloves
4 vanilla beans
Zest of 1 orange, cut into 3-inch strips

Combine the sugar and water in a medium saucepan. Stir and bring to a boil over high heat. Reduce the heat to very low and add the cloves. Split open the vanilla beans lengthwise, scrape in the seeds, then add the pods. Stir and simmer until all the sugar is dissolved and the mixture is slightly syrupy, about 2 to 3 minutes. Add the orange zest. Let cool to room temperature, then store the syrup, refrigerated, in an airtight container overnight. Leave the vanilla, orange zest, and cloves in the syrup to continue to develop flavors, but strain each portion as you use it.

Iced Tea

ICED TEA IS CREDITED AS AN AMERICAN INVENTION, ATTRIBUTED TO THE 1904 WORLD'S FAIR in St. Louis in the India Pavilion, but there are references to cold tea in cookbooks predating that event. Regardless of whether it was invented or just popularized at the World's Fair, it's a wonderfully refreshing beverage in warm weather.

Bottled, ready-to-drink iced teas are increasingly popular, but homemade iced tea is infinitely better, and quite easy to make. When you make it at home, you can experiment with teas, flavors, and levels of sweetness. You can also make ice cubes with leftover iced tea, which adds even more flavor to cold beverages.

Iced tea can be served straight up, sweetened, or mixed with milk, cream, lemon, or other fruits or spices as accompaniments. Because the tea is cold, it can take a while for sugar to dissolve, so simple syrups come in handy; infused syrups add another layer of flavor (see pages 238-241). Honey can also be used to sweeten iced tea.

There are several methods for making iced tea. Because the tea is usually served over ice, which dilutes it, the tea should be brewed at one-and-a-half times to twice the usual strength.

A cold-steeping method, in which the tea leaves are infused in cold water and refrigerated overnight, tends to produce a clearer, less cloudy tea with virtually no chance of oversteeping. Before using any method involving cold or room temperature water to infuse, give the leaves a quick "rinse" by pouring over hot water (at the temperature used for making hot tea with that style of leaf) and then immediately discarding the water.

Cloudy Tea

ICED TEA CAN SOMETIMES APPEAR CLOUDY, ALMOST OPAQUE. THIS DOES NOT MEAN THAT THERE is anything wrong with the tea. This is known as "creaming" and is the result of a precipitate being released by the tea leaves into the water. Many high-quality teas are prone to this. Northern Indian Assam teas, for instance, have a strong tendency to cream. It has no impact on flavor, but often a crystal-clear look is preferable for tea served iced. Nilgiri teas from southern India are particularly good for making iced teas as they tend to stay very clear. Sri Lankan (Ceylon) teas also work very well.

BASIC ICED TEA

ICED TEA IS BEST SERVED ON THE DAY IT IS MADE.

Makes about 1 quart/947 milliliters (4 servings)

4½ cups/1 liters water
3 tablespoons loose-leaf tea leaves (for 1½ strength tea)

Heat the water in a kettle or saucepan over high heat. If using green, oolong, or white tea leaves, heat to barely steaming, 175°F/80°C. If using black tea, bring to a rolling boil, 212°F/100°C. Add the tea leaves to the heated water.

Steep, covered, for the same length of time that you prefer when making the tea hot: 3 minutes for white, 2 minutes for green, 3 minutes for oolong, and 4 minutes for black tea (see table on page 44). Strain into a pitcher, discarding the leaves, and let cool to room temperature. Once cool, refrigerate, or serve. To serve, pour the tea into glasses filled with ice, with sweetener on the side.

NOTE: Cocktails and other tea beverages are better-served by stronger tea. See the variations for double- and triple-strength tea.

Variations

DOUBLE-STRENGTH ICED TEA: use 4 tablespoons loose-leaf tea leaves and proceed as directed.
TRIPLE-STRENGTH ICED TEA: use 6 tablespoons loose-leaf tea leaves and proceed as directed.

Try any of the following tea-and-fruit-combinations, most of which can be added when the tea is either hot or cold. If it is important to keep the items fresh-looking, then wait until cool. Fresh flower petals should be added after cooling.

- Ceylon black tea with plums, peaches, or blackberries
- Darjeeling tea with apples and pears
- Green tea with fresh mint and cinnamon
- White tea with rose petals
- Green tea with passion fruit and peaches

CHAI ICED TEA

CHILLED CHAI TEA CONCENTRATE MAKES A *pleasing warm-weather drink, which can be tailored to your tastes by varying the base tea, the simple syrup, or spiking it with rum or brandy. When multiplying for larger batches, you can stir it well in a pitcher rather than shaking each serving.*

Serves 2

1½ cups/360 milliliters Basic Iced Tea (this page),
  using black tea
¼ cup/60 milliliters chilled Masala Chai Concentrate
  (page 234)
Simple Syrup to taste (page 237)

Add ice to a cocktail shaker or lidded jar. Pour in the tea, chai concentrate, and simple syrup to taste. Shake vigorously, taste, and adjust sweetener level as needed. Shake after additions and pour into 2 tall glasses filled with ice.

Alternatively, pour the iced tea into 2 tall glasses filled with ice cubes, then add the simple syrup; pour in the chai concentrate without stirring—it makes a nice presentation, and will mix as you sip. Serve immediately.

LEMONADE ICED TEA

THIS COMBINES TWO FAVORITE SUMMER DRINKS: *lemonade and iced tea. You can also use this recipe as a base for a refreshing sorbet—just pour it into an ice-cream maker and follow the manufacturer's instructions for freezing.*

Serves 4

½ cup/100 grams granulated sugar
½ cup/120 milliliters hot water
½ cup/120 milliliters fresh lemon juice
4 cups/960 milliliters Basic Iced Tea (page 243), using black or green tea

In a pitcher, combine the sugar and hot water. Stir until the sugar dissolves. Stir in the lemon juice. Add the iced tea and stir gently.

To serve, pour into glasses filled with ice.

Variation
GINGERED LEMONADE ICED TEA: Replace the sugar and hot water with ¹/₂ cup/120 milliliters Ginger Simple Syrup (page 238).

ICED TEA FLOAT

THIS REFRESHING—AND NOVEL—WAY TO ENJOY *iced tea and ice cream is for fans of tea with milk. As the ice cream melts, it infuses the tea with a delicious creaminess.*

Serves 1

1½ cups/360 milliliters Basic Iced Tea (page 243), using black tea
1 scoop Dulce de Leche Tea Ice Cream (page 221) or vanilla ice cream

Pour the tea into a tall glass half-filled with ice. Top with a large scoop of ice cream and serve immediately.

Fruit Purées

FRUIT PURÉES ARE HANDY TO HAVE AROUND AND EASY TO MAKE, ESPECIALLY IN THE SUMMER. WHEN extra fruit is starting to get overripe, cut it into chunks and purée it in a blender or food processor with just enough simple syrup to allow it to liquefy. If the fruit has skins or fibers, strain the purée, and then freeze it in ice cube trays to have smaller quantities readily available. After they freeze solidly, you can pop out the cubes and store in a resealable freezer bag. You can also purée leftover canned fruits; just use some of the syrup the fruit was packed in rather than added simple syrup.

PARK PLAZA BLACKBERRY ICED TEA-ZER

VARY THE MUDDLED FRESH FRUIT BY WHAT'S SEASONALLY BEST AT THE TIME. ALTERNATIVELY, FRUIT *purées work beautifully, as do different styles of mint.*

Serves 1

1 cup/240 milliliters triple-strength Basic Iced Tea (page 243), using white or green tea

5 mint leaves, divided

Simple syrup, preferably Keemun-Spiced Plum (page 240), to taste

4 fresh blackberries, divided

¼ cup/60 milliliters ginger ale

In a cocktail shaker or lidded jar, muddle together a large splash of the tea, 4 of the mint leaves, a splash of simple syrup, and 3 of the blackberries. Fill with ice and add remaining tea and simple syrup to taste. Shake well and strain into a tall glass filled with ice. Top with the ginger ale and garnish with the remaining mint leaf and blackberry. Serve immediately.

Tea Creams

TEA CREAMS ARE A VARIATION ON ICED TEA BLENDS THAT INVOLVE SHAKING TOGETHER ICED TEA, one or more fresh fruit purées or muddled fruit, a touch of cream, and, optionally (depending on the sweetness of the fruits), some simple syrup. Alternatively, they can be made in a blender with crushed ice for a smoothie-like consistency. They can also be made with ice cream, yogurt, or sorbet. Lighter tea smoothies can be made using frozen chunks of fruit, rather than ice cream. When including fresh herb leaves in shaken drinks, crush them first (unless they are muddled in the drink) to release the flavorful oils. Because you are adding so many other dominant flavors, in order to not lose the tea, use at least double- or triple-strength iced tea.

PEACHY GREEN TEA CREAM

This tea cream was one of the first to be offered at the Cambridge, Mass., location of Tea-Tray in the Sky, and was one of the most popular.

Serves 1

1 cup/240 milliliters triple-strength Basic Iced Tea (page 243), using green tea

3 tablespoons peach or mango purée

1 teaspoon passion fruit purée or passion fruit syrup, or more to taste (optional)

2 tablespoons light cream

1 tablespoon plain or Ginger-Oolong Simple Syrup (page 238) or more to taste

3 basil leaves, lightly crushed (optional)

1 peach slice for garnish

Shake all ingredients except for the peach slice vigorously with ice in a cocktail shaker. Adjust sweetener or amounts of fruit purée to taste. Pour into a tall glass, ice and all, or strain into a coupe glass. Garnish with the peach slice on the rim.

KEEMUN BLACKBERRY TEA CREAM

Serves 1

1 cup/240 milliliters triple-strength Basic Iced Tea (page 243), using Nilgiri or Keemun tea

2 tablespoons blackberry purée

2 tablespoons light cream

1 tablespoon Keemun-Spiced Plum Simple Syrup (page 240), or more to taste

3 fresh mint leaves, lightly crushed

Shake all ingredients vigorously with ice in a cocktail shaker. Alternatively, use a blender, with or without added ice. Serve in a tall glass with a straw.

APRICOT-OOLONG TEA CREAM

Serves 1

1 cup/240 milliliters triple-strength Basic Iced Tea (page 243), using oolong tea

2 tablespoons apricot, peach, or plum purée

2 tablespoons light cream

1 tablespoon Ginger-Oolong Simple Syrup (page 238) or Keemun-Spiced Plum Simple Syrup (page 240) or more to taste

Shake all ingredients vigorously with ice in a cocktail shaker. Alternatively, use a blender, with or without added ice. Serve in a tall glass with a straw.

BLUEBERRY-BANANA SMOOTHIE

THIS IS A VARIATION ON THE TEA CREAM IDEA— *but dairy-free. The tea is steeped in soy milk and puréed with banana and frozen blueberries, making for a healthful start to the day. This satisfying breakfast shake is served at Starwood Hotels and was created by chefs Christoph Leu and Julia Tolstunova.*

Serves 3

1¼ cups/300 milliliters soy milk

1 tablespoon loose-leaf green tea leaves

¾ cup/180 milliliters orange juice, chilled

1 medium banana, sliced

12 ounces/340 grams frozen blueberries

In a medium saucepan, heat the soy milk over medium-high heat until just steaming (about 175°F/80°C). Remove from the heat and add the tea leaves. Steep, covered, for 4 minutes, then strain and discard the leaves. Let cool to room temperature, then refrigerate until chilled. May be prepared a day in advance.

Combine chilled soy infusion, orange juice, banana, and frozen blueberries in a blender and purée until smooth. Divide among 3 glasses and serve immediately.

TROPICAL CHAI BREEZE

THIS DELICIOUS DRINK WAS CREATED BY DOT *Jacobson, who was a finalist representing the Cambridge School of Culinary Arts in the 2009 New England Culinary Tea Competition. For a spirited iced tea, rum makes a nice addition (see Tropical Chai Rum Breeze, page 268).*

Serves 3

⅔ cup/115 grams finely diced fresh pineapple

⅔ cup/115 grams finely diced fresh mango

1 cup/240 milliliters Basic Iced Tea (page 243)
  using loose-leaf chai tea

1 cup/240 milliliters regular or light coconut milk

2 tablespoons granulated sugar, or more to taste

1 cup/240 milliliters ice cubes

Slices or chunks of pineapple and mango for garnish

Purée the pineapple in a blender until smooth. Add the mango and blend well. Add the tea, coconut milk, sugar, and ice cubes. Blend until thick and frothy.

Pour into 3 glasses, with additional ice if desired, and garnish with slices of fresh pineapple and mango.

NOTE: The chai iced tea used here should be regular iced tea made using loose-leaf chai tea, not the Iced Chai Tea made with Masala Chai Concentrate.

RED GRAPE *and* BLACK TEA LASSI

A LASSI IS AN INDIAN YOGURT SMOOTHIE. THIS *recipe was created by Israeli chef Sharone Artsi when he was living in Boston. Chef Artsi has family ties to Indian and Moroccan cuisines and studied at The Cambridge School of Culinary Arts in a program based largely on French cuisine. With a strong focus on health, diet, and nutrition, his passion turned towards healthy, fresh cuisine, which now includes the use of tea.*

Serves 2

1½ cups/360 milliliters milk

2 tablespoons loose-leaf Nilgiri or Assam tea leaves

1 cup/240 milliliters plain Greek-style yogurt

3 tablespoons granulated sugar

1 cup/150 grams red grapes, frozen

½ banana, sliced and frozen

In a medium saucepan, combine the milk and tea and heat over medium-high heat. As soon as the mixture begins to bubble, remove from the heat. Let steep, covered, for 10 minutes, then strain, discarding the leaves. Refrigerate until cold.

In blender, combine the infused milk, yogurt, sugar, grapes, and banana. Blend until smooth. Pour into 2 glasses and serve immediately.

NOTE: Place the grapes and banana slices in the freezer several hours (or days) before you plan to make this lassi.

Vodka Infusions

VODKA IS NEUTRAL ENOUGH NOT TO CONFLICT WITH THE TEAS AND OTHER INGREDIENTS THAT you choose to infuse, allowing for almost limitless creativity. Infused vodkas can be enjoyed on their own, or as part of a cocktail. Start with a good-quality vodka as the base of your infusions; added flavors should never be used to cover up flaws, but to highlight and balance the characteristics of different spirits.

Each infused vodka here is followed by a cocktail recipe using the infusion. Use them as inspiration for your own creations.

⤜ GREEN TEA VODKA ⤛

THIS INFUSED VODKA WORKS WELL AS THE BASE FOR FRUITY DRINKS. DRIED QUINCE CAN BE FOUND *at Asian markets, or dried apple may be substituted.*

Makes 1 liter

1 (1-liter) bottle vodka

1 vanilla bean, split in half lengthwise

½ cup/20 grams loose-leaf green tea leaves, such as Dragonwell, bancha, or sencha

¼ cup/40 grams dried peaches or apricots, diced into ¼-inch/6-millimeter pieces

¼ cup/40 grams dried quince, diced into about ¼-inch/6-millimeter pieces

2 tablespoons dried chamomile

Pour the vodka into a large pitcher. Scrape the vanilla bean seeds into the vodka; add the vanilla pod. Add the tea, dried fruit, and chamomile.

Let mixture sit for at least 30 minutes. When the flavor is at a concentration you like, strain the mixture through double layers of cheesecloth, or through a coffee filter, making sure to remove all bits of tea and fruit. Store in an airtight glass bottle, at room temperature or chilled.

STRAWBERRY BASIL MAR-TEA-NI

WHAT A LOVELY WAY TO CELEBRATE FRESH, *perfect berries at the height of their season—strawberries for grown-ups! The amount of simple syrup needed will vary depending on the sweetness of the fruit.*

Serves 1

3 strawberries, hulled and quartered

3 basil leaves, divided

2 ounces/60 milliliters Green Tea and Citrus Vodka (page 256)

½ ounce/15 milliliters Green Tea Simple Syrup (page 238), or more to taste

1 basil leaf, for garnish

Fill cocktail shaker halfway with crushed ice. Add the strawberries and 2 of the basil leaves. Crush the fruit and basil well with a muddler or the back of a heavy spoon. Add the vodka and syrup. Shake well and strain into a chilled martini glass. Garnish with a fresh basil leaf floated on top, if desired.

GREEN *-and-* WHITE VODKA

THIS VODKA WAS CREATED FOR THE RASPBERRY *Flir-tea-ni (page 252), but can also be enjoyed alone. We like Stolichnaya vanilla vodka, but any vanilla or plain vodka would be fine.*

Makes 1 liter

1 (1-liter) bottle vanilla vodka

½ cup/20 grams loose-leaf white peony tea leaves

¼ cup/40 grams dried sour cherries, or cherry blossoms if available

¼ cup/40 grams diced dried peaches

¼ cup/10 grams loose-leaf green tea leaves, such as bancha, sencha, or Dragonwell

Combine the vodka, white tea, dried cherries, and dried peaches in a large pitcher. Steep at room temperature for 1 hour, then add the green tea leaves and steep, covered, for 45 minutes more. When the flavor is at a concentration you like, strain the mixture through double layers of cheesecloth, or through a coffee filter, making sure to remove all bits of tea and fruit. Store in an airtight glass bottle, at room temperature or chilled.

RASPBERRY FLIR-TEA-NI

THIS COCKTAIL WAS CREATED FOR THE BROADWAY *show* Legally Blonde *when it came to Boston. The drink obviously had to be pink, fun, and frivolous! And, of course, it needed to be made with plenty of tea.*

Serves 1

1 ounce/30 milliliters Green-and-White Vodka (page 251)
1 ounce/30 milliliters Chambord liqueur
1½ ounces/45 milliliters half-and-half
½ ounce/15 milliliters white crème de cacao
Splash grenadine
1 raspberry for garnish

Shake all the ingredients except the raspberry vigorously in a cocktail shaker with ice. Strain into a chilled martini glass. Garnish with the fresh raspberry.

KEEMUN-CLOVE VODKA

THIS IS THE BASE VODKA FOR THE KEEMUN CREAM *cocktail and the French Mar-tea-ni (next page). If you are making the French Mar-tea-ni, it makes sense to use a French vodka, such as Grey Goose, but feel free to use any good-quality vodka. Chinese Keemun tea will impart an earthy richness and depth to this vodka.*

Makes 1 liter

1 (1-liter) bottle vodka
1 teaspoon whole cloves
½ teaspoon cracked black peppercorns
⅓ cup/15 grams loose-leaf Keemun tea leaves

Combine the vodka, cloves, pepper, and tea leaves in a large pitcher. Steep at room temperature for 45 minutes then taste. When the flavor is at a concentration you like, strain the mixture through double layers of cheesecloth, or through a coffee filter, making sure to remove all bits of tea and spices. Store in an airtight glass bottle, at room temperature or chilled.

FRENCH MAR-TEA-NI

TEA-INFUSED VODKA GIVES THE POPULAR FRENCH *Martini more depth and complexity than the original classic, not to mention a good dose of anti-oxidants. To meld with the earthiness of the tea-infused vodka, we changed the standard Chambord to crème de cassis, a black currant liqueur.*

Serves 1

2 ounces/60 milliliters Keemun-Clove Vodka (previous page)
1 ounce/30 milliliters pineapple juice
½ ounce/15 milliliters crème de cassis
Wedge of pineapple for garnish

Shake the vodka, pineapple juice, and crème de cassis vigorously in a cocktail shaker with ice. Strain into a chilled martini glass. Garnish with the wedge of fresh pineapple on the rim.

KEEMUN CREAM

THIS RICH TEA COCKTAIL IS EARTHY AND COMPLEX *and adds depth and interest to the sweet richness of Irish cream liqueur; the flavors meld to perfection.*

Serves 1

1 ounce/30 milliliters Keemun-Clove Vodka (previous page)
2 ounces/60 milliliters Irish cream liqueur, such as Bailey's
Whipped cream for garnish
Pinch ground cinnamon or mace for garnish

Fill a rocks glass with ice. Add the vodka and Irish cream liqueur. Stir. Garnish with a large dollop of whipped cream and dust lightly with cinnamon. Serve with a thin straw.

GREEN TEA *and* PEAR VODKA

DRIED LAVENDER IS AVAILABLE IN GOURMET *shops or markets that have more extensive selections of spices. Be sure to buy lavender intended for culinary use, not as pot-pourri. This vodka is very nice for those who enjoy sipping straight vodka. It's used as the base for the Lavender Pear Mar-tea-ni (this page).*

Makes 1 liter

1 (1-liter) bottle vodka

6 dried pear halves, coarsely chopped

3 tablespoons dried lavender

1 tablespoon lightly crushed black peppercorns

½ cup/20 grams loose-leaf green tea leaves, such as Dragonwell or sencha

Combine the vodka, pears, lavender, and pepper in a large pitcher. Steep at room temperature 20 minutes, then add the tea. Steep, covered, for 30 more minutes. When the flavor is at a concentration you like, strain the mixture through double layers of cheesecloth, or through a coffee filter, making sure to remove all bits of tea, spices, and fruit. Store in an airtight glass bottle, at room temperature or chilled.

LAVENDER PEAR MAR-TEA-NI

ANOTHER PARK PLAZA CLASSIC, THE FRUITY AND *floral aromatics on this cocktail are particularly enticing.*

Serves 1

1½ ounces/45 milliliters Green Tea and Pear Vodka (this page)

½ ounce/15 milliliters pear brandy

Lemon twist for garnish (optional)

1 sprig fresh lavender for garnish (optional)

Shake the infused vodka vigorously in a cocktail shaker with ice and pear brandy. Serve strained into a chilled martini glass. Garnish with the lemon twist and a sprig of fresh lavender, if desired.

GREEN TEA *and* CITRUS VODKA

THIS INFUSION WAS CREATED FOR THE STRAW-*berry Basil Mar-tea-ni (page 251), but consider it any time you might reach for a citrus vodka. Perhaps a cosmopolitan with that extra something special? It is a refreshing complement to many summer cocktails.*

Makes 1 liter

1 (1-liter) bottle vodka
Zest of 1 orange or tangerine in strips
Zest of 1 lime in strips
¼ cup/10 grams loose-leaf green tea leaves

Combine the vodka and citrus zests in a large pitcher. Steep at room temperature for 45 minutes then add the tea. Steep, covered, for another 30 minutes, then taste. When the flavor is at a concentration you like, strain the mixture through double layers of cheesecloth, or through a coffee filter, making sure to remove all bits of tea and fruit. Store in an airtight glass bottle, at room temperature or chilled.

GREEN TEA MARTINI

THIS MARTINI HAS BEEN A FAVORITE AT THE *Boston Park Plaza Hotel and Towers ever since tea cocktails were introduced there several years ago. The infused vodka base is so popular that it is kept behind the bar in a large, specialized dispenser for easy access.*

Serves 1

2 ounces/60 milliliters Green Tea Vodka (page 249)
Splash peach Schnapps
1 dried peach or apricot or 1 teaspoon dried
 cranberries for garnish

Shake the vodka and peach Schnapps vigorously in a cocktail shaker with ice. Strain into a chilled martini glass. Garnish with the dried fruit.

BLACK TEA-GINGER VODKA

THIS VODKA WAS CREATED FOR THE SPICED
Apple-tea-ni (this page), which adds a tea twist to the ever-popular appletini cocktail. It works very nicely in other mixed drinks as well. Consider using this vodka along with mango, apricot, or peach juices for a refreshing drink.

Makes 1 liter

1 (1-liter) bottle vodka

12 quarter-size slices fresh ginger

1 tablespoon whole cloves

6 dried pear halves, coarsely chopped

⅓ cup/15 grams loose-leaf black tea leaves, such as Ceylon or Chinese congou

Combine the vodka, ginger, cloves, and pears in a large pitcher. Steep at room temperature for 20 minutes, then add the tea leaves. Steep an additional 30 minutes, then taste. When the flavor is at a concentration you like, strain the mixture through double layers of cheesecloth, or through a coffee filter, making sure to remove all bits of tea, fruit, and spices. Store in an airtight glass bottle, at room temperature or chilled.

SPICED APPLE-TEA-NI

THIS DRINK WILL BE VERY FAMILIAR, WITH JUST
a slight twist, to lovers of the ever-popular appletini cocktail. It's a good way to introduce the uninitiated to the idea of tea cocktails!

Serves 1

2 ounces/60 milliliters Black Tea Ginger Vodka (this page)

1 ounce/30 milliliters sour apple Schnapps

Splash Grand Marnier or Cointreau liqueur

Lemon twist for garnish

Shake the vodka, Schnapps, and Grand Marnier vigorously in a cocktail shaker with ice. Strain into a chilled martini glass and garnish with a lemon twist.

OOLONG VODKA

THIS IS AN INTENSELY INFUSED VODKA WHICH *depends on the quality and style of the oolong used. We created it for the first* Sante Magazine *restaurant Symposium with Rou Gui, a rock oolong from the Wuyi Mountains in China which is noted for its smooth earthiness with a hint of smoke and notes of cinnamon. If that oolong is not available, substitute another fairly high-oxidation oolong. Consider adding a cinnamon stick to the infusion as well. Rou Gui is a loosely rolled, bold-leaf oolong; if you are using an oolong with a tight leaf roll, it will measure substantially less than the 1 cup/40 grams tea leaves called for in the recipe. In that case, measure the tea by weight (1½ ounces) instead of volume.*

Makes 1 liter

1 (1-liter) bottle vodka
1 cup/40 grams loose-leaf oolong tea leaves,
  1½ ounces by weight

Combine the vodka and the tea leaves in a large pitcher. Steep at room temperature for 6 hours. When the flavor is at a concentration you like, strain the mixture through double layers of cheesecloth, or through a coffee filter, making sure to remove all bits of tea. Store in an airtight glass bottle, at room temperature or chilled.

PEACH-OOLONG SAN-TEA-NI

THE FRUIT NOTES OF THE OOLONG ARE AMPLIFIED *by stone fruits, especially peach and apricot, so a splash of peach Schnapps in this cocktail melds beautifully.*

Serves 1

2½ ounces/75 milliliters Oolong Vodka (this page)
¾ ounce/20 milliliters peach Schnapps
¾ ounce/20 milliliters Simple Syrup (page 237)
Peach slice for garnish
Lemon twist for garnish

Shake the vodka, Schnapps, and simple syrup vigorously in a cocktail shaker with ice. Strain into a chilled martini glass and garnish with a peach slice and a lemon twist.

White Port Infusions

TEA FLAVORS COMPLEMENT THE RICHNESS OF WHITE PORT AND HELP TO BALANCE THE SWEETNESS with added complexity and aromatics. We have included some of our favorite tea-port infusions. These cocktails were all originally developed using Dow's Fine White Porto. Different ports will give you different results, so let your taste be your guide. Consider trying some of these combinations with a sweet sake instead of port.

WHITE PORT *with* GREEN TEA *and* FLOWERS

IN THIS INFUSION, LAVENDER ADDS FLORAL TONES AS WELL AS A BIT OF SPICINESS, AND CHAMOMILE *gives a sweet roundness, with the tea helping to cut back any excess sweetness from either the chamomile or the port itself. Lime-flowers, also known as* linden *or* tilleul, *have long been used for medicinal purposes. They are available more widely in Europe, where they are enjoyed for a lightly floral herbaceous flavor. If they are not available near you, order them online.*

Makes 750 milliliters

1 (750-ml) bottle sweet white port
2 tablespoons dried lavender
2 tablespoons dried chamomile
¼ cup/10 grams dried limeflowers
½ cup/20 grams loose-leaf green tea leaves, such as Lung Ching or Dragonwell

Place the port in a large pitcher. Add the lavender, chamomile, and limeflowers. Steep 30 minutes, then add the tea leaves. Steep an additional 20 minutes, then taste. When the flavor is at a concentration you like, strain the mixture through double layers of cheesecloth, or through a coffee filter, making sure to remove all bits of tea and herbs. Store in an airtight glass bottle, at room temperature or chilled.

WHITE PORT *with* BLACK TEA, GINGER, *and* LYCHEE

THE BOSTON PARK PLAZA HOTEL AND TOWERS *offers a tea-and-cheese VIP amenity in which a perfectly paired combination of a fine cheese and either a tea or tea cocktail are presented as a special gift to certain lucky guests. This tea cocktail was created as a part of this program to pair with Shropshire Blue, a wonderful English cheese.*

Makes 750 milliliters

1 (750-ml) bottle sweet white port
¼ cup/30 grams fresh or canned lychee fruit, coarsely chopped
2 tablespoons coarsely chopped crystallized ginger
4 quarter-size slices fresh ginger
½ cup/20 grams loose-leaf Chinese black congou tea leaves

Place the port in a large pitcher. Add the lychee, crystallized ginger, and fresh ginger and steep, covered, for 20 minutes. Add the tea leaves and steep an additional 20 minutes, then taste. When the flavor is at a concentration you like, strain the mixture through double layers of cheesecloth, or through a coffee filter, making sure to remove all bits of tea and fruits. Store in an airtight glass bottle at room temperature, or chilled.

Variation
WHITE PORT WITH BLACK TEA, APRICOT, AND LYCHEE: Replace the crystallized ginger with coarsely chopped dried apricots. This will result in a port with a little less bite to it, but with a rich, fruity complexity.

WHITE PORT *with* BLACK TEA, ROSE, *and* LAVENDER

THIS COCKTAIL WAS CREATED FOR MOTHER'S *Day at the Boston Park Plaza Hotel and Towers, using rich and full-bodied New Vithanakande tea from Sri Lanka, one of our favorites. Roses seemed a natural for Mom. Take care to buy flowers meant for culinary use, not sold as potpourri.*

Makes 750 milliliters

1 (750-ml) bottle sweet white port
½ cup/10 grams loosely packed fresh rose petals or ¼ cup/10 grams dried rose petals
¼ cup/10 grams loose-leaf black tea leaves, such as a Ceylon or Chinese congou
1 tablespoon dried lavender

Place the port in a large pitcher with the rose petals. Steep, covered, for 30 minutes. Add the lavender and tea leaves. Steep, covered, for an additional 30 minutes, then taste. When the flavor is at a concentration you like, strain the mixture through double layers of cheesecloth, or through a coffee filter, making sure to remove all bits of tea and flowers. Store in an airtight glass bottle, at room temperature or chilled.

TEA SANGRIAS MADE WITH FRUITY AND AROMATIC RIESLING WINE ARE WONDERFULLY REFRESHING in the summer and go particularly nicely with grilled or spicy foods. They can be served immediately, but they are even better when their flavors are allowed to meld and develop for a day. Although the idea may seem new, spirited tea punches were often enjoyed in Victorian times.

JASMINE TEA *and* BRANDIED FRUIT SANGRIA

ANY COMBINATION OF FRUITS WILL WORK WELL IN THIS SANGRIA. TRY EQUAL PARTS THINLY SLICED *oranges, apples, pears, plums, and peaches—or whatever combination you have handy. Ideally you want to give the fruit a day in the brandy, but 20 minutes will do in a pinch. Leave the fruit to macerate in the brandy while the tea cools. The fruit and brandy may be left for up to a week, so if you expect to make another batch soon, cut and soak extra now. This sangria will hold well refrigerated for 3 or 4 days.*

Serves 8

- 2 cups/300 grams thinly sliced fruit (any combination of oranges, apples, peaches, plums, and peaches)
- 1 cup/240 milliliters brandy, plus more as needed
- ¼ cup/10 grams loose-leaf jasmine tea leaves
- 6 cups/1.4 liters steaming water (about 175°F/80°C)
- 1 (750-ml) bottle Riesling, chilled
- 2 tablespoons Simple Syrup (page 237)

Place the sliced fruit in a nonreactive container and completely cover with the brandy. Let sit for at least 20 minutes, or ideally overnight.

Place the tea leaves in a large pitcher. Add the steaming water and steep, covered, for 2 minutes. Strain, discarding the leaves and returning the tea liquid to the container, and let cool completely. Add the chilled Riesling, brandied fruit, and simple syrup. Taste and add additional simple syrup and the brandy from the macerated fruit to taste. Serve over ice garnished with an orange slice.

DARJEELING and PEAR SANGRIA

THIS SANGRIA WILL HOLD WELL REFRIGERATED FOR 3 OR 4 DAYS. ANY DARJEELING WILL WORK HERE, *but a first flush Darjeeling plays up on the fruit flavors particularly well.*

Serves 8

1/4 cup/10 grams loose-leaf Darjeeling tea leaves

6 cups/1.4 liters boiling water (about 212°F/100°C)

1 (750-ml) bottle Riesling, chilled

3 pears, cored and thinly sliced

1 apple, cored and thinly sliced

1 cup apple juice, chilled

2 tablespoons Simple Syrup (page 237) or more to taste

Additional pear slices for garnish

Place the tea leaves in a large pitcher. Pour over the boiling water and steep, covered, for 3 minutes. Strain, discarding the leaves and returning the tea liquid to the pitcher. Let cool completely to room temperature.

Add the chilled Riesling, pears, apple, apple juice, and simple syrup to taste. Chill; if possible, give the flavors a day to meld before serving. Serve over ice garnished with slices of fresh pear.

GREEN TEA-COCONUT RUM

USE THIS INFUSION WITH SOME OF YOUR FAVORITE TROPICAL RUM-BASED DRINKS AS WELL AS THE *Plaza Citrus Tea-zer (next page). You could also use it to make a delicious rum cake. Let your imagination run with it.*

Makes 750 milliliters

1 (750-ml) bottle Malibu rum or other coconut rum

½ cup/35 grams coarsely chopped fresh lemongrass

⅓ cup/15 grams loose-leaf green tea leaves, such as sencha or Dragonwell

Place the rum and lemongrass in a large pitcher. Steep, covered, for 45 minutes, then add the tea leaves. Steep another 30 minutes, then taste. When the flavor is at a concentration you like, strain the mixture through double layers of cheesecloth, or through a coffee filter, making sure to remove all bits of tea and lemongrass. Store in an airtight glass bottle, at room temperature or chilled, for up to 6 weeks.

PLAZA CITRUS TEA-ZER

THIS BOSTON PARK PLAZA FAVORITE IS PERFECT *by the pool, on the beach, or at a barbecue. Try it—it may become a new summer favorite.*

Serves 1

1½ ounces/45 milliliters Green Tea-Coconut Rum (page 264)

3 ounces/90 milliliters grapefruit juice

½ ounce/15 milliliters Green Tea-zer Simple Syrup (page 238)

Splash Champagne

Lemon twist for garnish (optional)

Basil leaf for garnish (optional)

Shake the rum, grapefruit juice, and syrup vigorously in a cocktail shaker with ice. Strain into a chilled martini glass. Finish with a splash of Champagne and garnish with the lemon twist or basil leaf, if desired.

TEA-INFUSED BRANDY

THIS IS THE BRANDY THAT WE RECOMMEND *adding to the Park Plaza Tea-Nog (page 266) or Masala-Style Chai (page 235) to give a bit of a kick while offering another layer of flavors. Try using this the next time you make a Brandy Alexander.*

Makes 1 cup/240 milliliters

1 tablespoon loose-leaf Assam tea leaves

1 cinnamon stick

1 teaspoon cracked black peppercorns

3 quarter-size slices fresh ginger

1 cup/240 milliliters brandy

In a large glass measuring cup, combine the tea leaves, cinnamon, pepper, and ginger. Pour brandy over and steep 45 minutes or longer, to taste. When the flavor is at a concentration you like, strain the mixture through double layers of cheesecloth, or through a coffee filter, making sure to remove all bits of tea and spices. Store in an airtight glass bottle, at room temperature or chilled, for up to 6 weeks.

NOTE: This is a strong infusion as the brandy is not intended to be consumed straight, but for adding to very rich cocktails. Since it holds well, consider infusing a full bottle at a time to have around throughout the holidays.

PARK PLAZA TEA-NOG

THIS INCREDIBLY POPULAR COCKTAIL IS SERVED *only during the month of December at the Boston Park Plaza Hotel and Towers. Since pasteurized eggs might be difficult to get for many home cooks, we created this faster home version using store-bought eggnog rather than eggnog from scratch. If you prefer it non-alcoholic, omit the brandy.*

Serves 12

3 tablespoons loose-leaf Assam or Nilgiri tea leaves
1 quart/950 milliliters Masala Chai Concentrate (page 234)
2 quarts/1.9 liters eggnog, chilled
2½ cups/600 milliliters boiling water (about 212°F/100°C)
½ to 1 cup/120 to 240 milliliters Tea-Infused Brandy (page 265), or cognac or brandy (optional)
Grated nutmeg for garnish

Place the tea leaves in a medium bowl and pour the boiling water over them. Steep 4 to 5 minutes, covered, strain, and discard the leaves. Set aside to cool to room temperature.

In a large pitcher, blend together the Masala Chai Concentrate, eggnog, 1½ cups/360 milliliters of the cooled tea, and ½ cup/120 milliliters of the brandy, if using. Stir, taste, and add additional tea and brandy, if using, to taste. Serve chilled in a martini glass with a small sprinkle of nutmeg.

CHAI MARTINI

THERE ARE MANY WAYS TO CREATE A WONDERFUL *chai martini. All the ratios shown below can be adjusted according to your taste.*

Serves 1

2 ounces/60 milliliters Masala Chai Concentrate (page 234)
1 ounce/30 milliliters milk
1 ounce/30 milliliters Tea-Infused Brandy (page 265) or rum
Simple Syrup (page 237) to taste
Grated nutmeg for garnish

Combine chai concentrate, milk, brandy, and simple syrup in a shaker filled with ice; shake vigorously. Strain into a chilled martini glass and garnish with a dusting of freshly grated nutmeg.

GENEVRIER VERTE
(Green Juniper)

THIS RECIPE, CREATED BY MAX SOLANO, THE *mixologist for Emeril's Table 10, won first place in the Tea Cocktail Competition at the 2009 World Tea Expo in Las Vegas. This drink is as the creator intended, sized for a dramatic oversized martini glass. If you choose to use smaller glassware, adjust as needed. Keep in mind when you are making or creating cocktails, the gins are not interchangeable. Every gin has its own unique recipe. It's a lot more than just juniper berries! Max chose Hendrick's, which is a velvety gin that plays up the vanilla and clove, subtle with a touch of citrus to not overpower the delicate jasmine. Hendrick's is actually made with rose petals, so other floral additions would be a natural. This drink also includes Agwa Coca Leaf Liqueur which is made with Bolivian coca leaves.*

Serves 1

1½ ounces/45 milliliters double-strength Basic Iced Tea (page 243) using jasmine tea

1½ ounces/45 milliliters Hendrick's gin

¾ ounce/20 milliliters Agwa Coca Leaf Liqueur

¾ ounce/20 milliliters Vanilla-Clove Simple Syrup (page 241)

½ ounce/15 milliliters fresh lime juice

1 egg white

Cucumber slice for garnish

Mint sprig for garnish

Combine all ingredients except cucumber and mint sprig in a cocktail shaker filled with ice. Shake vigorously for 10 to 15 seconds. Strain into a chilled 7- to 9-ounce martini glass and garnish with cucumber slice and mint sprig.

NOTE: The vanilla-clove syrup needs to be made at least 1 day in advance, so plan accordingly.

APRICOT-OOLONG CHAMPAGNE COCKTAIL

THIS IS A VARIATION ON A BELLINI. CONSIDER *offering a selection of syrups and purées for your guests to choose from. You could coordinate your tea syrup-and-purée pairing with the dessert you are serving.*

Serves 1

1 teaspoon apricot or peach purée

1 tablespoon Ginger-Oolong Simple Syrup (page 238) or more to taste

Champagne

Place the apricot purée and the Ginger-Oolong syrup in the bottom of a champagne flute. Add the Champagne and serve immediately.

Variation

BLACKBERRY-KEEMUN: Use blackberry purée and Keemun-Spiced Plum Simple Syrup (page 240).

TROPICAL CHAI RUM BREEZE

THINK COOL, SPICY, FRUITY, AND CREAMY—WITH *the richness of rum! We may never drink another piña colada. This drink was created by Dot Jacobson of the Cambridge School of Culinary Arts.*

Serves 2

2 ounces/60 milliliters light rum
1½ cups/360 milliliters Tropical Chai Breeze (page 268)
Slices or chunks of pineapple and mango for garnish

Fill 2 tall glasses all the way with ice. Pour 1 ounce/30 milliliters of rum and ³/₄ cup/180 milliliters of the Tropical Chai Breeze into each glass. Stir well and garnish with slices of fresh pineapple and mango.

EARL GREY GIN

THE BERGAMOT OIL IN A GOOD EARL GREY IS A *terrific complement to the juniper in the Plymouth Gin, which has a natural earthiness and citrus bite. Mixologist Patricia Richards chose to play up the citrus notes throughout her drink. Plymouth is also known for its smoothness. Try this infusion straight up or mix it with tonic water and a squeeze of lime, or with your favorite gin-based recipes. It's used in the Earl Grey Mar-tea-ni (page 268).*

Makes 1 liter

1 tablespoon loose-leaf Earl Grey tea leaves
1 (1-liter) bottle gin, preferably Plymouth Gin

Combine tea and gin in a glass pitcher. Infuse overnight at room temperature. Stir and then strain well. Store in an airtight glass bottle, at room temperature or chilled.

EARL GREY MAR-TEA-NI

MIXOLOGIST PATRICIA RICHARDS OVERSEES THE *creation of specialty drinks and manages more than 25 bars at the Wynn and Encore Las Vegas properties, where she created this wonderful tea cocktail. The optional Frothee is an emulsifier that gives drinks a creamy head without the need for egg whites. It is available online and at most liquor stores. Agave syrup is a natural sweetener and can be found in many supermarkets with honey and other syrups.*

Serves 1

1½ ounces/45 milliliters Earl Grey Gin (this page)
½ ounce/15 milliliters limoncello liqueur
¼ ounce/7.5 milliliters organic agave syrup
³/₄ ounce/20 milliliters fresh lemon juice
³/₄ ounce/20 milliliters Simple Syrup (page 237)
1 squirt Frothee (optional)
Lemon slice, for garnish

Combine all ingredients except the lemon slice in a cocktail shaker with ice. Shake well and strain into a chilled coupe glass (an old-fashioned, rounded martini glass) or traditional martini glass. Garnish with a lemon slice.

ELDER EARL

THIS DRINK, A WONDERFUL BLENDING OF ELDER-
flower liqueur and Earl Grey tea, was created by Casey Wright while he was a student at Johnson and Wales University. The measures are sized for a very dramatic, oversized martini glass. If you intend to use different glassware, adjust the quantities accordingly. Casey enjoys garnishing this cocktail with a flamed orange peel, but for home convenience, a fresh orange twist will give you excellent results as well as playing off of the citrus tones of the Earl Grey.

Serves 1

1 ounce/30 milliliters vodka

1½ ounces/45 milliliters St. Germain elderflower liqueur

½ ounce/15 milliliters fresh lemon juice

½ cup/120 milliliters Basic Iced Tea (page 243), made with Earl Grey tea

1-inch/2.5-centimeter strip orange peel for garnish

Shake the vodka, liqueur, lemon juice, and tea in a cocktail shaker with ice. Strain into a chilled cocktail glass. Rub the rim of the glass with the orange peel, then twist and drop into the cocktail to serve.

THE EARL *of* HUM

THIS COCKTAIL BY Chicago-BASED MASTER
sommelier and mixologist Adam Seger features Earl Grey tea and Hum Botanical Spirits, a lightly sweetened rum-based infusion of ginger, hibiscus, and cardamom that he created. Adam is a "bar chef" who takes a culinary approach to creating drinks, and he has recently begun to play with teas in his cocktails. He calls the combination of bergamot, hibiscus, and cardamom in this drink "seductive."

To find Hum Botanical Spirits, go to www.humspirits.com or make your own version, starting with the Ginger Simple Syrup (page 238) made with the addition of 6 cardamom pods and 1 tablespoon dried hibiscus. Use 1 teaspoon of the syrup and 1½ ounces/45 milliliters of your favorite rum in place of the Hum.

Serves 1

1 teaspoon loose-leaf Earl Grey tea leaves

¾ cup/180 milliliters boiling water (about 212°F/100°C)

1½ ounces/45 milliliters Hum Botanical Spirit

Crystallized ginger for garnish

Place the tea leaves in a medium bowl and add the boiling water. Steep, covered, for 4 minutes. Strain into an Irish coffee mug, discarding the leaves. Add the Hum. Skewer the ginger and garnish. Serve hot.

VANILLA GREEN-TEA-NI

THIS COCKTAIL IS A SIMPLIFIED VERSION OF THE *drink created by chef Sharone Artsi that won first place in the 2009 New England Culinary Tea Competition. Artsi specializes in healthful foods. He said he started using tea as an ingredient not only because of its healthful and healing properties, but also for "the special flavor it contributes."*

Serves 1

½ ounce/15 milliliters Raspberry Tea Simple
   Syrup (page 239)
Granulated or sanding sugar, for rimming the glass
1½ ounces/45 milliliters Matcha Green Tea Simple
   Syrup (page 241)
1¼ ounces/37.5 milliliters vanilla vodka
1 ounce/30 milliliters almond milk
Fresh raspberries for garnish

Pour the raspberry syrup into a shallow dish. Dip the rim of the glass in the syrup and then dip into sugar, turning to coat the rim.

   Shake matcha syrup, vodka, and almond milk in a cocktail shaker with ice. Strain into the rimmed martini glass. Garnish with fresh raspberries.

UPCOUNTRY COMRADE

RUTH FELDMAN OF THE NEW ENGLAND CULINARY *Institute in Vermont created this lightly smoky and refreshing blend of maple, vodka, and just a hint of spice. Finding the Flag Hill Sugar Maple Liqueur may be challenging, but it should be available online (www.flaghill.com). Other maple liqueurs may be substituted. Russian Caravan tea is a mildly smoky black tea blend. If not readily available, substitute 1½ teaspoons full-bodied black tea leaves and ½ teaspoon Lapsang Souchong tea leaves.*

Serves 1

2 teaspoons loose-leaf Russian Caravan tea leaves
½ cup/120 milliliters boiling water (about 212°F/100°C)
2 ounces/60 milliliters vodka
1 ounce/30 milliliters Flag Hill Sugar Maple Liqueur
1 ounce/30 milliliters maple syrup, preferably grade B
1 lemon wedge
Maple sugar, for coating rim of glass
Pinch freshly ground black pepper

Put the tea leaves in a small bowl or cup. Pour over the boiling water and steep, covered, for 4 minutes. Strain, discarding the leaves, and cool to room temperature.

   Place 2 tablespoons of the steeped tea in a cocktail shaker filled with ice. Reserve remaining tea for another use. Add vodka, maple liqueur, and maple syrup to the shaker. Shake vigorously for 20 seconds.

   Lightly rub the rim of a cocktail glass with the lemon wedge. Dip rim in maple sugar, turning to coat the edges.

   Shake cocktail another 10 seconds and pour into the martini glass. Garnish with the black pepper and serve.

RED CHILE *and* HONEYED GINGER TEA COCKTAIL

THIS COCKTAIL WAS CREATED FOR DILMAH TEA *by Paul Brown, the executive chef of the Mantra Erskine Beach Resort in Australia. He used Dilmah's Green Tea and Ginger Tea, but for convenience, we adapted the recipe using green tea and Ginger Simple Syrup (page 238). The chef used Manuka honey from New Zealand, but you can use any darker honey, preferably creamed. Creamed honey is opaque—a thicker, spreadable honey produced through controlled crystallization. It can be found in many gourmet shops and online.*

Serves 1

GREEN TEA ICE CUBES

2 tablespoons loose-leaf green tea leaves

2 cups/480 milliliters room-temperature water

¼ cup/60 milliliters honey, preferably creamed honey

COCKTAIL

½ lime, cut into 4 wedges

6 fresh mint leaves

1 long red fresh chile (such as Thai), seeded

½ ounce/15 milliliters Ginger Simple Syrup (page 238)

Green Tea Ice Cubes

2 ounces/60 milliliters vodka

Mint sprig for garnish

TO MAKE THE ICE CUBES: Place the tea leaves and the water in a medium bowl. Let steep, covered, overnight. Strain and discard the leaves. Add the honey to the tea and stir until dissolved. Freeze the infusion in an ice tray.

TO MAKE THE COCKTAIL: Muddle the lime, mint, chile, and syrup in the bottom of a glass. Add the Green Tea Ice Cubes to fill. Add the vodka, stir slightly and serve. Garnish with a fresh mint sprig.

NOTE: The tea for this cocktail comes in the form of ice cubes, which need to be made a day in advance, so plan accordingly.

THE WHITE ROSE

CHRIS CASON OF TAVALON TEAS SHARED THIS *beautiful and aromatic drink with us. Rosewater is sold at specialty foods markets as well as Middle Eastern and Indian markets. You can also make your own by infusing fresh (food-grade) rose petals in water overnight.*

Serves 1

2 ounces/60 milliliters gin

¾ cup/180 milliliters Basic Iced Tea (page 243), made with white tea

1 teaspoon rosewater

1 tablespoon honey

Edible flowers, such as a rose petal or peony, for garnish (optional)

Combine the gin, tea, rosewater, and honey in a cocktail shaker filled with ice. Shake vigorously and strain into a martini glass. Garnish with edible flowers, if desired.

GLOSSARY

ACID—substance having a pH of less than seven, but in cooking more typically defined as an item having a sharp or sour flavor, such as wine, vinegar, or citrus. When substituting a tea for an acid, use a highly astringent tea, such as a first flush Darjeeling, steeped long enough to develop this astringency. Alternatively, the tea can be used to complement a more traditional acid source.

AFTERNOON TEA—the ritualized meal begun in England by Anna, the seventh Duchess of Bedford, in the 1700s as an added meal between luncheon and evening supper. Typically consists of tea, cakes, and small sandwiches and savories. Also called cream tea, referring to the classic clotted cream often served, or low tea, referring to the low parlor tables where tea was often served, as opposed to high tea or meat tea, which is a more substantial meal, or workman's supper, served at standard height or high tables.

AGONY OF THE LEAVES—refers to the twisting and unfolding of rolled tea leaves in hot or boiling water. Also the title of an excellent book by the late Helen Gustafson.

ASTRINGENCY—a tasting term referring to the drying, puckering sensation in the mouth that can result in a particularly cleansing or refreshing drink. May also be referred to as *bite*. Astringency offers an ideal foil for rich or heavy foods, cleansing the palate and balancing the experience.

BAKEY—a negative tasting term referring to an over-fired tea: tea fired at too high a temperature yields an overcooked taste.

BERGAMOT—a citrus tree grown largely in Turkey, Greece, and Italy whose fruit produces bergamot oil, used in perfumes and to flavor Earl Grey tea.

BING CHA—a flat, disk-shaped form for Pu-erh or other compressed teas.

BISCUITY—a tasting term referring to the pleasant flavor and aroma of a black tea reminiscent of English biscuits, sometimes also including maltiness.

BOLD—refers to leaves that are oversized for their grade.

BOP—Broken Orange Pekoe. A leaf size or grade that refers to the Orange Pekoe harvest (bud and two leaves) that have been broken during the rolling process. This added surface area of the broken leaf edges yields a stronger infusion than the whole leaf grades.

BRIGHT—tasting term referring to the look of the tea infusion (as opposed to dull). May also refer to a refreshing character on the palate (as opposed to muddy).

BRINE—a solution of salt, water, and seasonings used to preserve food. In culinary tea, the addition of tea to the solution not only alters the flavors and aromatics, but allows a modest reduction in the salt-to-water ratio used (see page 56).

BRISK—a tasting term referring to a light, clean, lively taste in the mouth. A balanced level of astringency.

BRUISE—to partially crush a food product or tea leaf in order to break the interior cell walls without tearing or breaking the exterior. This releases the enzymes, flavors, and aromatic oils. In tea processing, this step is used to stimulate oxidation of the leaves.

BUD—refers to the immature leaves or shoots of the tea plant that have not yet opened. May also be referred to as *tips* or *budset*.

BURNT—an off-taste indicative of faulty manufacture during the drying of the tea leaves.

CAMELLIA SINENSIS—botanical name for the tea plant. All true tea comes from one of the varieties of *Camellia sinensis*. Note that herbal infusions often incorrectly called herbal "tea" are not true tea and contain no actual *Camellia sinensis*.

CEYLON—teas grown on the island of Sri Lanka, just off the southern tip of India, and the name of that island prior to 1972.

CHA—the word for tea in Chinese and Japanese.

CHAI—the name for tea in Hindi, Russian, and several other languages. Within the United States it has become the accepted name for Indian masala-spiced tea.

CHAI-WALLA—an Indian tea vendor.

CHANOYU—the ritualized Japanese tea ceremony involving preparation, serving, and drinking of the powdered green tea, matcha.

CLEAN—tasting term referring to the appearance of the leaf as evenly graded with no stalk, debris, or incorrectly sized particles. Also used to refer to the absence of any off-tastes.

COLORY—a positive tasting term referring to depth and richness of color in the cup.

CONGOU—a generic name for Chinese black teas.

COURT BOUILLON—a broth, usually containing an acid, used for poaching fish. Tea may be substituted for the usual wine or vinegar or it may supplement it.

CREAM TEA—another name for afternoon tea, referring to the clotted cream usually served. Cream tea may omit the tea sandwiches or savories that would be expected as a part of afternoon tea.

CREAMED OR CREAMING—refers to the clouding that can form when steeped tea cools. Some teas (such as Assams) cream more than others (such as Nilgiris). This does not indicate anything wrong with the tea and does not affect flavor, but should be taken into account when choosing teas to use in cold beverages or similar applications, such as granita or tea aspic.

CRÈME PÂTISSIÈRE—pastry cream or custard made with eggs and milk or cream. It is ideal for infusing with tea.

CTC— Stands for crush-tear-curl or cut-tear-curl. A machine-processed tea which is heavily bruised and pulverized during the manufacture, resulting in uniform pellets of tea which look a lot like instant coffee. CTC-processed tea steeps quickly, yielding assertiveness rather than subtlety or finesse. CTC-processed leaves are often used in tea bags.

DULL—a negative tasting term, the opposite of a tea that is bright. The flavor is muddy and lacks clarity.

EARTHY—a positive taste profile found in many teas, especially Pu-erh teas.

EVEN—tea leaves or leaf pieces of uniform size as opposed to irregular, sometimes referred to as *neat*. The opposite of uneven or ragged. This is typically a sign of good manufacture and grading.

FANNINGS—a very small broken leaf grade of tea often found in tea bags.

FBOP—Flowery Broken Orange Pekoe. The exclusive harvest of one leaf and a bud, but with smaller broken leaves after the rolling process. The broken leaves increase the surface area for steeping and result in a more assertive liquor.

FOP—Flowery Orange Pekoe. The exclusive harvest of one leaf and a bud. Not as tightly rolled as an OP grade with a lighter profile than the more full-bodied or assertive broken grades.

FERMENTED—a term regularly used incorrectly when the process being referred to is actually oxidation. The only teas that undergo a true fermentation are Pu-erhs.

FIRING—when heat is applied to the withered and potentially oxidized tea leaves to prevent further (or any) oxidation and to dry the leaves. Firing sets the leaves at the desired level of oxidation, such as for oolong, green, or black tea.

FLAT—a tasting term referring to an unexciting or dull tea. May indicate poor firing, but it also could mean that the tea is stale or old, or the water used to steep the tea was de-oxygenated.

FLOWERING TEA—also referred to as a *display tea*. These consist of tea leaves and buds tied together, often around one or more dried flowers, and allowed to dry as a closed bulb. When the bulb is steeped, the leaves open, creating a very attractive display. Due to the visual focus of these teas, they should be steeped in clear glass teapots or wine goblets to be appreciated.

FLUSH—used most commonly with Darjeelings and certain Japanese teas to refer to a particular seasonal harvest, but can refer to any young shoots or new growth. A tea is "in flush" when the plants are not dormant.

FRESH—typically indicates a newly processed, well-stored tea, as opposed to *stale*. Can also indicate newly harvested, unwithered, and unprocessed leaves (see page 57).

FULL—having good body, as in *full-bodied* flavor.

GRADE—refers to the size of the leaf or leaf particle after manufacture.

HARSH—refers to a tea in which the balance is off and the briskness or astringency overwhelms the body, yielding an overly aggressive tea. The term is more commonly used to refer to the balance being off due to poor manufacture, as opposed to oversteeping.

HERBAL INFUSION—steeped herbs, leaves, flowers, and other botanicals that are not from the tea plant.

Often incorrectly referred to as herbal "tea," but does not contain any actual tea. Common herbal infusions include chamomile, rose hips, hibiscus, chicory, rooibos, ginger, and mint. Some of these may be used to flavor tea. Also called *tisanes*.

HIGH TEA—a term often misused to refer to afternoon tea. High tea (or "meat tea") is a hearty workman's supper, not the more formal afternoon tea. The name originates from the height of the tables (standard height, or "high") at which it was served, as opposed to the low parlor tables at which butlers more commonly served afternoon tea (or "low tea").

INFUSION—a tasting term for the resulting liquor after tea leaves have been steeped in water. May also refer to a liquid other than water in which tea or other solids have been steeped.

IRREGULAR—inconsistent sorting resulting in leaves or leaf pieces of uneven sizes, as opposed to *even*. This is usually undesirable because the uneven pieces will steep at different rates, but in some cases, as in certain Japanese teas, may occur intentionally to add complexity to the steeped brew.

LIQUOR—in the world of tea does not refer to alcohol, but the resulting infusion after a tea has been steeped.

MALTY—a tasting term for a desirable quality, with a hint of malt, found in certain well-made, rich, full-bodied black teas.

MAO CHA—the rough tea stage, or preliminary stage in Pu-erh production. See page 26.

MUDDY—dull or opaque tea resulting from excessive particulate matter in the brewed tea that was not removed by standard straining.

MUSCATEL—a desirable sweet, fruity, winey note found in certain well-made Darjeelings, especially second flush (summer harvest) Darjeelings.

MUSTY—typically used as a negative term to describe a result of improper drying, but may also be used as a positive term in describing Pu-erh teas.

NEAT—see *even*.

ORANGE PEKOE (OP)—a plucking term referring to the harvest of a bud and two leaves below it.

OXIDATION, OXIDIZED—the chemical changes that begin in the tea leaf after it has been bruised or rolled. These changes are responsible for the alteration of color, aromatics, strength, and briskness of the final tea. The level of oxidation plays a major role in defining the style of the tea.

POACHING—a "wet" cooking technique in which the main item being cooked is gently simmered in liquid. This liquid may be partially or completely tea in order to impart the flavor, color, and aromatics of the chosen tea to the dish. The liquid may be reduced at the end to make a sauce.

PROCESSED—refers to tea leaves that have undergone finishing techniques as opposed to the newly plucked fresh leaves.

PUNGENT—a positive tasting term referring to a tea with a bite or astringency without bitterness.

RAW—a Sheng Cha Pu-erh that has not yet been aged.

RICH—full-bodied, flavorful, satisfying.

RUB—a combination of spices, herbs, and in culinary tea, ground teas. Used as an external crust or dry marinade.

SELF-DRINKER—a tea with the right balance of flavor, aromatics, and body such that there is no need to blend it, flavor it, or alter it for ideal enjoyment.

SHENG CHA—the traditional style of Pu-erh, called raw, rare, or uncooked, that will develop by slow aging, whereby the color darkens and flavor smoothes out and gains richness and depth.

SHOU CHA—the style of Pu-erh known as cooked or ripe, in which the aging process is simulated through a process almost like composting to create a dark, rich "aged" Pu-erh in roughly three months instead of 10 years.

SINGLE ESTATE TEAS—noteworthy teas from a single source that do not need to be blended with other teas to create complexity or balance.

SOFT—can be used as a negative tasting term, as in lacking life, flat. May also be used as a positive term, as in smooth or lush.

STEWED—may refer to improper manufacture but is more commonly used to refer to tea that has been oversteeped.

TANNINS—polyphenols in tea responsible for the bitterness and astringency that yield a drying or puckering feeling in the mouth. Tannins are released more effectively in hot water which is why cooler steeping can yield a smoother, sweeter result in many teas.

THIN—a tasting term referring to a tea lacking in body or character.

TIP OR TIPPY—consisting of or including the bud or budset, or referring to the pointed edge of the budset. Evidence of a very exclusive plucking.

TISANE—see *herbal infusion*.

TOU CHA—small bird's-nest- or dome-shaped compressed tea forms. Commonly found with Pu-erh but may be made of other styles of tea as well.

T-SAC—one commonly available brand of tea filter bags (tea sacks) that can be filled with any loose-leaf tea desired. They are very handy not only for steeping tea, but also for making bouquet garni sachets or filling with any manner of dry ingredients.

TWO LEAVES AND A BUD—the classic plucking; also referred to as Orange Pekoe.

WIRY—a long leaf that is well twisted or rolled, lengthwise. A very elegant look that is indicative, ideally, of full flavor.

WITHER—the stage after plucking in which the leaves are allowed to rest, reduce in moisture content, and become more pliable.

WO DUI—the process developed by the Yunnan Kunming Tea Company of accelerated aging of Pu-erh to create Shou Cha style, or "cooked" Pu-erh.

YOUNG—a tasting term referring to early harvest teas with a green or astringent nature. May also be used to refer to a Sheng Cha (slow-aging Pu-erh) that has not yet been well aged.

SOURCES

THE FOLLOWING PRODUCT SOURCES WILL HELP YOU FIND SUPERB TEAS AND HARD-TO-FIND ingredients, but please look first to your local vendors. Developing a relationship with your local tea purveyors will allow you to see, feel, and taste the teas firsthand. They will also be happy to share their knowledge and access to their latest finds, some perhaps too limited in supply to make it into the Web site and catalogs of major distributors.

Cooking Supplies

COOKS SHOP HERE
www.cooksshophere.com
This dual resource has hard-to-find culinary supplies and is a great source for fine teas. Their tea-focused site can be found at www.teatrekker.com.

FRONTIER NATURAL PRODUCTS CO-OP
www.frontiercoop.com
A good source for spices, as well as culinary herbs and flower petals.

KING ARTHUR FLOUR
www.kingarthur.com
Good source for cocoa, nut flours, gelatin sheets, orange-flower water, and all things baking-related.

ORGANZA BAGG
www.organzabagg.com/flora.html
Source for culinary-grade flower petals, including lavender, rose, calendula, and more.

PENZEY'S SPICES
www.penzeys.com
Specialty spices and harder-to-find seasonings from around the world, including excellent paprikas.

THE SAN FRANCISCO HERB COMPANY
www.sfherb.com
Good source for spices and general culinary herbs and flower petals.

Sources for Tea

BARNES & WATSON FINE TEAS
206-625-9435; www.barnesandwatson.com

DILMAH TEA
www.dilmahtea.com
This innovative family-owned Sri Lankan tea company has lead the way in inspiring chefs to look to the culinary potential of teas. Their fine teas are not widely available in the U.S. yet, but they are readily

available in Europe, England, and Sri Lanka. Go to their website for information about availability, and to purchase their teas online.

GLENWORTH ESTATE, LTD.
(VIA QTRADE TEAS AND HERBALS)
949-766-0070; info@qtradeteas.com; www.qtradeteas.com
A source for many excellent teas, as well as the fine Nilgiri teas of Glendale Estates.

HARNEY AND SONS, LTD.
www.harney.com
Purveyor of many of the teas offered at fine hotels and restaurants.

IMPERIAL TEA COURT
imperial@imperialtea.com; www.imperialtea.com
Home of some of the finest Chinese teas on the market. Owner Roy Fong is currently expanding to domestic tea growth as well with a new tea farm in California, which will offer fresh tea leaves.

ITI/INTERNATIONAL TEA IMPORTERS
1629 Date Street, Montebello, CA 90640
tealand@msn.com
Source for exceptional Indian teas, as well as teas from around the world, and a source for the seminal tea works by James Norwood Pratt.

MARK T. WENDELL, IMPORTER
978-635-9200; www.marktwendell.com
U.S. Source for Hu-Kwa brand Lapsang Souchong tea.

NEW VITHANAKANDE ESTATES (SRI LANKA)
www.vithanakandeteas.com
These award-winning teas are available through select U.S. importers, including Qtrade (listed above) but for straight access to their teas contact them directly.

PEETS COFFEE AND TEA
800-999-2132; www.peets.com
Specialty tea shops with locations nationwide.

SERENDIPITEA
888-TEA-LIFE; www.seredipiTea.com

SHANGRI-LA TEAS
www.shangrilaicedtea.com; 1-800-487-9828
An excellent source for iced teas. They specialize in wholesale and food service supplying top-notch products as well as equipment, but their teas can also be purchased retail, directly through their website. Also, an additional source for the superb Nilgiri teas of Glendale Estate, India.

SILK ROAD TEAS
415-458-8624; www.silkroadteas.com

SIMPSON AND VAIL, INC.
800-282-8327; www.svtea.com

SPECIALTEAS, INC.
888-588-7553; www.specialteas.com

TEASOURCE
651-690-9822; www.teasource.com
Good selection of teas at excellent prices.

TEA TREKKER
413-584-5116; www.teatrekker.com
General source for fine teas, run by Mary Lou and

Robert Heiss, the authors of *The Story of Tea, A Cultural History and Drinking Guide.*

TEN REN TEA

800-650-1047; www.tenren.com

Source for Chinese teas with locations nationwide.

UPTON TEA IMPORTS

800-234-8327; www.uptontea.com

Excellent general source for teas, with particular focus on fine, hard-to-find Darjeelings. Also the U.S. source for the well-designed Chatsford teapots.

ZHONG GUO CHA

www.buygreattea.com

A source of superb Chinese teas.

Fresh Tea Leaves

CAMELLIA FOREST NURSERY, CHRISTINE PARKS

Tea Gardens at Camellia Forest Nursery

9701 Carrie Road

Chapel Hill, NC 27516

919-968-0504; www.camforest,com

teagardens1@bellsouth.net

This source can supply fresh tea leaves, plants or seedlings

TEA HAWAII & COMPANY, EVA LEE

PO Box 362, Volcano, Hawaii 96785

www.teahawaii.com

808-967-7637; teahawaii@gmail.com

Tea Hawaii can ship fresh tea leaves to your door from surrounding tea farms.

HAWAII TEA SOCIETY: BOB JACOBSON, PRESIDENT; JACOBS@HAWAIIANISP.COM

plants@hawaiiteasociety.org; www.hawaiiteasociety.org

A noteworthy organization involved in promoting tea propagation and culture in Hawaii, as well as a source for tea seedlings, offered at reasonable prices due to subsidization by the County of Hawaii Department of Research and Development. They are helping to bring more Hawaiian growers into the network to supply fresh culinary leaves.

SAKUMA BROTHERS FARM, RICHARD SAKUMA

Burlington, Washington

360-661-4248; richards@sakumabros.com; sakumamarketstand.com

Tea Accessories

ADAGIO TEAS

www.adagio.com

Source for IngenuiTEA tea maker and attractive glass teapots, as well as an assortment of teas. Publisher of teamuse.com, an excellent source for tea news, information, and discussions. Includes a monthly cooking-with-tea contest (see page 134 for a winning recipe).

A BIT OF BRITAIN

www.abitofbritain.com

Source for Brown Betty teapots.

EDGECRAFT

800-342-3255; www.edgecraft.com

Source for Chef's Choice SmartKettle

THE LONDON TEAPOT COMPANY

sales@ltpc.co.uk; www.chatsford.com

Source for Chatsford Teapots, classic-style pots with well-designed infuser baskets.

POSTCARD TEAS

9 Dering Street

New Bond Street

London W1S 1AG

+44 20 7629 3654

www.postcardteas.com

Source for Japanese green tea grinder (may be used with other teas to grind fine tea powders).

TEAVANA

www.teavana.com

Tea bars and retail counters throughout North America. A particularly good source for teaware and tea sets.

ZOJIRUSHI

800-264-6270; www.zojirushi.com.

Source for exceptional hot-water heaters.

Learning about Tea

TEA: A MAGAZINE

888-456-8651; www.teamag.com

The first consumer magazine dedicated to tea.

SPECIALTY TEA INSTITUTE

(a division of the Tea Association of the U.S.A, Inc.)

www.teausa.org

Offers in-depth certification-level classes on tea.

WORLD TEA EXPO TRADE CONVENTION

www.worldteaexpo.com

A great way to take brief tea seminars and classes, network, and check out the latest innovations in the industry.

INDEX